CAMPBELL'S
2701 QUIZ QUESTIONS

By John P. Campbell

Campbell's High School / College Quiz Book (Revised Edition)

Campbell's Potpourri I of Quiz Bowl Questions (Out of Print)

Campbell's Potpourri II of Quiz Bowl Questions (Revised Edition)

Campbell's Middle School Quiz Book #1 (Revised Edition)

Campbell's Potpourri III of Quiz Bowl Questions

Campbell's Middle School Quiz Book #2

Campbell's Elementary School Quiz Book #1

Campbell's 2001 Quiz Questions

Campbell's Potpourri IV of Quiz Bowl Questions

Campbell's Middle School Quiz Book #3

The 500 Famous Quotations Quiz Book (Out of Print)

Campbell's 2002 Quiz Questions

Campbell's 210 Lightning Rounds

Campbell's 175 Lightning Rounds

Campbell's 2003 Quiz Questions

Campbell's 211 Lightning Rounds

Omniscience[TM] *The Basic Game of Knowledge in Book Form*

Campbell's 2004 Quiz Questions

Campbell's 212 Lightning Rounds

Campbell's Elementary School Quiz Book #2

Campbell's 176 Lightning Rounds

Campbell's 213 Lightning Rounds

Campbell's Potpourri V of Quiz Bowl Questions

Campbell's Mastering the Myths Quiz Book

Campbell's 3001 Quiz Questions

Campbell's 2701 Quiz Questions

CAMPBELL'S
2701 QUIZ QUESTIONS

by John P. Campbell

PATRICK'S PRESS

Columbus, Georgia

Printed in the United States of America

CIP data suggested by the author

Campbell, John P., 1942-
Campbell's 2701 Quiz Questions

   Includes index.
   Summary: Questions and answers on a wide-range of topics, such as history, literature, geography, sports, the Bible, science, art, mythology, and religion, are arranged into thirty chapters.
   1. Questions and answers. [1. Questions and answers]
I. Title II. Title: Campbell's 2701 Quiz Questions.
III. Title: 2701 Quiz Questions
IV. Title: Two Thousand Seven Hundred and One Quiz Questions
AG195.C294b   1996   031'.02

ISBN (International Standard Book Number): 0-944322-23-9

First Edition
First Printing, April, 1996
Second Printing, February, 2000
Third Printing, December, 2003

ACKNOWLEDGEMENTS

I am once again very indebted to Rinda Brewbaker for her editing ability and suggestions.

I appreciate the help of Pam Coffield of Brookstone School and Billy Pickens of Auburn High School with all the math questions. I thank Dr. Jay Cliett of Georgia Southwestern College for reading all the material. I thank the following for their corrections and suggestions: Biology: Dr. Jack Carter, Georgia Southwestern College; Chemistry and Physics: Dr. Wayne Counts, Georgia Southwestern College; and Mathematics: Dr. Jay Cliett.

I also thank the consultants with the Muscogee County school system and various members of the Columbus College faculty who read some of the material.

I also thank Deborah Metivier and Connie Erb for their indexing.

I want to thank my mother, Mrs. John Campbell, for her support.

I would also like to thank Cornerstone Images of Columbus for their typesetting services.

TO

Students everywhere who seize the opportunity of academic quiz competition to give them a chance to show their talent:

"The world is always ready to receive talent with open arms."
—Oliver Wendell Holmes

PREFACE

This book is intended as quiz bowl material not only for the coach of an Academic Bowl team to use in conducting practices but also for individual team members to use as study material. The complete index complements this intention as the users of this book are able to find quickly material they wish to review.

Your suggestions and comments will be appreciated. Please send them to me care of PATRICK'S PRESS, Box 5189, Columbus, Georgia 31906.

John Campbell

CONTENTS

CHAPTER ONE

1) What is the official language of Austria?
   Answer: German.

2) Give the term that identifies a Jewish religious teacher.
   Answer: Rabbi.

3) Name the bone in the leg that is the longest and strongest bone in the human body.
   Answer: Femur (or thigh bone).

4) What is the difference when the square of 17 is subtracted from the square of 18?
   Answer: 35 (do NOT accept negative 35).

5) Which 2 continents do NOT border the world's largest ocean?
   Answer: Europe and Africa (the largest ocean is the Pacific).

6) Name the dominant painter of the 20th century who was born at Malaga, Spain, on October 25, 1881. He is known for his "Blue Period" painting *The Old Guitarist*.
   Answer: Pablo Ruiz Picasso.

7) Name the bull that prefers to smell fragrant flowers rather than to fight in a Munro Leaf story.
   Answer: Ferdinand.

8) Which term for a kind of government is derived from the Greek for "rule of the people"?
   Answer: Democracy.

9) In terms of *pi*, what is the circumference of a circle with a diameter of 5?
   Answer: 5 *pi*.

10) In 1993, the AP became the 1st U.S. news organization to return to which Asian country 18 years after a war involving the U.S. ended there?
    Answer: Vietnam (the AP is the Associated Press).

11) Name Alaska's chief river, the 5th longest in North America.
    Answer: Yukon River.

12) Which term designates the period in American history following the Civil War from 1865 to 1877?
    Answer: Reconstruction.

13) Which state, nicknamed "The First State," became the first to install video cameras on school buses statewide in 1994?
    Answer: Delaware.

14) Name the geometric solid with 2 congruent, parallel, and circular bases.
    Answer: Cylinder.

15) Identify the country whose Bay of Fundy has tides that sometimes rise and fall more than 50 feet.
    Answer: Canada.

16) Which word from the Italian for "alone" designates a musical piece played or sung by one person?
    Answer: Solo.

17) Give the acronym for the 1993 trade agreement with Mexico and Canada.
    Answer: NAFTA (North American Free Trade Agreement).

18) Identify the group of Indians in Florida that the U.S. government forced to move west in the early 1800s.
    Answer: Seminoles.

19) Identify the smallest state in area west of the Appalachian Mountains.
    Answer: Hawaii.

20) Of hepatitis, chicken pox, AIDS, or cancer, which one is a noncommunicable disease?
    Answer: Cancer (noncommunicable means one that is not caused by germs and cannot be transmitted from one person to another).

21) Which word, meaning "crude oil," completes the full name of OPEC, the Organization of _____ Exporting Countries?
    Answer: Petroleum.

22) In which year, the first of the U.S. Civil War, was the first transcontinental telegram sent on October 24?
    Answer: 1861 (sent from California to Washington, D.C.).

23) Identify the dense, sticky liquid in the mouth, nose, throat, and lungs.
    Answer: Mucus.

24) What is the average measure of the angles of a triangle?
Answer: 60 degrees.

25) Which word beginning with the letter *T* identifies a set of 3 related novels, plays, or operas?
Answer: Trilogy.

26) Identify the American silversmith made famous by Henry Wadsworth Longfellow for his 1775 ride.
Answer: Paul Revere.

27) Which planet and element are named for a god known for his speed?
Answer: Mercury.

28) Which American was the oldest signer of both the Declaration of Independence and the Constitution?
Answer: Benjamin Franklin.

29) Arrange the following numbers in order from smallest to largest: 9/10, 7/13, 2/5, 9/19 (nine-tenths; seven-thirteenths; two-fifths; nine-nineteenths).
Answer: 2/5, 9/19, 7/13, 9/10.

30) Identify the annual award given to the author of the U.S.'s most distinguished piece of children's literature.
Answer: Newbery Medal.

31) Which words are capitalized in the following sentence: "During the spring, John read 3 books about French heroes for his history class"?
Answer: During, John, French.

32) In which state did Baron von Steuben begin drilling General Washington's infantry in 1778 at Valley Forge?
Answer: Pennsylvania.

33) Identify the flowerless plant that consists of a fungus and an alga living together as a single unit.
Answer: Lichen.

34) Which term is used in math to identify the quantity inside a root symbol?
Answer: Radicand (do NOT accept radical).

35) Identify the Dutch painter who is known for cutting off part of his ear.
Answer: Vincent Van Gogh.

36) Name the first African-American to win the Wimbledon men's singles tennis championship.
Answer: Arthur Ashe.

37) Spell the word used to designate the thick mucus that develops in the lungs during an asthma attack, cold, or other respiratory infection.
Answer: P-H-L-E-G-M.

38) Which part of the brain controls the coordination of the muscles?
Answer: Cerebellum.

39) Who was named chancellor of Germany on January 30, 1933?
Answer: Adolf Hitler.

40) Does a *spelunker* fly airplanes, collect stamps, climb rocks, or explore caves?
Answer: Explore caves.

41) In which state is Vicksburg, the river port that fell to the Union Army on July 4, 1863, after a 47-day siege?
Answer: Mississippi.

42) Name the balsa raft on which Thor Heyerdahl sailed to prove that Polynesians could have originated in South America.
Answer: *Kon-Tiki.*￼

43) What does an equestrian ride?
Answer: A horse.

44) Give the measures of both the complement and the supplement of an angle of 78 degrees.
Answer: 12 degrees (complement) and 102 degrees (supplement).

45) Which name identifies the 130 armed Spanish ships defeated by the British in 1588 in the English Channel?
Answer: Armada.

46) Which mineral on the Mohs Scale of hardness is the hardest at a rating of 10?
Answer: Diamond.

47) Identify the state where Mark Twain's novel *The Adventures of Tom Sawyer* is set in the fictional town of St. Petersburg. This state's capital is Jefferson City.
Answer: Missouri.

48) Name 3 of the 4 blood types.
Answer: A, B, AB, O.

49) What percentage is the equivalent of 7/20?
Answer: **35% (or 35).**

50) In which novel does Jo's music-loving sister Beth die young and her older sister Meg marry John Brooke?
Answer: *Little Women.*

51) Which word designates that the author of a work is unknown, as is the case with the book *Go Ask Alice*?
Answer: **Anonymous.**

52) From which country did President Kennedy demand that Soviet missiles be removed after he set up a naval "quarantine" in 1962?
Answer: **Cuba.**

53) Which state, called "The Silver State," is located entirely in the Pacific time zone but doesn't border the Pacific Ocean?
Answer: **Nevada.**

54) What is 500% of 30?
Answer: **150.**

55) Which Charles Dickens character asks the workhouse-master for more gruel?
Answer: **Oliver Twist.**

56) Which poetic device features the repetition of an initial sound in phrases such as "A telling tale of terror"?
Answer: **Alliteration.**

57) Which body organ supplies the blood with oxygen and removes carbon dioxide from it?
Answer: **Lungs.**

58) Which South American country has 2 capitals, one of which is Sucre?
Answer: **Bolivia (its actual, but unofficial, capital is La Paz).**

59) What name is given to a polynomial that is the sum of two terms?
Answer: **Binomial.**

60) Name the oldest permanent settlement established in the U.S. by Europeans.
Answer: **St. Augustine (Florida).**

61) Name the French king who served from 1643 to 1715.
Answer: **Louis XIV.**

62) Which element, whose symbol is Hg, does any alloy called an amalgam contain?
Answer: Mercury.

63) Name the legislative body formed in Virginia in 1619 that was the start of self-government in America.
Answer: House of Burgesses.

64) Give in simplest form the trinomial that is the product of the following 2 binomials: the quantity $a + 4$ and the quantity $2a - 3$.
Answer: $2a^2 + 5a - 12$.

65) Name the arm of the Mediterranean Sea between Greece and Turkey where many Greek islands are found.
Answer: Aegean Sea.

66) Identify the pair of organs that filter out waste products from the blood and maintain the body's salt and water balance.
Answer: Kidneys.

67) Of Bach, Beethoven, Brahms, or Mozart, which one, a child prodigy, began composing at age 5 and wrote *The Magic Flute*?
Answer: Wolfgang Amadeus Mozart.

68) Name the early theory, disproved in 1668, that life can spring from nonliving matter.
Answer: Spontaneous generation (or abiogenesis).

69) What is the largest of 3 consecutive odd integers, the smallest of which is x?
Answer: $x + 4$ (or $4 + x$).

70) Which word designates the action taken by Congress to remove government officials on charges of wrongdoing?
Answer: Impeachment.

71) Name the world conqueror who according to Greek legend cut the Gordian knot with a single stroke of his sword.
Answer: Alexander the Great.

72) How many complete presidential terms did Franklin Roosevelt serve?
Answer: 3.

73) Name the American author of the stories *Rip Van Winkle* and *The Legend of Sleepy Hollow*.
Answer: Washington Irving.

74) What is the principal square root of 289?
Answer: 17.

75) Which invention brought wealth and fame to chemist Alfred Nobel, the founder of the Nobel prizes?
Answer: Dynamite.

76) The name of which U.S. state is derived from the Indian words for "Great Water" or "Father of Waters"?
Answer: Mississippi.

77) Name the American astronomer after whom an orbiting space telescope launched in 1990 is named.
Answer: Edwin Hubble.

78) Identify the South American liberator after whom Bolivia was named.
Answer: Simón Bolívar.

79) Name the supreme deity in Roman mythology.
Answer: Jupiter.

80) Name the famous geyser located in Yellowstone National Park.
Answer: Old Faithful.

81) Name the Swedish capital, where all Nobel Prizes except for the Nobel Peace Prize are awarded.
Answer: Stockholm.

82) Which word ending in -*archy* means "absence of any form of political authority"?
Answer: Anarchy.

83) Name the document the king of England approved in 1215 in the meadow at Runnymede.
Answer: Magna Charta (or Magna Carta).

84) How many lines of symmetry does a square have?
Answer: 4.

85) Which American inventor is remembered for saying, "Mr. Watson, come here. I want you!"
Answer: Alexander Graham Bell.

86) At how many degrees longitude is the Greenwich, or prime, meridian?
Answer: 0 degrees.

87) Identify the U.S. capital city that served as the first capital of the Confederacy.
Answer: Montgomery (Alabama).

88) Identify the fictional character whose address is 221 B Baker Street.
Answer: Sherlock Holmes.

89) A trapezoid has bases of lengths 3 and 9. If the area of the trapezoid is 48, what is its height?
Answer: 8.

90) Which flower featured in a Vincent Van Gogh painting is the state flower of Kansas?
Answer: Sunflower (Van Gogh's painting is entitled _Sunflowers_).

CHAPTER TWO

1) Name the 1898 war whose last surviving U.S. veteran died in 1992.
   Answer: Spanish-American War.

2) Of U.S. Presidents James A. Garfield, Chester A. Arthur, William McKinley, and John F. Kennedy, which one was NOT assassinated?
   Answer: Chester A. Arthur (Abraham Lincoln was the other President to be assassinated).

3) What name is given to the red, green, and sometimes brown simple organisms that contain chlorophyll and live in water?
   Answer: Algae.

4) What field of mathematics involves the study of operations and relationships among numbers by using variables such as x and y?
   Answer: Algebra.

5) Which nursery rhyme character "had so many children she didn't know what to do"?
   Answer: "Old woman who lived in a shoe" (or "Old woman").

6) Name the oldest national park in the U.S., one whose attractions include about 200 geysers.
   Answer: Yellowstone National Park.

7) Name the Tennessean Bill Clinton chose as his vice president.
   Answer: Al Gore.

8) What name is often used for Siddhartha Gautama, the religious figure whose birth in India about 563 B.C. is commemorated on April 8?
   Answer: Buddha (the founder of Buddhism).

9) What name identifies a geometric solid with exactly one circular base and exactly one vertex?
   Answer: Cone.

10) Of the U.S. states Idaho, Montana, Wyoming or Minnesota, which one does NOT border Canada?
    Answer: Wyoming.

11) Of hyperbole, simile, metaphor, or personification, which figure of speech is an extravagant exaggeration NOT meant to be taken literally?
Answer: Hyperbole.

12) Name the North European sea bordered by Scandinavian countries on the west and the former Soviet Union on the east.
Answer: Baltic Sea.

13) When combined, the postal abbreviations of which 2 states spell the word *game*?
Answer: Georgia and Maine.

14) Factor the following binomial into the product of 2 binomials: $4a^2 - 9$.
Answer: $(2a + 3)(2a - 3)$, or $(2a - 3)(2a + 3)$ [READ: the quantity of two a plus three times the quantity of two a minus three, or vice versa).

15) Name the premier of the Soviet Union from 1957 to 1964. He was in office during President Kennedy's term and the Cuban missile crisis.
Answer: Nikita Khrushchev.

16) Identify the deformed dwarf of German folklore who spins straw into gold in exchange for the miller's daughter's first child.
Answer: Rumpelstiltskin (Rumpelstilzchen).

17) Name the canal that opened in New York in 1825 to link the Hudson River with a Great Lake.
Answer: Erie Canal.

18) Name the Bolshevik leader of the 1917 October Revolution in Russia for whom St. Petersburg was renamed.
Answer: Vladimir I. Lenin (city was renamed Leningrad).

19) Which one of the following secretes enzymes and hormones used in digestion: pancreas, parathyroid, pharynx, or pituitary?
Answer: Pancreas.

20) Which word, derived from the French for "to the valley," designates a mass of loosened snow that slides down a mountain slope?
Answer: Avalanche.

21) Name the king of England who agreed to the Magna Carta in 1215.
Answer: King John.

22) What name is given to the group of heads of departments who serve as the President's official advisors?
Answer: Cabinet.

23) Which country did Manuel Noriega once head? He began serving a 40-year U.S. prison sentence in 1992.
Answer: Panama.

24) One-half of what number equals one-fifth of one-fifth?
Answer: 2/25 (two twenty-fifths).

25) Name the Viking who colonized Greenland about A.D. 986.
Answer: Eric the Red (Erik Thorvaldsson).

26) Name the world's largest lake.
Answer: Caspian Sea.

27) Of Iowa, Missouri, Wisconsin, and Kansas, which one is EAST of the Mississippi River?
Answer: Wisconsin.

28) Name the English explorer sailing for the Dutch who has a North American river, bay, and strait named for him.
Answer: Henry Hudson.

29) If a heart beats at a rate of 30 beats per quarter minute, what is the average time in seconds between 2 consecutive beats?
Answer: 1/2 second.

30) Which term is used to designate June 21-22, the longest day of sunlight of the year in the Northern Hemisphere?
Answer: Summer solstice.

31) Name the American inventor who said, "Genius is one percent inspiration and ninety-nine percent perspiration."
Answer: Thomas Edison.

32) In which famine-stricken African country were U.N. relief efforts being coordinated in Mogadishu, its capital, in the 1990s?
Answer: Somalia.

33) Of Idaho, Washington, Oregon, and California, which one does NOT border the Pacific Ocean?
Answer: Idaho.

34) If 2 angles of a triangle measure 40 degrees and 60 degrees, what is the measure of the 3rd angle?
Answer: 80 degrees.

35) Identify the lowest point in North America, located near Badwater at 282 feet below sea level.
Answer: Death Valley (in California).

36) Name the English naturalist who established the theory of organic evolution.
Answer: Charles Darwin.

37) Of Abraham Lincoln, George Washington, Franklin Roosevelt, and Thomas Jefferson, which one is NOT carved in granite on Mount Rushmore?
Answer: Franklin Roosevelt (Theodore Roosevelt is the 4th).

38) In which country is Stonehenge, the circular group of stones considered by some to be man's first celestial observatory?
Answer: England.

39) Identify the famous means of public transportation used on the hills of San Francisco.
Answer: Cable car.

40) Identify the colorless, odorless, tasteless gas that makes up about 78% by volume of dry air.
Answer: Nitrogen.

41) Which month is named for the Roman god of beginnings or openings?
Answer: January (named for Janus).

42) In which country of the United Kingdom is the legendary Loch Ness monster said to live?
Answer: Scotland.

43) What is the Spanish word for "a brief nap or rest taken after the noonday meal"?
Answer: Siesta.

44) What is the sum of the identity element of addition and the identity element of multiplication?
Answer: 1.

45) Which epithet follows the name of Peter I and Catherine II of Russia and Alexander III, the king of Macedonia?
Answer: The Great.

46) Identify "The Wolverine State," whose name is derived from an Indian word for "big lake."
Answer: Michigan.

47) Identify the type of forest in which the dominant trees shed their leaves during certain seasons and grow new ones.
Answer: Deciduous forest.

48) Which canal connects the Mediterranean Sea with the Red Sea?
Answer: Suez Canal.

49) What is the principal square root of 169?
Answer: 13.

50) Name 2 of the first 3 letters of the Greek alphabet.
Answer: Alpha, Beta, and Gamma.

51) How many permanent seats are there on the U.N. Security Council?
Answer: 5.

52) To which vitamin complex does folic acid belong?
Answer: Vitamin B Complex (folic acid is one of its 8 constituents).

53) Over which continent, the 5th largest, did an ozone "hole" reappear earlier in 1992 than ever before?
Answer: Antarctica.

54) If one card is randomly picked from a deck of 52 playing cards, what is the probability that this card will be a red face card?
Answer: 3/26.

55) From which country did the U.S. acquire the Louisiana Purchase, signing the treaty on May 2, 1803?
Answer: France.

56) Identify Tom's aunt with whom he lives in Mark Twain's *The Adventures of Tom Sawyer*.
Answer: Aunt Polly.

57) What name is given to a species that has no living members?
Answer: Extinct.

58) Spell *aquatic*, which means "growing or living in or upon the water."
Answer: A-Q-U-A-T-I-C.

59) Which meteorological instrument is used to measure atmospheric pressure?
Answer: Barometer.

60) Which one of the following is NOT a woodwind instrument: clarinet, harpsichord, piccolo, or oboe?
Answer: Harpsichord (it is a keyboard instrument).

61) A *caucus* is a private meeting of leaders of a political party. Spell the word *caucus*.
Answer: C-A-U-C-U-S.

62) What term is used for someone who, like Mozart, writes music?
Answer: Composer.

63) Which adjective indicates that a person can speak 2 languages with equal or nearly equal facility?
Answer: Bilingual.

64) What is 5 raised to the second power?
Answer: 25.

65) Name the Greek author of the *Odyssey*, an epic poem that begins 10-years after the fall of Troy and recounts the wanderings of Odysseus.
Answer: Homer.

66) Spell the past form of the verb *to lie* that completes this sentence: He _____ on the beach for hours.
Answer: L-A-Y.

67) In which work by Mark Twain does Jim run away from the Widow Douglas's place?
Answer: *The Adventures of Huckleberry Finn*.

68) Name the Carthaginian general who crossed the Pyrenees and the Alps to fight the Romans in the 3rd century B.C.
Answer: Hannibal.

69) What is the value of the expression x cubed minus three x squared plus x minus two when x equals negative 2?
Answer: –24 (negative 24).

70) Identify the hardest substance produced by animal bodies, one that makes up the smooth, hard, outer layer of the teeth.
Answer: Enamel.

71) Which South American country is more than 10 times as long as it is wide?
Answer: Chile.

72) In 1793, who invented a machine for separating cotton fiber from the seed?
Answer: Eli Whitney.

73) How many musical instruments accompany a choir or chorus singing *a cappella*?
Answer: None (*a cappella* means to sing without the accompaniment of musical instruments).

74) Give the greatest common factor for the numbers 24 and 40.
Answer: 8.

75) How many atoms of hydrogen are there in 3 molecules of water?
Answer: 6.

76) Which French emperor, born on the island of Corsica in 1769, died in exile in 1821?
Answer: Napoleon Bonaparte (or Napoleon).

77) Name the architectural style of the great cathedral of Notre Dame in Paris.
Answer: Gothic.

78) Name the American Revolutionary War hero who was hanged as a spy by the British.
Answer: Nathan Hale.

79) In which field did Toni Morrison win a 1993 Nobel Prize?
Answer: Literature.

80) Which novel by Charles Dickens includes the opening line "It was the best of times, it was the worst of times . . . "?
Answer: *A Tale of Two Cities.*

81) Which country is the location of Mount Aconcagua, the highest mountain in the Western Hemisphere?
Answer: Argentina.

82) Which disease develops if the pancreas secretes too little insulin?
Answer: Diabetes (or diabetes mellitus).

83) Name the American who wrote *Poor Richard's Almanac(k).*
Answer: Benjamin Franklin.

84) A diameter of a circle separates the circle into two congruent arcs. What are these arcs called?
Answer: Semicircles.

85) Name the famous New England poet who wrote these lines:
    "Some say the world will end in fire, / Some say in ice."
    Answer: Robert Frost (in "Fire and Ice").

86) Name Alaska's largest city in population.
    Answer: Anchorage.

87) Name the seat of King Arthur's Round Table where he met
    with his Knights.
    Answer: Camelot.

88) Through which one of the following South American coun-
    tries does the Tropic of Capricorn NOT pass: Chile, Ecuador,
    Argentina, or Paraguay?
    Answer: Ecuador.

89) What is the lowest common denominator of the fractions
    3/5, 7/8, and 9/10?
    Answer: 40.

90) During which war was Washington, D.C., captured and
    burned by the British?
    Answer: War of 1812.

CHAPTER THREE

1) Which animal is known as the "king of the beasts"?
   Answer: Lion.

2) Spell the word *parallel*.
   Answer: P-A-R-A-L-L-E-L.

3) Which term is used to designate the average weather conditions of a region, considered over a long period of time?
   Answer: Climate.

4) What is the reciprocal of the reciprocal of 1?
   Answer: 1.

5) Name the first female member of the U.S. Supreme Court.
   Answer: Sandra Day O'Connor.

6) If you are a *docile* person, are you obedient, rebellious, intelligent, or amusing?
   Answer: Obedient.

7) How many provinces are there in Canada: 6, 8, 10, or 12?
   Answer: 10.

8) Give the nickname of the U.S.S. *Constitution*, which was launched in 1797 in Boston.
   Answer: "Old Ironsides."

9) How many hours does it take to make a 16-mile trip while travelling at an average speed of 5 miles per hour?
   Answer: 3⅕ (or 3 hours 12 minutes, or 3.2 hours, or 16/5 hours).

10) Which term designates the point on the surface of the earth directly above the focus of an earthquake?
    Answer: Epicenter (or focal point).

11) Which astronomer, co-author of a book on evolution, helped popularize science with his PBS series *Cosmos*?
    Answer: Carl Sagan (he and his wife, Ann Druyan, wrote *Shadows of Forgotten Ancestors: A Search for Who We Are*).

12) The spasmodic contraction of which large, powerful, dome-shaped muscle at the base of the chest cavity causes a hiccup?
    Answer: Diaphragm.

13) Which of the following does NOT name a bone in the human body: hammer, anvil, steppe, or stirrup?
Answer: **Steppe (steppe is a dry, treeless grassland; the hammer, anvil, and stirrup are bones in the middle ear).**

14) What is the area in square inches of a square with a perimeter of 20 inches?
Answer: **25 (square inches).**

15) Name the organisms such as rust, that lack chlorophyll and feed off of other plants or animals.
Answer: **Fungus (fungi is the plural).**

16) In which Massachusetts town near Lexington did colonists fire "the shot heard round the world" in 1775?
Answer: **Concord.**

17) Which name is shared by an NFL team and the participants in the California gold rush of the late 1840s?
Answer: **49ers.**

18) Which American colony was started on the Savannah River by James Oglethorpe?
Answer: **Georgia.**

19) Which one of the following South American countries does NOT border the Pacific Ocean: Bolivia, Ecuador, Peru, or Colombia?
Answer: **Bolivia.**

20) Identify the most noble of the knights of the Round Table, whose name today identifies a person who is pure and unselfish.
Answer: **Galahad.**

21) Name the Belgian village where Napoleon suffered a decisive defeat in 1815.
Answer: **Waterloo.**

22) Spell the present participle of the verb *to lie* to complete the following sentence: "He was _____ on the beach when I approached him."
Answer: **L-Y-I-N-G.**

23) In which organ of the human body are the aqueous humor and vitreous humor?
Answer: **Eye.**

24) How many square yards of carpet are required to cover a rectangular floor 9 feet by 12 feet?
Answer: **12.**

25) Identify the tendon at the back of the leg that connects the bone of the heel to the muscles of the calf. It is named for the Greek hero of the Trojan War.
Answer: Achilles' tendon.

26) Which literary work features Amy, the youngest of 4 girls, and Beth, her sister, who dies?
Answer: *Little Women* (by Louisa May Alcott).

27) Name the American explorer who is credited with the discovery of the North Pole on April 6, 1909.
Answer: Robert Edwin Peary.

28) In which William H. Armstrong novel does a coon dog's master steal a ham and sausage to feed his starving family?
Answer: *Sounder.*

29) What is the measure in degrees of an interior angle of an equiangular triangle?
Answer: 60.

30) On which date in which month is a U.S. President usually inaugurated at noon?
Answer: January 20 (on January 21 when the date falls on a Sunday).

31) Spell *appositive*, the name given to a word that explains another word.
Answer: A-P-P-O-S-I-T-I-V-E.

32) Which word is used to designate a proposed solution to a scientific problem? Scientists then use experimentation to test this proposal.
Answer: Hypothesis.

33) Which word designates the highest natural adult male singing voice?
Answer: Tenor.

34) Find the amount of interest that an investment of $150 earns in one year at a rate of 14% per year.
Answer: $21 (or 21).

35) In which country were tombs in the Valley of the Kings damaged in a 1992 earthquake?
Answer: Egypt.

36) Name the Washington, D.C., institution that includes the National Museum of American History and the National Air and Space Museum.
Answer: Smithsonian Institution (or Smithsonian; or Smithsonian Institute, an unofficial

term according to *Webster's New World Dictionary*).

37) Who is called the "Father of the U.S. Constitution"?
Answer: James Madison.

38) Identify 2 of the 3 chemical elements in carbohydrates.
Answer: Carbon, hydrogen, and oxygen.

39) During which war is Esther Forbes's *Johnny Tremain* set?
Answer: American Revolutionary War.

40) Identify the body of water at the extremity of South America between Tierra del Fuego and the mainland that is named after the Portuguese explorer who passed through it to reach the Pacific Ocean.
Answer: Strait of Magellan.

41) Which word beginning with the letter *P* designates a thin board on which an artist mixes his paints?
Answer: Palette.

42) Which term is used in geology to designate the central portion of the earth, consisting of a solid inner and a liquid outer part?
Answer: Core.

43) During which war did Francis Scott Key write "The Star-Spangled Banner" in 1814?
Answer: War of 1812.

44) What time is it in the state of Washington when it is 7:00 a.m. in Georgia?
Answer: 4:00 a.m.

45) The Pope said in 1992 that the Church had erred in condemning which Italian astronomer for holding that the Earth was not the center of the universe?
Answer: Galileo.

46) In which state is Redwood National Park?
Answer: California.

47) In which city is St. Paul's Cathedral, a church redesigned by Christopher Wren after the Great Fire in 1666?
Answer: London.

48) Which word is used in science to designate the remains of animals and plants that have lived and died on earth?
Answer: Fossils.

49) What is the volume of a right circular cylinder whose height is 10 feet and whose base has a radius of 2 feet?
Answer: 40 *pi* cubic feet.

50) Name the inventor of the light bulb who was awarded a posthumous Bachelor of Science degree in 1992.
Answer: Thomas Edison.

51) Hazel O'Leary, a U.S. secretary of energy, fined staff workers 25 cents when they used any word made from the initials of an agency's name in her presence. What is such a word as NATO called?
Answer: Acronym.

52) Identify the peninsula bordering the Red Sea where U.S. forces fought in the 1990s.
Answer: Arabian Peninsula.

52) What name is used to designate the scientific study of heredity?
Answer: Genetics.

53) Identify the South American capital city and port whose name means "good winds" in Spanish.
Answer: Buenos Aires (in Argentina).

54) How many fifths are in 12.4?
Answer: 62.

55) What is the capital of Ecuador?
Answer: Quito.

56) Which term is used to designate the leader of Canada: president, lord, prime minister, or chancellor?
Answer: Prime minister.

57) Identify the Old Testament book whose name means "beginning."
Answer: Genesis.

58) What name is given to the blood vessels that carry oxygen-rich blood away from the heart to the rest of the body?
Answer: Artery.

59) The abbreviation *anon.*, for "anonymous," is used to indicate unknown authorship of a novel or painting. Spell the word *anonymous*.
Answer: A-N-O-N-Y-M-O-U-S.

60) Name the American humorist who wrote *A Connecticut Yankee in King Arthur's Court*.
Answer: Mark Twain (or Samuel L. Clemens).

61) Which gland is the so-called "Master Gland" of the human body's endocrine system?
Answer: Pituitary gland (or hypophysis).

62) Name the mythological pair, the abductor and the alleged abductee, who caused the Trojan War.
Answer: Paris and Helen.

63) Norman leader William the Conqueror landed in England with his army in 1066. What language from across the English Channel did he bring with him?
Answer: French.

64) If 3 numbers have an average of 66, and two of them are 90 and 100, what is the third number?
Answer: 8.

65) Which U.S. President initiated a series of radio talks called "Fireside Chats" on March 12, 1933?
Answer: Franklin D. Roosevelt.

66) Which part of the earth's atmosphere, a region of electrically charged particles, reflects radio signals back to earth?
Answer: Ionosphere.

67) What name is given to the annual address the U.S. President delivers to Congress on the state of the nation?
Answer: State of the Union (message or address).

68) Name the body's largest internal organ, sometimes called "The Master Chemistry Lab" because it performs at least 500 functions.
Answer: Liver.

69) What is the only positive number whose square is its double?
Answer: 2.

70) Complete the title of Patricia MacLachlan's Newbery Medal award-winning book, *Sarah, Plain and* _____.
Answer: *Tall.*

71) In which South American country did Francisco Pizarro conquer the Incan empire?
Answer: Peru.

72) What is the grammatical function of the noun *state* in the following sentence: "Alaska is our largest state"?
Answer: Predicate noun (or predicate nominative; or subject complement).

73) In which work by Daniel Defoe is Friday rescued from death at the hands of cannibals?
Answer: *Robinson Crusoe.*

74) What is the principal square root of the product of 3, 6, and 2?
Answer: 6.

75) Name the longest and largest artery in the human body.
Answer: Aorta.

76) In which work by Fred Gipson does Travis have to shoot his dog?
Answer: *Old Yeller.*

77) Which word designates both "anything being hunted" and "a place where building stone, marble, or slate is excavated"?
Answer: Quarry.

78) In which state was the Battle of Gettysburg fought from July 1-3, 1863?
Answer: Pennsylvania.

79) Which American pen name comes from a riverboat term meaning "Two fathoms," for a depth of 12 feet?
Answer: Mark Twain.

80) How many members are there in the U.S. House of Representatives: 135, 235, 335, or 435?
Answer: 435.

81) Name the small, 6-legged animals that make up the largest class of arthropods.
Answer: Insects.

82) Which kind of animal is Misty in Marguerite Henry's *Misty of Chincoteague*?
Answer: Pony (or horse).

83) Which capital city on the Severn River is the home of the U.S. Naval Academy?
Answer: Annapolis.

84) In how many minutes can an automobile travelling at an average speed of 60 miles per hour make a 30-mile trip?
Answer: 30 minutes.

85) Which of the following is a satire written in the form of a story: *The Red Pony, Robinson Crusoe, Gulliver's Travels,* or *Romeo and Juliet*?
Answer: *Gulliver's Travels* (by Jonathan Swift).

86) Name the first secretary of the Treasury, whose portrait appears on the $10 bill.
Answer: Alexander Hamilton.

87) Which President was in office when the 49th and 50th states became a part of the Union in 1959?
Answer: Dwight Eisenhower.

88) Name the oldest man to serve as President of the United States.
Answer: Ronald Reagan.

89) Identify the percussion instrument and the geometric figure that have the same name.
Answer: Triangle.

90) If you are *lethargic*, are you lacking in energy, food, money, or intelligence?
Answer: Energy.

CHAPTER FOUR

1) Which 2 countries, separated since WWII, became reunited on October 3, 1990?
   Answer: East Germany and West Germany.

2) Which igneous rock is named in the official nickname of the state of New Hampshire?
   Answer: Granite (it's "The Granite State").

3) What is the capital of the U.S. state in which Charleston and Greenville are two of the most populous cities?
   Answer: Columbia (South Carolina).

4) Give the 3 measures of the interior angles of an isosceles right triangle.
   Answer: 45, 45, and 90 (or 45 degrees, 45 degrees, and 90 degrees).

5) Name the Norse who explored Vinland in North America about A.D. 1000.
   Answer: Leif Ericsson (Leif Eriksson).

6) In which work by Harriet Beecher Stowe is Simon Legree the chief villain?
   Answer: *Uncle Tom's Cabin.*

7) Is a *synopsis*, a speech, a summary, a medical procedure, or a group of persons?
   Answer: A summary.

8) Complete the title of the Frances Hodgson Burnett novel, *The Secret* _____, on which the 3-time Tony Award-winning play with the same title is based.
   Answer: *Garden.*

9) What is the value of x in the equation $4x + 4 = 4$?
   Answer: 0.

10) Which term designates the part of the skull that encloses the brain?
    Answer: Cranium (or braincase).

11) Which Middle Eastern country, whose capital is Amman, shares its name with a river emptying into the Dead Sea?
    Answer: Jordan.

12) Which word for a kind of reptile comes from 2 Greek words meaning "terrible lizard"?
Answer: Dinosaur.

13) Which birds traditionally leave San Juan Capistrano on St. John's Day, October 23, and return on St. Joseph's Day, March 19?
Answer: Swallows.

14) What term other than diameter designates a line segment whose endpoints lie on a circle?
Answer: Chord.

15) Name the mythological king in Asia Minor who had the power to turn everything he touched into gold.
Answer: Midas.

16) Which continent is considered to be the birthplace of Western civilization?
Answer: Europe (in Greece about 2,500 years ago).

17) A lithotripter is a device used to dissolve kidney stones with ultrasound. What does the Greek root *litho-* mean, as in *monolith*, the term for a granite mountain near Atlanta?
Answer: Stone (the mountain is Stone Mountain).

18) Which general psychological term designates a "loss of memory"?
Answer: Amnesia.

19) Which U.S. President was known as "Old Hickory"?
Answer: Andrew Jackson.

20) According to Benjamin Franklin's *Poor Richard's Almanac*, what makes a man "healthy, wealthy, and wise"?
Answer: "Early to bed and early to rise."

21) Which European country is known for raising tulips and other bulb flowers?
Answer: The Netherlands (or Holland).

22) In which capital city is the Prado Museum located?
Answer: Madrid.

23) Name the strip of land bordering the Mediterranean Sea granted autonomy by the 1994 Israeli/Palestinian peace accord.
Answer: Gaza Strip.

24) Which term is used to name the perimeter of a circle?
Answer: Circumference.

25) Which of the Great Lakes borders the states of Michigan, Wisconsin, and Minnesota?
Answer: Lake Superior.

26) Which word is used to designate the two air passages leading from the trachea to the lungs?
Answer: Bronchi.

27) Which word is used to identify the distance east or west on the Earth's surface, measured in degrees from the prime meridian?
Answer: Longitude.

28) Which term designates "the dome-shaped hut made of packed ice or snow that Eskimos use as a home"?
Answer: Igloo.

29) 27 is what percent of 90?
Answer: 30%.

30) Name the hormone that produces an energy spurt at times of danger.
Answer: Adrenalin.

31) Identify the complex maze where the mythological Minotaur was confined.
Answer: Labyrinth.

32) What name did an English chemist coin for Vitamin C because of its acidic qualities?
Answer: Ascorbic acid.

33) Which term is used to designate the one-celled organisms that can aid in human digestion but also cause infections?
Answer: Bacteria.

34) Simplify the square root of 24.
Answer: 2 square root of 6 (or 2 times the square root of 6).

35) Name the large peninsula in northeastern Canada that is part of Newfoundland.
Answer: Labrador.

36) Identify the body of water between England and France that connects the Atlantic Ocean and the North Sea.
Answer: English Channel.

37) To which city was the U.S. capital moved in 1790 before it was moved to Washington, D.C., in 1800?
Answer: Philadelphia.

38) For which Aztec emperor, who ruled from 1502 to 1520, is an Arizona group of ancient Indian dwellings named?
Answer: Montezuma (the dwellings are called the Montezuma Castle).

39) Identify the great winged horse of Greek mythology.
Answer: Pegasus.

40) What is the human body's largest organ in terms of area?
Answer: Skin.

41) Members of the U.S. Supreme Court are appointed for what period of time: 6 years, 12 years, 24 years, or life?
Answer: Life.

42) Name the Astrid Lindgren character who is super-strong and lives in Villa Villekulla.
Answer: Pippi Longstocking.

43) What name have historians given to the period in European history from the end of the Roman Empire to the 1500s?
Answer: Middle Ages (or Medieval period; do NOT accept Dark Ages).

44) Which 3 consecutive integers add up to 27?
Answer: 8, 9, and 10.

45) On which date, month, day, and year is Christopher Columbus credited with the discovery of the New World?
Answer: October 12, 1492.

46) Give the term for "a casual reference to a literary or historical figure or event that the reader is expected to know."
Answer: Allusion.

47) Identify the hero of a play by Sir James Barrie about a little boy who refuses to grow up.
Answer: Peter Pan.

48) Give the meaning of the suffix *-itis* as in the word tonsillitis.
Answer: Inflammatory disease or inflammation (or disease).

49) If a person works 40 hours a week and takes 3 weeks of vacation in a 52-week year, how many hours does he spend on the job in one year?
Answer: 1,960 hours.

50) Name the section of the air passage in the throat that contains the vocal cords and is sometimes called the voice box.
Answer: Larynx.

51) In which country did the Industrial Revolution begin during the 1700s?
Answer: Great Britain (or England).

52) How many senators are in the U.S. Congress?
Answer: 100.

53) Which Italian city is known for its canals and the gondolas that carry people through it?
Answer: Venice.

54) What year is represented by the Roman numerals MLXVI?
Answer: 1066.

55) In which country did Johannes Gutenberg print the first Bible from movable type, the Gutenberg Bible?
Answer: Germany.

56) During which decade of the 20th century did WWI occur?
Answer: 1910s (1914-1918; or 2nd decade).

57) Which British author, whose real name is Charles Lutwidge Dodgson, wrote *Alice in Wonderland*?
Answer: Lewis Carroll.

58) Identify the only continent smaller than the European continent.
Answer: Australia.

59) Identify the system of ancient Egyptian writing in which figures or objects were used to represent words or sounds.
Answer: Hieroglyphics.

60) Which bird is used as a symbol for those who work for peace?
Answer: Dove.

61) Which one of the following pronouns is not a third person pronoun: us, they, him, she?
Answer: Us.

62) Which word from the Greek for "general education" designates "a work that contains information on all branches of knowledge"?
Answer: Encyclopedia.

63) What name is used to designate the projection of the larynx more prominent in men than in women?
Answer: Adam's apple.

64) Give the 6 positive factors of 18.
Answer: 1, 2, 3, 6, 9, and 18.

65) Identify the smallest U.S. state in area.
   Answer: Rhode Island.

66) Name one of the 2 double-reed instruments in an orchestra.
   Answer: Bassoon or oboe.

67) According to the proverb, from which animal's mouth does one get something from a reliable source?
   Answer: Horse's mouth.

68) Spell the singular form of the plural noun *alumni* traditionally used for male graduates.
   Answer: A-L-U-M-N-U-S.

69) Give the number of vertices of a cube.
   Answer: 8.

70) Give the Latin name for the constellation known as "the twins."
   Answer: Gemini.

71) Identify "The Land of Enchantment," the Southwestern U.S. state that is fifth largest in area.
   Answer: New Mexico.

72) Which term for "rebirth" identifies the period in European history between the 1300s and the 1600s?
   Answer: Renaissance.

73) What is the astronomical term for "the distance that light traverses in a vacuum in one year, a distance of approximately 9.5 trillion km, or 6 trillion miles"?
   Answer: Light-year (at the speed of approximately 299,793 km/sec).

74) What is the total surface area of a cube with an edge of length two units?
   Answer: 24 square units.

75) In E.B. White's *Stuart Little*, what kind of an animal is Stuart Little, the second son of Mr. and Mrs. Frederick C. Little?
   Answer: Mouse (George is the oldest child).

76) Which of the following can NOT be a linking verb: smell, seem, throw, or taste?
   Answer: Throw.

77) Who won a $25,000 prize in 1927 for being the first person to fly nonstop from New York to Paris?
   Answer: Charles Lindbergh.

78) Whose name completes the following line in Dickens' *A Christmas Carol*: "And so, as _____ observed, God Bless Us, Every One!"
Answer: "Tiny Tim."

79) What name is given to the line on a weather map connecting locations with the same barometric pressure?
Answer: Isobar.

80) Which word for "a spiritual being" names the world's highest falls, those located in Venezuela?
Answer: Angel Falls.

81) Name the lowest male singing voice.
Answer: Bass (voice).

82) In which year, the year after George Washington was first inaugurated, did the U.S. conduct its first census?
Answer: 1790 (1990 was the bicentennial of this event).

83) Identify the aquatic mammals whose name completes the title of Scott O'Dell's novel *Island of the Blue* _____.
Answer: *Dolphins*.

84) Solve for T: T minus four equals T divided by five.
Answer: Five.

85) Give the word for "a story in which a person, abstract idea, or event has a hidden or symbolic meaning," such as Bunyan's *Pilgrim's Progress*.
Answer: Allegory.

86) Which famous British explorers met in Africa in 1871 when one of them was missing and the other found him?
Answer: David Livingstone and Henry M. Stanley.

87) What drug is usually taken for diabetes?
Answer: Insulin.

88) What is the world's largest living animal?
Answer: Blue whale.

89) What name is given to a polygon that has all angles congruent and all sides congruent?
Answer: Regular (polygon).

90) Identify the Greek or Roman god whose symbol is a three-pronged spear called a trident.
Answer: Poseidon or Neptune.

CHAPTER FIVE

1) Which of the Great Lakes is the largest?
   Answer: Lake Superior.

2) Spell the possessive plural of country.
   Answer: C-O-U-N-T-R-I-E-S'.

3) Identify the state whose Outer Banks were damaged by Hurricane Emily in 1993.
   Answer: North Carolina.

4) What is the name of the point with coordinates (0,0) in a two-dimensional coordinate plane?
   Answer: Origin.

5) In which city are basketball tournaments played in the Hoosier Dome?
   Answer: Indianapolis (Indiana, nicknamed the "Hoosier State").

6) A postage stamp depicting a red ribbon was issued in 1993 to encourage awareness of which disease?
   Answer: AIDS (World Aids Day is December 1).

7) In which city did a snow cancel a major league baseball game between the Astros and the Rockies in 1993?
   Answer: Denver (Colorado).

8) Identify the largest island in North America.
   Answer: Greenland (it is also the world's largest island).

9) What number has the property that 7 more than 3 times the number is 40?
   Answer: 11.

10) Which woman distinguished herself at the 1778 Battle of Monmouth by carrying water and by replacing her husband in firing his cannon?
    Answer: ("Sergeant") Molly Pitcher (or Mary Hays McCauley).

11) Name the scientist who allegedly discovered the principle of gravity by watching an apple fall to the ground.
    Answer: Isaac Newton.

12) Identify the Canadian province whose name means New Scotland.
   Answer: Nova Scotia.

13) Identify the mythological life-giving drink of the gods.
   Answer: Nectar.

14) What is the perimeter of a rectangle with dimensions 11 feet by 9 feet?
   Answer: 40 feet.

15) How many teeth are in an adult human?
   Answer: 32.

16) Which term is used in science to designate bands of light appearing in the night sky, especially in polar regions?
   Answer: Aurora.

17) In which bay did Francis Scott Key observe the bombardment of Fort McHenry?
   Answer: Chesapeake Bay.

18) The 50th anniversary of the surprise Japanese attack on Pearl Harbor was marked in 1991 in which state where the U.S.S. *Arizona* Memorial is located?
   Answer: Hawaii.

19) Which term designates the band of colors visible when light passes through a prism?
   Answer: Spectrum.

20) Name both the largest or smallest of the 7 classification groups developed by Carolus Linnaeus.
   Answer: Kingdom (largest) and species (smallest).

21) What word is used for both "an area of military activity" and "an auditorium for viewing films and staged shows"?
   Answer: Theater.

22) According to the saying, what speaks louder than words?
   Answer: Actions.

23) Identify the following as a *simple*, *complex*, or *compound* sentence: "The book that is lying on the table belongs to my brother."
   Answer: Complex.

24) What is the sum of the measures of any 2 interior angles of an equilateral triangle?
   Answer: 120.

25) Which word designates "the study of the weather, atmosphere, and climate of the earth"?
Answer: Meteorology.

26) During which decades of the 20th century did WWII occur?
Answer: 1930s and 1940s (1939-1945; Or 4th and 5th decades).

27) Name the author of these children's books: *Superfudge*, *Tales of a Fourth Grade Nothing*, and *Fudge-A-Mania*.
Answer: Judy Blume.

28) Which term using the Latin root for "earth" is used to designate an enclosure in which small animals or small plants are kept?
Answer: Terrarium.

29) What is the measure of one of the central angles of a regular octagon?
Answer: 45 degrees.

30) Which term designates the soft, flexible tissue that protects the joints in the human body from shock?
Answer: Cartilage.

31) What is the capital of the country in which Melbourne is the second-largest city?
Answer: Canberra (Australia).

32) In which state was the Battle of Yorktown fought on October 17, 1781, to end the Revolutionary War?
Answer: Virginia.

33) Which ancient Chinese philosopher, known for his wisdom, wrote *The Analects*?
Answer: Confucius (or K'ung Fu-tse).

34) What is the sum of $2x^2 + 3x - 5$ and $x^2 - x + 7$?
Answer: $3x^2 + 2x + 2$.

35) What part of speech is the word *ouch*?
Answer: Interjection.

36) Mischievous students are frequently punished. Spell the word mischievous.
Answer: M-I-S-C-H-I-E-V-O-U-S.

37) According to the Bible, who became a high official in Egypt after interpreting dreams for the Pharaoh?
Answer: Joseph.

38) Who presides over the United States Senate?
Answer: The Vice President of the U.S. (or the present Vice President).

39) Which metallic element, whose symbol is Ag, is considered to be the most perfect known conductor of electricity and heat?
Answer: Silver.

40) What is the more common name for the star called Polaris?
Answer: North Star.

41) In which country was the Parthenon, the Doric temple of Athena, built on the Acropolis?
Answer: Greece.

42) Which term is used in music to designate any instrument whose sound is produced by striking or hitting?
Answer: Percussion.

43) Spell the singular form of the plural noun *criteria*.
Answer: C-R-I-T-E-R-I-O-N.

44) Give the year in which *Back to the Future, Part II* is set, or the year designated by the Roman numerals MMXV.
Answer: 2015.

45) Identify the first great Revolutionary War battle fought near Boston on June 17, 1775.
Answer: Battle of Bunker Hill (or Breed's Hill, where it was actually fought).

46) What term is used in meteorology to designate the dividing surface between 2 distinct air masses?
Answer: Front.

47) Which author, the subject of the biography *Dreams of Exile*, began his first novel, *Treasure Island*, at age 30?
Answer: Robert Louis Stevenson (the biographer is Ian Bell).

48) In Greek legend, which slave was not harmed by a lion in the arena because he had removed a thorn from the lion's paw?
Answer: Androcles.

49) Of length, width, area, and volume, which one is measured in cubic units?
Answer: Volume.

50) Which government body has the power to try and convict an impeached President?
Answer: Senate (2/3 vote is required for conviction).

51) Which term is used to designate all the plants of a specified region or time?
Answer: Flora.

52) What is another name for the snowman also called the "Yeti"?
Answer: Abominable Snowman.

53) What name designates the American Revolutionary War volunteers who together were ready to fight at a moment's notice?
Answer: Minutemen.

54) Of length, width, area, and volume, which one is measured in square units?
Answer: Area.

55) Who surrendered to whom at Appomattox Court House on April 9, 1865, to end the Civil War?
Answer: Robert E. Lee surrendered to Ulysses S. Grant.

56) Identify the mechanical device for fixing the speed at which a piece of music is to be played by marking time at a steady beat.
Answer: Metronome.

57) Name the 2 identical fat twins Alice meets in Lewis Carroll's *Through the Looking Glass.*
Answer: Tweedledum and Tweedledee.

58) In which U.S. state does the Mackinac Bridge link the upper and lower peninsulas?
Answer: Michigan.

59) Which term designates a long narrative poem about a legendary hero, such as Homer's *Odyssey*?
Answer: Epic.

60) In which Southern U.S. state is Marguerite Henry's novel *Misty of Chincoteague* set?
Answer: Virginia.

61) Which street in lower Manhattan in New York City is the main financial center of the U.S.?
Answer: Wall Street.

62) Which organization did Juliette Gordon Low found in Savannah, Georgia, in 1912?
Answer: Girl Scouts of America.

63) Which king founded the Persian empire: William, Cyrus, Hannibal, or Caesar?
Answer: Cyrus (the Great).

64) If a girl can walk 2½ miles in 2½ hours, how far can she walk in 5 hours at the same speed?
Answer: 5 miles.

65) Give the word for the "study of insects."
Answer: Entomology.

66) Which dinosaur, whose name means "tyrant-lizard king," was allegedly the most feared meat-eating dinosaur of its time?
Answer: Tyrannosaurus rex (or T-rex).

67) In what city does the United Nations have its headquarters?
Answer: New York City.

68) Identify the Alaska peak that is the highest in North America.
Answer: Mount McKinley.

69) What is the value of 2 raised to the zero power?
Answer: 1.

70) In which city is Fort Sumter located?
Answer: Charleston (South Carolina).

71) What is the more formal name for a kingdom or form of government having a king or queen who inherits the position and rules for life?
Answer: Monarchy.

72) Identify the mythical person of Hamelin, Germany, for whom the leader of the horses in the novel *Misty of Chincoteague* is named.
Answer: Pied Piper.

73) Which name identifies the mythological giant with one eye in the middle of its forehead?
Answer: Cyclops (Cyclopes).

74) If negative 7*b* equals 35, what does 14*b* equal?
Answer: Negative 70.

75) Which part of the human brain is the largest and controls the senses, thought, and conscious activities?
Answer: Cerebrum.

76) Name the Civil War ironclad called "a cheese box on a raft."
Answer: *Monitor*.

77) Which term is used to designate all the animals of a specified region or time?
Answer: Fauna.

78) What term is used in mathematics to designate the most frequently appearing number in a series of numbers?
Answer: Mode.

79) Which planet, the smallest in the solar system, was discovered by an astronomer in 1930?
Answer: Pluto (discovered by Clyde Tombaugh).

80) In which city is George Selden's *The Cricket in Times Square* set?
Answer: New York City.

81) Identify the Brazilian city whose name literally means "River of January."
Answer: Rio de Janeiro.

82) What is the length of one term of office for a member of the U.S. House of Representatives?
Answer: 2 years.

83) What is the name for the offspring of a lion and a lioness?
Answer: Cub.

84) What term refers to the ratio of the vertical change to the horizontal change between two points plotted on a line?
Answer: Slope.

85) Which American is remembered for saying in an August 28, 1963, speech at the Civil Rights "March on Washington": "I have a dream . . . ."?
Answer: Martin Luther King Jr.

86) Name the only country with which South Korea shares a border.
Answer: North Korea.

87) Identify the world's smallest bird, whose name comes from the sound made by its wings.
Answer: Hummingbird.

88) What is the minimum age set by the Constitution to be elected President of the United States?
Answer: 35 years of age.

89) 690 millimeters equals how many centimeters?
Answer: 69 centimeters.

90) If a person is *drowsy*, is he aggressive, quiet, talkative, or sleepy?
Answer: Sleepy.

CHAPTER SIX

1) Which New England state is located between New York and Rhode Island?
   Answer: Connecticut.

2) Name the great bell in the Parliament clock tower in London.
   Answer: Big Ben.

3) Name one of the 2 winners of the 1993 Nobel Peace Prize, who together negotiated the end of apartheid in South Africa.
   Answer: F.W. de Klerk or Nelson Mandela.

4) What is the square of the square of 1/2?
   Answer: 1/16.

5) Identify Captain Smollett's ship in *Treasure Island* that bears the same name as the island shared by Haiti and the Dominican Republic.
   Answer: Hispaniola.

6) What is the abbreviation for deoxyribonucleic acid, the constituent of living cell nuclei that determines individual hereditary characteristics?
   Answer: DNA.

7) Which state is the site of Yosemite Falls, the highest falls in North America?
   Answer: California.

8) Which country defeated the Arab forces in the Six-Day War of June 1967?
   Answer: Israel.

9) What percentage is the equivalent of 4/5?
   Answer: 80%.

10) Give the term for any of the many large divisions of Canada.
    Answer: Province.

11) Is Somalia on Africa's east, west, north, or south coast?
    Answer: East.

12) What is the basic unit of capacity or volume in the metric system?
    Answer: Liter.

13) In which European country is Roald Dahl's James Henry Trotter living when the novel *James and the Giant Peach* opens?
Answer: England.

14) If one family of 5 children is randomly selected, what is the probability that all 5 children in the family are females?
Answer: 1/32 (Or one out of thirty-two; do NOT accept "one to thirty-two").

15) Which of the following words identifies "a region near a place": *vicinity, severity, morality,* or *obesity*?
Answer: Vicinity.

16) Because of their brightly colored uniforms, what name was given to the British soldiers during the Revolutionary War?
Answer: Redcoats.

17) Name the English author of *Just So Stories, The Jungle Book,* and *Captains Courageous.*
Answer: Rudyard Kipling.

18) Name the black woman, an escaped slave, who conducted more than 300 slaves to freedom on the "Underground Railroad."
Answer: Harriet Tubman.

19) What is the more common name for *pertussis,* an acute infectious disease of the respiratory system?
Answer: Whooping cough.

20) Which kind of animal is Shiloh in a novel of the same name by Phyllis Reynolds Naylor?
Answer: Dog (a beagle).

21) Give the 2-word scientific name for the day in the Northern Hemisphere on which the sun shines for the fewest hours of the year, either December 21 or 22.
Answer: Winter solstice.

22) Which of the following verb forms cannot be used with the auxiliary verb *has*: swum, went, drunk, or raised?
Answer: Went (should be *gone*).

23) Which German mechanical engineer developed an internal combustion engine that uses oil as fuel? This kind of engine, used in heavy trucks and buses, is named for him.
Answer: Rudolf Diesel.

24) If carpeting costs $10 per square yard, what is the cost of carpeting a rectangular floor with dimensions 10 feet by 9 feet?
Answer: $100.

25) Which organization, founded by William Booth, rings bells in malls for donations at Christmas time?
Answer: Salvation Army.

26) Which word is used to describe an invasion that begins in the water and ends on land: hydraulic, supersonic, subterranean, or amphibious?
Answer: Amphibious.

27) Which planet has the most moons and is the 2nd largest planet in the solar system?
Answer: Saturn.

28) In which sea is the island of Corsica, the birthplace of Napoleon?
Answer: Mediterranean Sea.

29) How many square inches are there in a square foot?
Answer: 144 (square inches).

30) Of the 2 landlocked countries of South America, which one has its capital at Asunción?
Answer: Paraguay.

31) Which month-long European athletic event did American Greg LeMond win for the third time in 1990?
Answer: Tour de France.

32) Which Northern U.S. state has more inland water than any other state?
Answer: Alaska.

33) To which major blood group—A, B, AB, or O—does the universal donor belong?
Answer: O (because it contains no antigens).

34) Which number is next in the following geometric sequence: 1,4,16,...?
Answer: 64.

35) Which city is called "The Birthplace of the U.S." because the Declaration of Independence and the Constitution were adopted there?
Answer: Philadelphia.

36) In which Western state did Democrat Ben Nighthorse Campbell become the first Native American to win a U.S. Senate seat since 1929? This state's name is Spanish for "colored red."
Answer: Colorado.

37) What name does Alec Ramsay call the wild stallion in Walter Farley's novel *The Black Stallion*?
Answer: The Black.

38) Identify the imaginary line that runs through southern Greenland and the northern parts of Canada, Alaska, and Russia.
Answer: Arctic Circle.

39) Which author lived in a cabin he built in the woods on Walden Pond in Massachusetts?
Answer: Henry David Thoreau.

40) The moon is a satellite of Earth. What is the spelling of the word *satellite*?
Answer: S-A-T-E-L-L-I-T-E.

41) The system of taxonomy developed by Linnaeus used a binomial name from which language?
Answer: Latin.

42) In which U.S. state is Walt Morey's novel *Gentle Ben* set, primarily in Orca City?
Answer: Alaska.

43) What term designates "a natural, narrow channel that connects two larger bodies of water"?
Answer: Strait.

44) If a segment 80 inches long is divided into two smaller ones with ratio 3 to 2, what is the length of the smaller segment?
Answer: 32 inches.

45) Which French explorer, whose name identifies a lake, founded the Canadian city of Quebec?
Answer: Samuel de Champlain.

46) Name the first modern-day black professional baseball player to enter the major leagues, signed by the Brooklyn Dodgers in 1947.
Answer: Jackie Robinson.

47) Identify the breakfast food made from grain and named after the Roman goddess of agriculture.
Answer: Cereal (after Ceres).

48) Which U.S. city uses the phoenix as its symbol to represent the city's rebirth after the 1906 earthquake?
Answer: San Francisco.

49) What is the largest prime factor of 105?
Answer: 7.

50) Identify the major religion of the Middle East that observes a month of fasting called Ramadan.
Answer: Islam (or the Muslim religion).

51) Name Canada's westernmost province.
Answer: British Columbia.

52) Which one of the following pronouns is not plural: us, them, everyone, few?
Answer: Everyone.

53) Which geographical term designates "the broad, treeless plains of the arctic regions, having a permanently frozen subsoil"?
Answer: Tundra.

54) If x is a positive integer and x raised to the x power equals x, what is the value of x?
Answer: 1.

55) Which U.S. capital on the Susquehanna River was named after a Quaker whose son founded the city?
Answer: Harrisburg (Pennsylvania).

56) Identify the chain of huge underground caves in southeastern New Mexico.
Answer: Carlsbad Caverns.

57) Name Paul Bunyan's gigantic blue ox.
Answer: Babe.

58) Which medal is awarded for outstanding illustrations in children's books?
Answer: Caldecott Medal.

59) Name the hot, dry winds that frequently fan major firestorms in California and share their name with a Mexican general.
Answer: Santa Ana winds.

60) Which North Carolina city was awarded the first of 2 NFL expansion franchises?
Answer: Charlotte (its team began play in 1995 as the Panthers).

61) Which group of Caribbean islands, including St. Thomas and St. John, did the U.S. buy from Denmark in 1917?
Answer: Virgin Islands (for $25,000,000).

62) Name either the mythological father or son who escaped from the labyrinth by tying feathers joined with wax to their arms and flying away.
Answer: Daedalus or Icarus.

63) Identify the contagious fungal infection causing cracks in the feet.
Answer: Athlete's foot.

64) If 2 legs of a right triangle have lengths 1 and 5, what is the exact length of the hypotenuse?
Answer: Square root of 26.

65) Who was the first Roman Catholic U.S. President?
Answer: John Kennedy.

66) What name is given to the place where 2 or more bones in the human body meet?
Answer: Joint.

67) Identify the capital of the 2nd largest U.S. state in area.
Answer: Austin (Texas).

68) What is the 2-word term designating the highest expertise in the martial arts?
Answer: Black belt.

69) What name is given to the point of intersection of two sides of a polygon?
Answer: Vertex.

70) How many labors was the mythological Hercules required to perform?
Answer: 12.

71) In which state is Fred Gipson's *Old Yeller* set?
Answer: Texas.

72) Name "The Birdwoman" who accompanied Lewis and Clark on their expedition.
Answer: Sacagawea.

73) Which Charleston, South Carolina, school, whose name means "a stronghold," was Shannon Faulkner the first woman to attend?
Answer: The Citadel.

74) If twice the diameter of a circle is 12 feet long, how long is the radius of the same circle?
Answer:　3 feet.

75) On which temperature scale is 212° the boiling point for water?
Answer:　Fahrenheit (for Gabriel Daniel Fahrenheit; most countries uses Celsius scale).

76) When one country imposes penalties to cut a trade imbalance, are such penalties referred to as *leverages*, *sanctions*, *entitlements*, or *perks*?
Answer:　Sanctions.

77) Who served as the first chief justice of the U.S. Supreme Court?
Answer:　John Jay.

78) What term containing the Greek root for "name" designates either of 2 words with the same sound and often the same spelling but different meanings?
Answer:　Homonym.

79) What is the pastime or occupation of sportsmen who are sometimes called anglers?
Answer:　Fishermen.

80) Which person nominated for the Nobel Peace Prize in 1994 was one of the 3 delegates sent by President Clinton to Haiti in the same year?
Answer:　(Former President) Jimmy Carter.

81) Into which planet did fragments of a giant comet named Shoemaker-Levy 9 slam with great force in July 1994?
Answer:　Jupiter.

82) Which author, who created the classic *The Chronicles of Narnia*, is the subject of the play *Shadowlands*?
Answer:　C.S. Lewis.

83) In which European capital did celebrations on August 25, 1994, mark the day 50 years ago when Nazi occupation crumbled and Charles de Gaulle proclaimed victory?
Answer:　Paris.

84) Give the 8th term of the sequence whose first 7 terms are the following: 1, 2, 3, 5, 8, 13, 21.
Answer:　34.

85) Which European mountain is the highest in the Alps?
Answer:　Mont Blanc.

86) Which of the following identifies the calendar used in the U.S. and other Western nations: Octavian, Mercadian, Gregorian, or Julian?
Answer: Gregorian.

87) Of loon, kiwi, emu, or dodo, which bird is extinct?
Answer: Dodo.

88) Which of the following gods or goddesses are INCORRECTLY paired as Roman and Greek equivalents: Jupiter / Zeus; Bacchus / Dionysus; Apollo / Apollo; or Diana / Aphrodite?
Answer: Diana / Aphrodite (Venus / Aphrodite is the correct pairing).

89) How many cubic feet are there in a cubic yard?
Answer: 27 (cubic feet).

90) Identify the prime minister whose surname designates the military rank between captain and lieutenant colonel.
Answer: John Major (of Great Britain).

CHAPTER SEVEN

1) Which name identifies both the device used to draw a circle and the device that determines the direction of the north magnetic pole?
   Answer: Compass.

2) A sudden neck twist can trigger the third leading cause of death in the U.S. Name this affliction caused by a blockage or rupture of a blood vessel to the brain.
   Answer: Stroke.

3) A 14-year-old from Tennessee correctly spelled "kamikaze" to win the 66th National Spelling Bee. Spell *kamikaze*.
   Answer: K-A-M-I-K-A-Z-E.

4) If a train traveling at a constant speed of 35 mph takes 26 hours to travel from Chicago to New York, how fast must the train travel to make the trip in 20 hours?
   Answer: 45½ mph.

5) Name the bay that lies between India and Myanmar, formerly called Burma.
   Answer: Bay of Bengal.

6) In which decade did the U.S. launch its first successful satellite, the *Explorer*?
   Answer: 1950s (on January 31, 1958).

7) Identify the system developed by Samuel Morse to send coded signals over wire.
   Answer: Telegraph.

8) Criticized for its handling of the Hurricane Andrew disaster, which federal agency was quickly on hand after the 1994 Los Angeles earthquake to coordinate disaster relief?
   Answer: Federal Emergency Management Agency (accept FEMA).

9) What sort of line has an undefined slope?
   Answer: Vertical (line).

10) Name the folk hero of the Southwest who allegedly dug the Rio Grande and invented tarantulas as a joke on his friends.
    Answer: Pecos Bill.

11) Because the rocket sent to study the moon in 1994 disappeared when the encounter was over, it was named for which miner's daughter who is "lost and gone forever" according to a folk song?
Answer: Clementine.

12) What word, meaning "pertaining to finances," is used to name the business year as opposed to the calendar year: *caustic, ecumenical, fiscal* or *frugal?*
Answer: Fiscal.

13) Which country celebrates its founding as a British colony on January 26, the 1788 date when a shipload of convicts arrived at Botany Bay? It is south of the equator.
Answer: Australia (on the same day, they went to Port Jackson, present-day Sydney).

14) A gasoline gauge registers 1/8 full. After 12 gallons are added to the tank, the gauge registers 7/8 full. What's the capacity of the tank?
Answer: 16 gallons.

15) Henry Clay first said in a Senate speech on February 7, 1839, "I'd rather be right than be president." Name the "Bluegrass State" which he represented.
Answer: Kentucky.

16) In which ancient empire were 2 Christian martyrs named Valentine said to have been beheaded on the Flamian Way, one on February 14, A.D. 269?
Answer: Rome (the other, in a later but unknown year).

17) Which body elected John Quincy Adams as U.S. President on February 9, 1825, after no candidate received an electoral majority in the national election of 1824?
Answer: House of Representatives.

18) For which entertainer did the Navy announce in 1994 it was naming its new class of cargo ships to thank him for years of entertaining U.S. troops?
Answer: Bob Hope.

19) Give the standard number of separate bones in the human skeleton, the equivalent of 14 squared plus 10.
Answer: 206.

20) Identify the mythological hero who caused the death of the Sphinx by answering her riddle.
Answer: Oedipus.

21) What is the scientific name for man in the binomial system, using genus followed by species?
Answer: *Homo sapiens.*

22) Who assumed the English throne on the death of King George VI on February 6, 1952?
Answer: Elizabeth II.

23) The last survivor of the 6 servicemen pictured in the Pulitzer Prize-winning WWII photo that was the model for a Marine memorial in Arlington, Virginia, died in 1994. On which island were these servicemen raising the flag when the photo was taken?
Answer: Iwo Jima (photo was model for the Marine Corps War Memorial).

24) If a drug costs $1.50 in Britain, how much would it cost at a 60% increase in the U.S.?
Answer: $2.40.

25) Give the 3 letters that identify the important plant nutrients commonly provided by fertilizers.
Answer: N-P-K (Nitrogen, phosphorus, and potassium).

26) In 1995, the first dancers' strike in the 218-year history of the Bolshoi Theater resulted in the firings of some of the company's biggest stars. In which country is the Bolshoi located?
Answer: Russia (the strike was over the resignation of the artistic director).

27) Which phrase, like "to smoke a peacepipe," is drawn from Indian custom and means "to stop fighting, to lay down arms, to make peace"?
Answer: Bury the hatchet.

28) Name the only Cabinet title not including the word *secretary*.
Answer: Attorney general.

29) Find the arithmetic mean of the following data set: 4, 5, 9, 4, 1, 10, 5, 1, 6.
Answer: 5.

30) Who became the emperor of Japan in 1989 upon the death of Emperor Hirohito?
Answer: Emperor Akihito.

31) *American Heritage* magazine once featured what may be the first photographic portrait of Abraham Lincoln, a photo taken in 1843 while he was serving in the legislature in which state nicknamed the "Land of Lincoln"?
Answer: Illinois.

32) Which Amendment to the U.S. Constitution, ratified on February 10, 1967, provides for presidential succession and disability?
Answer: 25th Amendment.

33) Which city was awarded the 28th NBA franchise, the first outside the U.S.? The franchise played its first season in 1995-96 in the SkyDome, also the home of the American League's Blue Jays.
Answer: Toronto.

34) Find the modes of the following data set: 4, 5, 9, 4, 1, 10, 5, 1, 3.
Answer: 1, 4, 5 (NOTE: must have all three, but they may be given in any order).

35) According to a 1994 article in the *Journal of the AMA*, caffeinated coffee's contribution to osteoporosis can be negated by consuming which element found in milk?
Answer: Calcium.

36) Which spiral galaxy outside the Milky Way and over 2 million miles away can be seen without a telescope by people in the Northern Hemisphere?
Answer: Andromeda (only 2 other galaxies can be seen without a telescope).

37) A senator of Texas was acquitted of ethics charges in 1994 when prosecutors said they could not proceed without a ruling permitting the admission of key evidence. Spell *proceed.*
Answer: P-R-O-C-E-E-D.

38) What phrase from baseball did President Clinton use at his 1994 State of the Union address to describe the mandatory life sentence he favors for 3-time violent felons?
Answer: "Three strikes (and you're out)."

39) According to the AHA, the number of Americans with high blood pressure has dropped to about 50 million in the early 1990s, from about 63 million in 1983. Is high blood pressure called psoriasis, hypertension, anemia, or gingivitis?
Answer: Hypertension.

40) Which country did President Nixon visit in 1972, even though it was not then diplomatically recognized by the U.S.? He arrived in its capital, known for its Tiananmen Square, on February 21.
Answer: People's Republic of China.

41) Name the U.S. state whose forests on the Olympic Peninsula are among the rainiest areas of the earth.
Answer: Washington.

42) Which Asian country was chosen to host the 1998 Winter Olympics to be held in Nagano?
Answer: Japan (in 1972, Japan hosted the Winter Games in Sapporo).

43) Which day of the week completes the name of _____ *Evening Post*, the publication for which Norman Rockwell painted many covers depicting American life?
Answer: *Saturday.*

44) What is the area of a rhombus whose base is 12 inches and whose corresponding height is 8 inches?
Answer: 96 square inches.

45) Which California city was chosen as the host city for the 1996 Republican National Convention? It lies close to the Mexican border, not far from Tijuana.
Answer: San Diego (Democrats chose Chicago).

46) Give either of the 2 acceptable degree readings for north on a compass.
Answer: 0 or 360 (east is 90; south is 180; west is 270).

47) Who hosted the 1994 Oscars? She was the 1st black star to host the awards show solo and the 1st woman to emcee it without a co-host.
Answer: Whoopi Goldberg.

48) On February 19, 1942, President Franklin D. Roosevelt issued the executive order for the legal detention of which group of Americans?
Answer: Japanese-Americans.

49) By what factor is the area of a circle multiplied if its radius is doubled?
Answer: 4.

50) Which country on the North Sea borders both France and Germany?
Answer: Belgium.

51) In 1994, a 146-year-old opera house in Barcelona with the world's 2nd largest operatic stage was destroyed by fire. In which Italian city is La Scala, the world's largest operatic stage?
Answer: Milan.

52) Which planet was discovered by a Lowell Observatory astronomer in Arizona, on February 18, 1930? Charon is its one known satellite.
Answer: Pluto (found by Clyde Tombaugh at Flagstaff, AZ).

53) Name the Nobel Peace Prize winner whose birthday was first observed as a federal holiday on the third Monday in January in 1986.
Answer: Martin Luther King Jr.

54) One-half of one number is the same as three times a second number. Twice the second added to the first is 80. Find the numbers.
Answer: 60 and 10 (must have both).

55) In which year did investors begin panic selling of stocks on October 24, dumping more than 13 million shares?
Answer: 1929 (October 24 became known as "Black Thursday").

56) In 1994, protesters dumped which product into Washington, D.C., streets to protest the use of the new genetically engineered hormone BST, or bovine somatotropin?
Answer: Milk.

57) Name King Arthur's sword, which, according to one legend, the Lady of the Lake retrieved from a lake and gave to Arthur.
Answer: Excalibur.

58) Complete the following proverb: "Don't put the _____ before the horse," meaning "do things in the correct order."
Answer: "cart."

59) What is the source of all light that comes from a comet?
Answer: Sun.

60) Which country launched the ground war called "The Mother of All Battles" on February 23, 1991, in leading the Allies against Iraq?
Answer: United States.

61) On January 23, 1849, which of the following was the first U.S. woman to receive a medical degree: Elizabeth Blackwell, Shirley Chisholm, Sally Ride, or Betsy Ross?
Answer: Elizabeth Blackwell.

62) According to the 22nd amendment, ratified on February 27, 1951, how many terms may a U.S. president serve?
Answer: 2 terms.

63) In which Rocky Mountain capital city did a $4 billion airport replace Stapleton Airport in 1995 after numerous delays? This city is known as "the Gateway to the Rockies."
Answer: Denver (Denver International).

64) Expressed in simplest terms, what is square root of 2 times square root of 8?
Answer: 4.

65) Name the antislavery newspaper published by Frederick Douglass, the Maryland-born leading spokesman of American blacks in the 1800s. Its title is another name for Polaris, or the Pole Star.
Answer: *North Star*.

66) Which geographical term designates "a more or less conical hill or mountain from which steam, gasses, ashes, or molten rocks are ejected" during periods when it is active?
Answer: Volcano.

67) According to the proverb, what door is it silly to lock or close after the horse has been stolen, meaning "it's silly to take precautions after the damage has already been done"?
Answer: Barn door.

68) Identify the stringed instrument whose name is a homonym for a verb used with *on* to mean "to dwell upon, or talk about to an excessive degree."
Answer: Harp ("to harp on").

69) Expressed in simplest terms, what is the square root of 12 times the square root of 1/12?
Answer: 1 (do NOT accept square root of 1).

70) Name the wedge-shaped writing invented by the Sumerians.
Answer: Cuneiform.

71) Which of the following is NOT a shade of green: *chartreuse, emerald, jade,* or *sienna*?
Answer: Sienna (a reddish-brown).

72) Identify the largest Indian tribe in the U.S., with 200,000 members and with the largest reservation in the U.S., covering 17 million acres in Arizona, New Mexico, and Utah.
Answer: Navajo (Navaho).

73) In which mountain range in Turkey, bearing the same name as the second sign of the zodiac, was the world's oldest tin mine discovered in 1994?
Answer: Taurus Mountains.

74) What is the slope of the line with the equation $2x - 3y = 2$?
Answer: 2/3.

75) In 1994, eleven Branch Davidians were acquitted of murder in the 1993 raid that left 4 federal agents dead near Waco in which state?
Answer: Texas.

76) What is the term for one of two or more atoms of the same element with different atomic weights?
Answer: Isotope.

77) Which of the following words has an Atlanta broadcaster popularized to indicate "an abundant supply of" traffic problems: *antithesis, blight, labyrinth,* or *plethora*?
Answer: Plethora (as in "a plethora of wrecks").

78) Give the Spanish name for sun-dried bricks used to make dwellings in the southwestern United States and in Mexico.
Answer: Adobe.

79) With a tenfold increase of motion for every increase of 1 on the Richter scale, how much more powerful is an earthquake registering 6 than one measuring 4?
Answer: 100 times.

80) By Presidential proclamation, October 31 is National UNICEF Day. Give the name of this U.N. agency.
Answer: United Nations Children's Fund (accept United Nations International Children's Emergency Fund).

81) Which stadium in which city was known as "The House That Ruth Built" when it was opened in 1923?
Answer: Yankee Stadium in New York City.

82) Name the Nebraska-born Congressman from Michigan who filled in as Vice President when Spiro Agnew resigned his post.
Answer: Gerald Ford.

83) Name 2 of the 3 Canadian provinces with 2-word names.
   Answer: British Columbia, New Brunswick, and Nova Scotia.

84) What number increased by 30% of itself equals 39?
   Answer: 30.

85) Which 1989 addition in the central courtyard of the museum in Paris called the Louvre takes trained Alpine mountain climbers to clean?
   Answer: Glass pyramid.

86) Name the parasitic disease, widespread in tropical and subtropical areas, that is the leading tropical killer in history. It is transmitted by the bite of the female *Anopheles* mosquito.
   Answer: Malaria.

87) Which term designates "the public square or marketplace of an ancient Roman city"?
   Answer: Forum.

88) Which word completes this proverb adapted from the Sermon on the Mount: "Don't hide your light under a _____"?
   Answer: "bushel."

89) What is 3 times the square of 6?
   Answer: 108.

90) Who succeeded King William IV of Great Britain in 1837?
   Answer: Queen Victoria.

CHAPTER EIGHT

1) Give the acronym for acquired immune deficiency syndrome.
   Answer: AIDS.

2) Name the writer and publisher of the following aphorisms: "God helps them that help themselves" and "The heart of the fool is in his mouth."
   Answer: Benjamin Franklin (accept Franklin's pen name "Poor Richard," or Richard Saunders).

3) Which country is sometimes referred to as the "Subcontinent of Asia"? This country was a British colony from the late 1700s until it became an independent country in 1947.
   Answer: India.

4) Identify the only positive integer whose cube root equals its square root.
   Answer: One (1).

5) A Supreme Court Justice announced in 1994 that he could no longer support the death penalty for any crime. What word completes the term _____ *punishment* to designate the death penalty?
   Answer: Capital.

6) Give the more common name for a tsunami, or the kind of natural disaster that killed at least 36 people in Nicaragua in 1992.
   Answer: Tidal wave (resulting from an offshore earthquake at sea or volcanic eruption.)

7) Name the Rudyard Kipling novel about a teenager's adventures on a New England fishing boat.
   Answer: *Captains Courageous*.

8) In which kind of competition did the U.S.'s Bobby Fischer defeat Boris Spassky in 1992 in Yugoslavia despite U.N. sanctions imposed because of fighting in its former republic of Bosnia?
   Answer: Chess.

9) Find the 2 numbers whose sum is 7 and whose difference is 9.
   Answer: 8 and negative 1.

10) In 1992, which country elected Fidel Ramos as president to succeed Corazon Aquino in an election riddled with vote tampering accusations?
Answer: Philippines.

11) Which Mideast country gave $10 million to the Red Cross, the single largest donation since Hurricane Andrew struck? Operation Desert Storm freed this country from Iraq.
Answer: Kuwait.

12) "I am the last President of the United States," said President James Buchanan in December 1860, following which state's secession from the Union?
Answer: South Carolina's.

13) On May 12, 1992, a record 32 people reached the summit of the world's tallest mountain. Name this mountain.
Answer: Mount Everest (at 29,108 feet, located in Nepal and Tibet).

14) What is a 15% tip on a bill of $14.80?
Answer: $2.22.

15) In 1992, in which country did the world's oldest known bound book, a 1,600-year-old Book of Psalms, go on display at the Coptic Museum? This country is known for having the world's longest river.
Answer: Egypt (the river is the Nile).

16) Name the Louisiana crop that was most heavily damaged by Hurricane Andrew, with $90 million in losses. Louisiana grows 20% of the nation's supply of this sweet grass.
Answer: Sugar cane.

17) Name Robert Louis Stevenson's fictional doctor who is concerned with the problems of good and evil in his laboratory in London.
Answer: Dr. Henry Jekyll.

18) What term is used to designate a tax, or duty, on imports or exports?
Answer: Tariff.

19) Which word is used to designate "the condition of the atmosphere at any particular moment or place, with respect to wind, pressure, temperature, and humidity"?
Answer: Weather.

20) Name the historic London residence of monarchs where, in 1992, women took part for the first time in the 155-year-old changing of the guard as members of a Royal Air Force band.
Answer: Buckingham Palace.

21) Don Wetzel, who pioneered the ATM bank card, was listed in *Money* magazine's "hall of fame" for innovations. What does ATM stand for?
Answer: Automatic teller machine.

22) In 1992, in which state did Dianne Feinstein and Barbara Boxer win U.S. Senate seats? It has the most representatives in the U.S. House.
Answer: California.

23) Name the largest New England state in area.
Answer: Maine.

24) Which number is the 7th term in following sequence: 1, 2, 4, 7, 11, 16, . . .?
Answer: 22.

25) In which Asian nation, where Hindi is an official language, do more than one million children work up to 18 hours a day in carpet factories?
Answer: India.

26) Name the British naturalist who wrote *On the Origin of Species*.
Answer: Charles Darwin.

27) The name of which secret kingdom completes the title of Katherine Paterson's book *Bridge to* _____?
Answer: *Terabithia*.

28) Who became the king of England following the Battle of Hastings in 1066?
Answer: William (or William I or William the Conqueror).

29) What is the sum of the prime factors of 14?
Answer: 9 (2 + 7).

30) Name the Bosnian capital and former Winter Olympics site where Europe's bloodiest fighting since WWII occurred in the 1990s. It was formerly a part of Yugoslavia.
Answer: Sarajevo.

31) Archaeological finds of 1992, coupled with those of years earlier, make Sepphoris, 4 miles from Nazareth, the richest site of mosaics in which country?
Answer: Israel.

32) Name the city in whose harbor the "Star-Spangled Banner" was written and in which it was sung for the first time on October 19, 1814.
Answer: Baltimore.

33) Name the "Gopher State" to which Garrison Keillor returned in 1992 to perform his monologue about the fictional town of Lake Wobegon after a 5-year, self-imposed exile.
Answer: Minnesota.

34) What is negative 2 times negative 2 times negative 2?
Answer: Negative 8.

35) In 1965, when new voting districts were drawn to give blacks and Hispanics a voting majority in nearly 2 dozen more House districts, under which President was the Voting Rights Act, the basis for this redistricting, passed?
Answer: Lyndon Johnson.

36) What term for "first formed" is given to the living matter of cells?
Answer: Protoplasm.

37) The Hawaiian island of Kauai is known as the "Garden Island." Spell *Hawaiian*.
Answer: H-A-W-A-I-I-A-N.

38) Name the Greek god of the sea.
Answer: Poseidon.

39) Which planet is known as the Red Planet?
Answer: Mars.

40) In 1992, from which Caribbean country did Russia withdraw the last of its military units that had been on the island since the 1962 missile crisis?
Answer: Cuba.

41) How many months of the year have exactly 30 days?
Answer: 4 (September, April, June, and November).

42) Give the surname of the child named Virginia who was the first child of English parents born in the New World.
Answer: (Virginia) Dare.

43) Which state led by Governor Pete Wilson is called the "Golden State"?
Answer: California.

44) How many square feet are there in a square yard?
Answer: 9.

45) Name the Dallas billionaire whom citizens placed on all 50 state ballots in 1992 despite his contention that he was not a candidate.
Answer: H. Ross Perot.

46) What is the term for a natural hot spring that periodically ejects a spurt of water and steam?
Answer: Geyser.

47) Give the title of E.B. White's book whose first line is "Where's Papa going with that ax?"
Answer: *Charlotte's Web.*

48) Name the Roman god of war.
Answer: Mars.

49) If you misspell 20 words from a list of 80, what percentage of the words did you spell correctly?
Answer: 75%.

50) Which South American country did Portuguese explorer Pedro Alvares Cabral discover on April 22, 1500, after allegedly being blown off course on an expedition to India?
Answer: Brazil.

51) In 1992, which student newspaper announced George Bush as the winner of its poll that had picked the correct winner in the last 9 presidential elections?
Answer: *Weekly Reader* (first published in 1928 under the title *My Weekly Reader*).

52) Identify the 36th U.S. President, one whose middle name is Baines.
Answer: Lyndon B. Johnson.

53) Which desert east of Los Angeles was the epicenter of a 1992 earthquake, the strongest to hit the state in 40 years?
Answer: Mojave Desert.

54) What is the exact circumference of a circle with a diameter of 1?
Answer: *Pi.*

55) Steve McAuliffe is the husband of the teacher killed in which spacecraft explosion?
Answer: *Challenger* (Christa McAuliffe was the teacher).

56) The summer of 1992 was the third coolest in the U.S. since records were first kept in 1895. Name the Philippine volcano whose eruption may have caused some of the temperature drop.
Answer: Mount Pinatubo (the 1992 summer was also the third wettest in the U.S.).

57) What word designates a government pardon of political offenders and comes from the same Greek root as a word for "a total loss of memory"?
Answer: Amnesty (*amnesia* means "a loss of memory").

58) Which mythological god, called *Jove* by the Romans, was given the title of *Optimus Maximus*?
Answer: Jupiter (*Optimus Maximus* means "best and greatest").

59) Identify the branch of biology dealing with the animal kingdom and animal life.
Answer: Zoology.

60) Name the 2 women who have held the British crown in the twentieth century.
Answer: Victoria and Elizabeth (II).

61) Which presidential candidate did 11-year-old Grace Bedell persuade to grow a beard, telling him she would then encourage her brothers to vote for him in the 1860 election?
Answer: Abraham Lincoln.

62) In which Virginia town did Lord Cornwallis surrender more than 7,000 English and Hessian soldiers to George Washington on October 19, 1781?
Answer: Yorktown.

63) Into which body of water does the Missouri River directly empty at its mouth?
Answer: Mississippi River.

64) What percentage of 65 is 39?
Answer: 60%.

65) Name the state where a movie cameraman was rescued in 1992 from Kilauea, a volcano on the southeastern slope of Mauna Loa.
Answer: Hawaii.

66) Name the 2nd planet from the sun.
Answer: Venus.

67) Complete the title of the 1943 film _____ *Come Home* with the name of the only animal, a collie, profiled in *Jane and Michael Stern's Encyclopedia of Pop Culture*.
Answer: Lassie (the film starred Elizabeth Taylor and Roddy McDowall).

68) In 1975, Elizabeth Seton became the first native-born American to be canonized. Does to be *canonized* mean to be executed, buried with a 21-gun salute, declared a saint, or installed as a public official?
Answer: Declared a saint.

69) If the product of 2 consecutive negative integers is 12, what's the larger integer?
Answer: Negative 3.

70) Which country detonated its first atomic bomb on September 22, 1949?
Answer: Soviet Union.

71) Give the nationality of Alfred Nobel, the inventer of dynamite and the founder of the Nobel prizes.
Answer: Swedish.

72) In which decade did Charles Lindbergh make the first solo trans-Atlantic flight on May 20-21, flying from New York to Paris?
Answer: 1920s (1927).

73) Despite protests, Gov. Pedro Rosello signed a bill in the early 1990s making English the official language in which predominantly Spanish-speaking U.S. territory?
Answer: Puerto Rico.

74) President Bush once proposed cutting the pay of top federal officials, including himself, by 10%. What would he have earned with a cut of 10% of his salary of $200,000?
Answer: $180,000.

75) Name the landmark 1973 abortion case that was narrowly upheld by the Supreme Court in 1992, an action denounced by both pro-choice and pro-life forces.
Answer: *Roe v. Wade.*

76) Two California campgrounds were briefly closed in 1992 after officials found a mouse that died of the same deadly disease that destroyed a fourth of the population of Europe in the 1300s. Name this deadly disease.
Answer: Bubonic plague (also known as the Black Death).

77) Which type of sentence has one independent clause and one or more dependent (subordinate) clauses?
Answer: Complex.

78) Which instrument did Italian virtuoso Niccolò Paganini play with such dexterity and technical brilliance that he was thought to be in league with the devil?
Answer: Violin.

79) Medical scientists have recommended that the familiar gauge of measuring fever be discarded for a morning oral reading of 99 degrees and an evening reading of 100 degrees. What has been accepted as the normal temperature since 1868?
Answer: 98.6 degrees.

80) Which U.S. President joined Leonid Brezhnev in issuing the Moscow Communiqué in 1972 during the first ever presidential visit to Moscow?
Answer: Richard Nixon.

81) Which college in Cambridge, Massachusetts, held its first commencement exercises on September 23, 1642?
Answer: Harvard.

82) Who became the first president of the Republic of Texas on October 22, 1836? The most populous city in Texas is named for him.
Answer: Sam Houston.

83) On October 23, 1989, which Eastern European country declared itself independent 33 years after the Soviets crushed a revolt against Communist rule? Its capital is Budapest.
Answer: Hungary.

84) What name is given to 2 angles whose measures have a sum of 180 degrees?
Answer: Supplementary angles.

85) In which U.S. state do all citizens receive a share of the state's oil wealth? Its motto is "North to the Future."
Answer: Alaska.

86) For which German-born inventor is the gas burner used for heating substances in science laboratories named?
Answer: Bunsen (burner).

87) One who writes poetry is called a poet. What is the term for one who writes plays?
Answer: Playwright (accept dramatist).

88) Some cities protested the laying off of city employees for a day to reduce the budget deficit. Spell *deficit*.
Answer: D-E-F-I-C-I-T.

89) In lowest terms, what is the mixed number for 24 over 9?
Answer: 2⅔.

90) In which country did the German Luftwaffe wage its heaviest daylight bombing on September 15, 1940, a date said to have been the turning point against Hitler's siege of the country when the Royal Air Force downed 185 enemy planes?
Answer: Britain (in the Battle of Britain).

CHAPTER NINE

1) Which 2 farm animals are mentioned in the nursery rhyme about Little Boy Blue?
   Answer: Sheep and cow.

2) In which state did Governor Ross Barnett personally bar a black student, James Meredith, from entering the university in 1962? Its capital is Jackson.
   Answer: Mississippi.

3) Name the first U.S. President to ride in an auto (1902), go underwater in a submarine (1905), and fly in an airplane (1910). A WWII President shares his surname.
   Answer: Theodore Roosevelt.

4) Completely factor the following: $2t^2 - 50$.
   Answer: $2(t + 5)(t - 5)$ [order does not matter].

5) In a 1992 U.N. speech, ousted President Jean-Bertrand Aristide denounced the Vatican as the only state in the world to recognize the government that overthrew him. Name Aristide's Caribbean country, part of the island of Hispaniola.
   Answer: Haiti.

6) What name is given to a raised bank of silt or other material deposited by running water along a river?
   Answer: Levee (levée; accept natural levee).

7) Give the word from Revelation 16:16 for "a place where the final battle between the forces of good and evil will be fought."
   Answer: Armageddon.

8) "Cleanliness is next to godliness" is a saying often mistakenly attributed to the Bible. Name the founder of Methodism who actually said it.
   Answer: John Wesley.

9) How many degrees are there in one-half of a quadrant of a circle?
   Answer: 45 degrees.

10) In which square in Beijing did the People's Army open fire on unarmed protestors on June 4, 1989?
    Answer: Tiananmen Square.

11) Give the months in which Mother's Day and Father's day are celebrated.
Answer: May and June, respectively.

12) The Presidential election of 1800 is the only one to have resulted in a tie in the electoral college. Name one of the 2 men who received 73 votes each.
Answer: Thomas Jefferson or Aaron Burr.

13) Which Canadian city in Alberta hosted the 1988 Winter Olympic Games?
Answer: Calgary.

14) What is the probability that all 4 children in a randomly selected 4-child family will be girls?
Answer: 1/16 (do NOT accept "one to sixteen").

15) Name the African National Congress leader whose praise for the Chinese government during a speech at Beijing University drew an icy silence from students whose comrades were shot down or beaten at Tiananmen Square in 1989.
Answer: Nelson Mandela.

16) Name the light-sensitive tissue in the inner eyeball that acts as the principal focus of the eye's lens.
Answer: Retina.

17) In which state is Washington Irving's short story entitled "Rip Van Winkle" set in the Catskill Mountains?
Answer: New York.

18) Give the term for "obstructive, lengthy speechmaking," such as a 15-hour speech protesting a tax bill in the U.S. Senate.
Answer: Filibuster.

19) Which Greek of the 5th-4th century B.C. is known as the "Father of Medicine"?
Answer: Hippocrates.

20) In which century did Costa Rica, El Salvador, Guatemala, Honduras, and Nicaragua declare independence from Spain on September 15?
Answer: 19th century (in 1821).

21) The Canadian flag was mistakenly flown upside down in opening ceremonies of Game 2 in the 1992 World Series. What is pictured on the Canadian flag?
Answer: Maple leaf (President Bush and the Marines who carried the flag apologized).

22) Name the 2 Democrats who served as U.S. President from 1933 to 1953.
Answer: Franklin Roosevelt and Harry S Truman.

23) Identify the U.S. state whose motto is "Liberty and Union, Now and Forever, one and inseparable." Its capital is named after a German chancellor.
Answer: North Dakota (its capital is Bismarck).

24) President William Taft served on the U.S. Supreme Court after his term of office. How many justices make up this court, or how many months is 3/4 of a year?
Answer: 9.

25) Which major-league baseball team was purchased by a Japanese-led group in 1992? The team is known as the Mariners.
Answer: Seattle (Mariners).

26) What name is given to the area of earth piled up at the mouth of a river? Its name is derived from the Greek letter whose triangular shape it resembles.
Answer: Delta.

27) From which Jonathan Swift book does the word *Lilliputian* for "a very small person" come?
Answer: *Gulliver's Travels.*

28) Which term for a title, brief description, or key accompanying an illustration or map also identifies a person whose deeds are talked about in his own time?
Answer: Legend.

29) What is the value of 2 to the 5th power?
Answer: 32.

30) On September 28, 1542, explorer Juan Rodriguez Cabrillo became the European discoverer of California when he sailed into the harbor of which southern California city named for a saint?
Answer: San Diego.

31) Give the grammatical term for "a word that expresses emotion and has no grammatical relation to other words in the sentence."
Answer: Interjection.

32) The Great Seal of the United States was first used on a document in September 1782. Give the English translation of its inscription *E pluribus unum.*
Answer: Out of many, one (accept "one out of many" or "from the many, one").

33) Spell the name of the country in which Mount Pinatubo erupted in 1991.
Answer: P-H-I-L-I-P-P-I-N-E-S.

34) If negative 9*b* equals 108, what does 2*b* equal?
Answer: Negative 24.

35) In 1992, from which country's oil sales abroad did the U.N., in its first seizure of a country's money, confiscate $1 billion to compensate victims in Kuwait, pay for U.N. weapons inspections, and give aid to dissident Kurds and Shiites?
Answer: Iraq's.

36) What name is given to hot liquid rock beneath the earth's surface from which igneous rock is formed?
Answer: Magma.

37) A black man considered by others to be subservient to whites is often referred to as an Uncle Tom, a reference to the leading character in *Uncle Tom's Cabin*. Who wrote this novel?
Answer: Harriet Beecher Stowe.

38) Name the American primitive painter born Anna Mary Robertson who began late in life painting gaily colored pictures of the countryside.
Answer: Grandma Moses.

39) Identify the muscular tube through which food passes from the lower part of the pharynx to the stomach.
Answer: Esophagus (accept gullet).

40) Which 13-letter word beginning with the letter *R* designates the joining of East and West Germany, a 1990 event following the removal of the Berlin Wall?
Answer: Reunification.

41) Which Olympic sport features the butterfly and the Australian crawl?
Answer: Swimming.

42) On which day in June 1777 did John Adams introduce the resolution that gave the U.S. flag 13 stripes and 13 stars?
Answer: June 14 (Flag Day).

43) Which Wonder of the Ancient World was probably built by King Nebuchadnezzar near modern Baghdad in Iraq and irrigated by water from the Euphrates River?
Answer: Hanging Gardens of Babylon.

44) What number has the property that 6 more than 4 times the number is 54?
Answer: 12.

45) In which Midwest city is the Gateway Arch?
Answer: St. Louis.

46) What color results when yellow and red pigments are mixed?
Answer: Orange.

47) Identify the following sentence as *simple, compound, complex*, or *compound-complex*: Grapefruit and oranges are usually plentiful and at times may even be cheap.
Answer: Simple.

48) Artist Frederic Remington is known for his paintings and sculptures of cowboys and Indians, particularly his statue *Bronco Buster*. Name the brownish alloy comprised primarily of copper and tin of which this statue is made.
Answer: Bronze.

49) In lowest terms, what is the mixed number for 38 over 6?
Answer: 6⅓.

50) In September 1919, which U.S. President collapsed aboard a train after making 40 speeches in behalf of the Treaty of Versailles?
Answer: Woodrow Wilson.

51) According to the Warren Commission's final report in 1964, who "acted alone" in killing President Kennedy?
Answer: Lee Harvey Oswald.

52) Identify the office building housing the Democratic Party headquarters where on June 17, 1972, several men were arrested during a break-in, an incident that led to the resignation of President Nixon.
Answer: Watergate.

53) When President Carter oversaw the Camp David Accords with Egypt and Israel on September 17, 1978, in which U.S. state was the agreement signed?
Answer: Maryland (site of Camp David).

54) Arrange the following numbers in order from smallest to largest: 2/3, 5/11, 7/13, 3/7 (two-thirds; five-elevenths; seven-thirteenths; three-sevenths).
Answer: 3/7, 5/11, 7/13, 2/3.

55) Which black leader, head of the Rainbow Coalition, directed Bill Clinton's 300-event voter registration drive in 1992?
Answer: Jesse Jackson.

56) What is the name for the smallest particle showing all the physical and chemical properties of a compound?
Answer: Molecule.

57) Orson Welles's October 30, 1938, broadcast of a radio drama about an extraterrestrial invasion caused near panic. On which H.G. Wells novel was this radio broadcast based?
Answer: *The War of the Worlds.*

58) Which word designating his nationality also identifies the 20 rhapsodies written by composer and pianist Franz Liszt?
Answer: Hungarian.

59) To which of the 3 classes of rock does granite belong?
Answer: Igneous.

60) The U.N. opens its annual regular sessions of the General Assembly on the third Tuesday of September. Name this organization's 15-member body charged with maintaining international peace.
Answer: Security Council (its permanent members are China, France, United Kingdom, Russia, and the U.S.).

61) Leap years are defined as those years evenly divisible by 4, except centennial years, which are not leap years unless divisible by 400. Name the next year in which a non-leap year presidential election will be held.
Answer: 2100 (only 3 years have seen a U.S. President elected in a non-leap year).

62) Name the state across which General Sherman began his 300-mile march of destruction on November 16, 1864, during the Civil War.
Answer: Georgia.

63) Name the largest island on the West Coast of North America.
Answer: Vancouver Island.

64) How many more events are in a decathlon competition than in a biathlon?
Answer: Eight (8).

65) Which element, whose symbol is Pb, was found in the water systems of some cities at levels 14 times higher than the allowable level? Absorption of this element, once commonly found in paint, has been found to cause brain disorders and retardation.
Answer: Lead.

66) Give the number of oxygen and carbon atoms in a carbon dioxide molecule.
Answer: Two oxygen atoms and one carbon atom.

67)   Give the pen name of the short story writer whose real name
      is William Sydney Porter. He allegedly adopted the name
      from a prison guard after entering prison on April 25, 1898.
      Answer: O. Henry.

68)   Of the Greek heroes who survived the Trojan War, which
      one was the last to return home?
      Answer: Odysseus (Ulysses).

69)   If a square picture frame has a perimeter of 8.32 inches, and
      the sides of the frame are .04 inches thick, what is the
      perimeter of the inside of the frame?
      Answer: 8 inches.

70)   In which 19th-century year did Congress declare war on
      Great Britain on June 18?
      Answer: 1812.

71)   In which U.S. state capital was the world's largest Coca-
      Cola sign lit in 1990 at the site of the company's world head-
      quarters?
      **Answer: Atlanta (the sign is 30 feet high by 26 feet
      wide).**

72)   Who was the President of the Confederate States of America
      during the Civil War?
      Answer: Jefferson Davis.

73)   In which North African country bordering the Red Sea and
      Libya did the British begin an offensive at El Alamein in
      October 1942?
      Answer: Egypt.

74)   Convert 36% to its decimal equivalent.
      Answer: .36 (point 36 or 36 hundredths).

75)   In a slap at the U.S., the U.N. General Assembly supported
      a 1992 resolution seeking to repeal the U.S. trade embargo
      against which Communist-ruled nation that is the Carib-
      bean's largest country in area?
      Answer: Cuba.

76)   Which 2 elements make up more than 74% of the rocks in
      the earth's crust?
      Answer: Oxygen (46.6%) and silicon (27.7%).

77)   English poet Alfred, Lord Tennyson became the state poet of
      England in 1850. What title designates the official poet of a
      country?
      Answer: Poet Laureate.

78) Of which island was Odysseus king? Cornell University is located in a town of the same name.
Answer: Ithaca.

79) To which of the 3 classes of rock does coal belong?
Answer: Sedimentary.

80) Name the country of President Anwar el-Sadat, who was assassinated in 1981 while reviewing a military parade commemorating his country's 1973 war with Israel.
Answer: Egypt.

81) What is your condition if, according to the saying, you travel to the Land of Nod?
Answer: You are asleep.

82) Name the dual-cities airport in Texas that the FAA expects to handle more traffic than Chicago's O'Hare by the year 2000 and to become the first to top 1 million takeoffs and landings in a year.
Answer: Dallas-Ft. Worth.

83) Name the U.S. state whose panhandle is located between Washington and Montana.
Answer: Idaho.

84) What is the sum of the prime factors of 42?
Answer: 12 (2 + 3 + 7).

85) Name the hereditary disease that causes poor clotting of the blood. Some victims of this disease received AIDS-tainted blood during the 1980s and 1990s.
Answer: Hemophilia.

86) According to a 1992 medical journal report, 1,470 children in the U.S. died from Reye's Syndrome because of the government's nearly 5-year delay in requiring warnings on bottles of which medication?
Answer: Aspirin.

87) *Scrooged* is a 1988 film based on which work by Charles Dickens?
Answer: *A Christmas Carol.*

88) Which statue by French sculptor Frédéric Auguste Bartholdi was dedicated on October 28, 1886, on Bedloe's Island?
Answer: *Statue of Liberty*, or *Liberty Enlightening the World.*

89) If an angle is inscribed in a semicircle, what is the angle's measure?
Answer: 90 degrees.

90) In which year, the last of WWII, was the U.N. formally established in San Francisco on October 24?
Answer: 1945.

CHAPTER TEN

1) Which adjective commonly precedes *corn*, *pea*, *roll*, and *"Georgia Brown"*?
   Answer: Sweet.

2) Name the two politicians who in 1960 held the first 4 national televised debates.
   Answer: John Kennedy and Richard Nixon.

3) Name the U.S. state whose panhandle is located between Oklahoma and New Mexico.
   Answer: Texas.

4) Expressed in fractional form, what is the average of one fifth and one-seventh?
   Answer: Six over thirty-five.

5) Name the Eurasian country whose ship was accidentally struck in 1992 by a U.S. missile during NATO war games in the Aegean Sea, killing 5 sailors. Its capital is Ankara.
   Answer: Turkey (missiles were fired from *USS Saratoga*).

6) Which element has the same name as a planet?
   Answer;   Mercury.

7) Name the smallest unit of an element that still retains the properties of that element.
   Answer: Atom.

8) Name the 3-headed dog who guarded the Gate of Hades in Greek mythology.
   Answer: Cerberus.

9) How many degrees are between northeast and southwest on a compass?
   Answer: 180 degrees.

10) Which Portuguese-born explorer was killed by natives in 1521 before the expedition he headed completed the first circumnavigation of the world?
    Answer: Ferdinand Magellan.

11) Each year, some people and businesses do not file a tax return with the IRS. What does the abbreviation IRS stand for?
    Answer: Internal Revenue Service.

12) House of Representative members spend millions to send quantities of pieces of mail to their constituents. What term from the Latin word *francus* designates the free mail privileges granted to Congress?
Answer: Franking (to frank).

13) Name the continent off whose coast the Great Barrier Reef is located.
Answer: Australia.

14) What positive number is the smallest one-digit even cube of an integer?
Answer: Eight (8).

15) Which country pressured Britain in 1993 to forego plans to make Hong Kong's elections more democratic before returning the territory to it in 1997?
Answer: China.

16) Which Mexican peninsula is the site of a 111-mile-wide crater which some scientists believe is evidence that a giant meteorite was responsible for the extinction of dinosaurs?
Answer: Yucatan Peninsula.

17) Name William Golding's book featuring Jack, Piggy, and Ralph in a story about survival on a deserted island.
Answer: *Lord of the Flies*.

18) Name the water plant whose fibers were used by the ancient Egyptians to make a writing material.
Answer: Papyrus.

19) Name the element contained in all organic compounds.
Answer: Carbon.

20) Which Greek philosopher, convicted of corrupting the youth of Athens, drank poisonous hemlock to carry out his sentence of death?
Answer: Socrates.

21) Which "unsinkable" luxury liner sank in 1912 after hitting an iceberg, with the loss of over 1500 of the 2224 persons aboard?
Answer: The *Titanic*.

22) On April 26, 1865, after a long search, which assassin was shot by federal troops in a barn on the farm of Richard Garrett near Port Royal, Virginia?
Answer: John Wilkes Booth (who assassinated President Lincoln).

23) Identify the oldest public building in Washington, D.C., whose cornerstone was laid on October 13, 1792. It is known for its Oval Office and Rose Garden.
Answer: White House (designed by architect James Hoban).

24) What is the sum of the degree measures of 2 complementary angles?
Answer: 90 degrees.

25) In which city in which country was a torch ignited by an archer's flaming arrow to signal the beginning of the 1992 Summer Olympic Games?
Answer: Barcelona, Spain.

26) The Mesabi Range in Minnesota, first leased for mining in 1890, is famous for its iron deposits. What 3-letter word, a homonym for a conjunction, designates rock or earth with silver, iron, or other metals in it?
Answer: Ore.

27) U.S. Representative Ted Weiss from New York, whose district included Greenwich Village, was known as the "conscience of Congress." Spell *conscience*.
Answer: C-O-N-S-C-I-E-N-C-E.

28) Name the mythological Titan who was punished by having to support the sky on his shoulders for all eternity.
Answer: Atlas.

29) If carpeting costs $3 per square foot, what will it cost to carpet a rectangular floor with dimensions 10 feet by 9 feet?
Answer: $270.

30) On May 3, 1979, who became Britain's first female prime minister in its 700 years of parliamentary history?
Answer: Margaret Thatcher.

31) Name the *Arabian Nights* hero for whom a genie found in a lamp builds a splendid palace.
Answer: Aladdin.

32) In which state did Molly Pitcher distinguish herself by carrying water to soldiers in combat and by later replacing her husband in loading and firing cannon at the Battle of Monmouth on June 28, 1778?
Answer: New Jersey.

33) In which U.S. state are the Painted Desert and the Petrified Forest National Park?
Answer: Arizona.

34) The hundred's digit of 1992 is how much larger than the one's digit of 1492?
Answer: 7.

35) Name the European country that became in 1992 the first nation to indefinitely suspend nuclear testing. Prime Minister Mitterrand was its head at the time.
Answer: France (in 1995, France began testing again under President Jacques Chirac).

36) Identify the imaginary line that marks the place on the earth's surface where each new calendar day begins.
Answer: International Date Line.

37) Which number completes the following phrase, "Section _____" for "a military discharge for mental incompetence or military inaptitude"?
Answer: Eight.

38) Which government agency engaged in sending volunteers to help developing nations raise their living standards did presidential candidate John Kennedy initiate in a campaign speech at the University of Michigan in 1960?
Answer: Peace Corps (formally proposed 19 days later).

39) Which of the following planets is the closest to the Earth: Mercury, Saturn, Venus, or Mars?
Answer: Venus.

40) Which religious leader in Wittenberg, Germany, nailed his 95 theses to the door of a palace church in October 31, 1517, beginning the Reformation in part by denouncing the selling of papal indulgences?
Answer: Martin Luther.

41) In which domed stadium do the NFL's Atlanta Falcons play their home games?
Answer: Georgia Dome.

42) Name the military leader and president of Columbia University who was elected U.S. President in 1952.
Answer: Dwight David Eisenhower.

43) Which state bordering both California and Oregon entered the Union on October 31, 1864?
Answer: Nevada (as the 36th state).

44) Give the measures of both the complement and the supplement of an angle of 88 degrees.
Answer: 2 degrees (complement) and 92 degrees (supplement).

45) In 1992, to which Asian country did Japan's Emperor Akihito express sorrow but not formally apologize for war atrocities before and during WWII?
Answer: China (during an unprecedented visit).

46) Name the curved bone of the human skeleton that connects the breastbone with the shoulder blade.
Answer: Collarbone (accept clavicle).

47) Which number completes the following phrase, "_____ sense" for "a power of perception beyond the 5 senses"?
Answer: Sixth.

48) What name is given to a jury that does not reach a verdict?
Answer: Hung jury.

49) If the area of a circle is one *pi*, what is the circumference of the circle in terms of *pi*?
Answer: 2 *pi*.

50) Including the controversial 1992 Congressional pay amendment, how many amendments are there to the U.S. Constitution?
Answer: 27.

51) In which South American country have gold prospectors endangered the world's largest Stone Age tribe by invading an Indian reservation in the Amazon rain forest?
Answer: Brazil (an estimated 20,000 Yanomami Indians live there).

52) Name the Vermont-born 21st U.S. President, who succeeded to the presidency following the death of James Garfield.
Answer: Chester A. Arthur.

53) In which state did Mount Spurr erupt in 1992, sending ash across the southern part of the state, including Valdez and Anchorage?
Answer: Alaska.

54) If a jet plane travels at an average velocity of 995 kilometers per hour, how many hours are required for it to travel a distance of 7,960 kilometers?
Answer: 8 hours (accept 8).

55) Name the President from the "Show Me State" whose folksy wisdom in the 1948 presidential election was quoted by both parties in the 1992 presidential race.
Answer: Harry S Truman.

56) Give the medical term for the leg bone commonly called the shin bone.
Answer: Tibia.

57) Which term designates "a narrative poem with 2- to 4-line stanzas suitable for singing"?
Answer: Ballad.

58) Identify the Trojan princess who spurned Apollo after he gave her the gift of prophecy.
Answer: Cassandra (also called Alexandra).

59) Which name designates the distorted map projection made with parallel straight lines instead of curved lines for latitude and longitude?
Answer: Mercator (Projection; Mercator's Projection; named after Gerardus Mercator).

60) In which country was the labor union known as Solidarity granted legal status in 1989? Its capital is Warsaw.
Answer: Poland.

61) What name is given to the kind of verb that can express action without taking an object?
Answer: Intransitive verb.

62) Prior to Ronald Reagan, who was the only U.S. President to serve past the age of 70?
Answer: Dwight Eisenhower.

63) Which term designates "a narrow strip of land connecting 2 larger bodies of land"?
Answer: Isthmus.

64) Find the product of 23 and 27.
Answer: 621.

65) Name the animal classified as *Canis lupus*, which was spotted in 1992 for the first time since 1926 in Yellowstone National Park.
Answer: Gray wolf (or timber wolf).

66) In the sexual reproduction of plants, the nuclei of 2 different cells join together and form a new cell. This new cell is called which of the following: diatom, zygote, sperm, or egg?
Answer: A zygote.

67) Which poem by Henry Wadsworth Longfellow includes the line, "on the eighteenth of April in Seventy-five"?
Answer: "Paul Revere's Ride."

68) Which 18th-century composer, whose only opera *Fidelio* was performed at the opening of Vienna's reconstructed opera house on November 6, 1955, became deaf in his late 40s?
Answer: Ludwig van Beethoven.

69) Which word designates both "printed music that shows the whole of a composition" and "a group of 20"?
Answer: Score.

70) Name the first permanent English settlement in America.
Answer: Jamestown (Virginia).

71) What name is now given to the Badge of Military Merit created by George Washington in 1782? It is awarded to those wounded or killed in combat.
Answer: Purple Heart.

72) President-elect Bill Clinton named a woman as the first female to head the Justice Department. What title is given to its head?
Answer: Attorney general.

73) What name is given to the strait or land bridge that once stretched from Siberia to Alaska across which American Indians probably came to this country from Asia?
Answer: Bering Strait or Bering Land Bridge.

74) If 2 legs of a right triangle measure 4 and 5, what is the length of the hypotenuse?
Answer: Square root of 41.

75) Which African country did the U.S., France, and Britain ask to extradite 2 airline bombing suspects? This country on the Mediterranean is bordered by 6 countries, including Chad, Niger, and Algeria.
Answer: Libya.

76) *Pioneer 10*, which marked its 20th year in space in 1992, was the first space probe to fly past which planet between Mars and Saturn, doing so in 1973?
Answer: Jupiter.

77) Name the American poet and short story writer who died in Baltimore in 1849 and whose epitaph reads "Quoth the Raven nevermore."
Answer: Edgar Allan Poe.

78) Name the author of the 1937 Pulitzer Prize novel, *Gone with the Wind*.
Answer: Margaret Mitchell.

79) Identify the 3rd smallest planet, the 4th from the sun.
Answer: Mars.

80) On which continent did President Franklin Roosevelt and Prime Minister Winston Churchill meet at Casablanca on January 14, 1943, to decide the course of WWII?
Answer: Africa (Casablanca is in Morocco).

81) What other name is given to the Day of Atonement, the holiest Jewish observance?
Answer: Yom Kippur.

82) Which Cabinet department of the U.S. government works to develop the nation's natural resources?
Answer: Department of the Interior.

83) Name one of the 2 European countries on the Iberian Peninsula.
Answer: Spain or Portugal.

84) What percentage is the equivalent of 2/25?
Answer: 8%.

85) In 1992, which city received the official Olympic flag from Barcelona exactly 2 years from the day it was awarded the 1996 Olympics?
Answer: Atlanta (September 18, 1990).

86) What name is given to the class of vertebrates including frogs, toads, and salamanders?
Answer: Amphibians (accept amphibious).

87) Is the word *daughter* an appositive, direct object, indirect object, or objective complement in the following sentence: I never knew her daughter Mary?
Answer: Direct object.

88) Identify the Roman and Greek god of light, poetry, medicine, the arts, and healing.
Answer: Apollo.

89) How many zeroes are in $3.97 trillion?
Answer: 10.

90) Which U.S. city did British forces invade and burn on August 24-25, 1814?
Answer: Washington, D.C.

CHAPTER ELEVEN

1) Which country always marches first in the Olympic procession in honor of the original Olympics held in its country?
   Answer: Greece.

2) How many years is the term of a U.S. senator?
   Answer: 6.

3) Which word is used to designate "a piece of land jutting out into the water"?
   Answer: Peninsula.

4) What is the perimeter of a square with one side measuring 7 meters?
   Answer: 28 meters.

5) From which country is Prince Khalid, leader of the Gulf War's Arab forces, who criticized Gen. Norman Schwarzkopf in 1992 for taking all the credit for the victory over Iraq? His country's capital is Riyadh.
   Answer: Saudi Arabia.

6) What name is given to the path a heavenly body travels around a second larger body?
   Answer: Orbit.

7) Which punctuation mark is found at the end of every direct inquiry?
   Answer: Question mark (accept interrogation mark or point).

8) How many years did the Trojan War last?
   Answer: 10 years.

9) Find the area in square inches of a rectangle 42 inches by 15 inches.
   Answer: 630 square inches.

10) In which country were 11 members of the Israeli Olympic Team killed in an Arab terrorist attack on the Olympic Village in Munich in 1972?
    Answer: Germany (it was West Germany at the time).

11) Identify the bridge dedicated at Lake Havasu City, Arizona, in October 1971. It is now Arizona's 2nd most popular tourist attraction.
    Answer: London Bridge.

12) In which state was U.S. President William McKinley fatally shot in September 1901, while attending the Pan American Exposition in Buffalo?
Answer: New York.

13) Which 2 countries are on the Scandinavian Peninsula? Their capitals are Stockholm and Oslo.
Answer: Sweden and Norway.

14) What is the largest prime factor of 125?
Answer: 5.

15) In 1992, in which nation did voters reject constitutional reforms designed to put an end to 200 years of English-French squabbling and to keep the country's 10 provinces united? It was called the Charlottetown Accord.
Answer: Canada.

16) What are Quadrantids, Lyrids, Delta Aquarids, Perseids, and Orionids—all of which appear at set times as the earth passes through particles left from the breakup of comets?
Answer: Meteor showers.

17) What type of poem is the following: "There was an old man of Tralee, / Who was bothered and bit by a flea, / So he put out the light, / Saying, "Now he can't bite, / For he'll never be able to see"?
Answer: Limerick.

18) Which word originally naming the mythological horn of plenty today designates "an abundant, overflowing supply"?
Answer: Cornucopia.

19) Name the German-born American scientist who announced his general theory of relativity in 1907.
Answer: Albert Einstein.

20) In which century did Juan Ponce de León discover Florida and claim it for the King of Spain?
Answer: 16th century (on April 2, 1513).

21) Identify the youth organization whose motto is "Be Prepared" and whose method used to teach its members is "learning by doing."
Answer: Boy Scouts.

22) Name the "Terrapin State," which was the 7th to ratify the Constitution, doing so on April 28, 1788. It is also the home of the U.S. Naval Academy.
Answer: Maryland.

23) Name the only U.S. state bordered by only one other state.
Answer: Maine.

24) What is 2 plus 9 divided by 3 minus 4 times 2?
Answer: Negative three (NOTE: to solve this problem, the student must follow the proper order of operations).

25) Which U.S. President was responsible for almost physically doubling the U.S. in area by the purchase he made from France in 1803?
Answer: Thomas Jefferson.

26) Identify the sea creature whose name is derived from the Greek for "eight-footed."
Answer: Octopus.

27) What is the rhyme scheme of the following: "There was an old man of Tralee, / Who was bothered and bit by a flea, / So he put out the light, / Saying, "Now he can't bite, / For he'll never be able to see"?
Answer: aabba.

28) In which country did Alabama-born Jesse Owens win 4 gold medals at the 1936 Olympic Games?
Answer: Germany (in Berlin).

29) A rectangular solid has a length of 8 inches, a width of 6 inches, and a height of 3 inches. Find the total surface area of the rectangular solid.
Answer: 180 square inches.

30) Spell the word that designates an ancient Egyptian king such as Ramses II, whose wife's tomb was reopened after being closed to the public for 50 years.
Answer: P-H-A-R-A-O-H (the tomb is that of Nefertari).

31) Which American League team brought the World Series to Canada for the first time in a matchup with the National League's Atlanta Braves in 1992?
Answer: Toronto Blue Jays.

32) Who was the youngest man ever elected U.S. President?
Answer: John Kennedy (at age 43).

33) The Central American country that borders South America declared itself independent from Colombia on November 3, 1903. Name this country.
Answer: Panama.

34) The numbers 4,004; 11; 515; and 5,665 remain unchanged when their digits are written in reverse order. What are such numbers called?
Answer: Palindromic numbers (accept palindromes).

35) In which capital city in which state is the Peach Bowl college football game played?
Answer: Atlanta, Georgia.

36) The man who received the world's first animal-to-human liver transplant in 1992 died in the same year. From which animal did he receive his liver?
Answer: Baboon.

37) In Judy Blume's novel *Superfudge*, in which major city do the Hatchers live before deciding to move to Princeton, New Jersey?
Answer: New York City.

38) Which nocturnal bird of prey is associated with Athena, the Greek goddess of wisdom?
Answer: Owl.

39) Which chemical compound added to municipal water systems for the prevention of tooth decay was linked in 1992 to increased hip fractures in the elderly?
Answer: Fluoride.

40) In which century was transcontinental telephone service inaugurated in San Francisco when the inventor of the telephone said once again, "Mr. Watson come here. I want you"?
Answer: 20th century (in January 1915).

41) Name the domed stadium in Toronto in which the Blue Jays play their home games.
Answer: SkyDome.

42) On September 13, 1788, which U.S. city did Congress choose as the center of the U.S. government? It was originally called New Amsterdam.
Answer: New York City (U.S. capital, 1789-1790).

43) Which state meets Colorado, Arizona, and Utah at a point called Four Corners?
Answer: New Mexico.

44) What is 120% of 200?
Answer: 240.

45) Name 2 of the 3 major vice presidential candidates during the 1992 campaign.
Answer: Al Gore, Dan Quayle, and James Stockdale.

46) Identify the narrow, winding tube in the human body where digestion is completed and nutrients are absorbed by the blood.
Answer: Small intestine.

47) What Robert Cormier book about a school candy sale is sometimes targeted for censorship in schools?
Answer: *The Chocolate War.*

48) Identify the nationality of Guiseppe Verdi, the composer of *Aïda* and *La Traviata*.
Answer: Italian.

49) As of October 31, 1992, President Bush had spent $18 million on national TV advertising during the presidential race, Ross Perot had spent $5 million more than Bush, and Bill Clinton had spent $14 million less than Perot. How much had Clinton spent?
Answer: $9 million.

50) Name the king and queen of Spain who supported the trips of Christopher Columbus to the New World and gave him the title "Admiral of the Ocean Sea."
Answer: King Ferdinand and Queen Isabella.

51) Name the national oath first recited in 1892 as part of the 400th anniversary of Columbus's voyage to the Americas.
Answer: "Pledge of Allegiance."

52) Congress passed the Volstead Act of 1919 to stop the sale of alcoholic beverages in this nation. By what common name is this banning of alcohol better known?
Answer: Prohibition.

53) Which 2 bodies of water are directly connected by the Erie Canal?
Answer: Lake Erie and the Hudson River (it also connects the Great Lakes and the Atlantic Ocean).

54) Solve for *T*: Three *T* minus five equals *T* divided by two.
Answer: Two.

55) In which city did Mayor Tom Bradley step down in 1993 after 20 years as head of the nation's second-largest city?
Answer: Los Angeles (he was the first black mayor of this city).

56) Which term that comes from a word for "dog" identifies the sharp pointed teeth used for tearing and shredding meat?
Answer: Canines.

57) Name the California-born author who won the Pulitzer Prize for poetry in 1924, 1931, 1937, and 1943, and is closely identified with the region of New England.
Answer: Robert Lee Frost.

58) With which occupation is Frank Lloyd Wright most closely identified?
Answer: Architecture.

59) Identify the group of organic compounds called the "building blocks of proteins" by scientists.
Answer: Amino acids (accept alpha amino acids).

60) Name the British leader who met with President Roosevelt and Generalissimo Chiang Kai-shek at a conference in Cairo, Egypt, in 1943 to discuss the defeat of Japan.
Answer: Winston Churchill (the conference opened on November 22).

61) Name the 1977 Pulitzer Prize-winning author of *Roots*.
Answer: Alex Haley.

62) Four of the first 6 U.S. Presidents came from Virginia. Name these 4 Presidents.
Answer: George Washington, Thomas Jefferson, James Madison, and James Monroe.

63) Complete the name of the Union army unit headed first by Gen. George McClellan and later by Gen. Ambrose Burnside by giving the name of the river bordering Washington, D.C.
Answer: Potomac (Army of the Potomac; Lincoln replaced McClellan on November 5, 1862).

64) 160 is what percent of 400?
Answer: 40 percent.

65) In which city in which state is the Sugar Bowl college football game played?
Answer: New Orleans, Louisiana.

66) The scientific observation of weather is said to have begun about 1600 when an Italian scientist measured air temperature with a thermometer he invented. Name him.
Answer: Galileo.

67) Identify the noun of apposition in the following sentence: "Mr. Whitney, our conglomerate's manager of operations, recently attended a conference in London."
Answer: Manager.

68) Name the only major Roman god who was physically imperfect. He was the son of Jupiter and Juno, and some say he was born lame and thrown into the sea by his mother.
Answer: Vulcan.

69) Which integer is the product of the cube root of 64 and the positive square root of 64?
Answer: Thirty-two (32).

70) Name the leader who is purportedly the world's richest woman. In 1992, this monarch volunteered to pay taxes on her personal income, said to be $50 million annually.
Answer: Queen Elizabeth II.

71) Which former U.S. President, governor, professor, diplomat, and builder of homes for Habitat for Humanity is the author of two poems published in the *Georgia Journal* in 1992?
Answer: Jimmy Carter (his poetry book *Always a Reckoning* was published in 1994).

72) In which town did abolitionist John Brown stage a raid in October 1859 to try to free the nation's Negroes and establish an independent Negro Republic?
Answer: Harpers Ferry (Virginia, present-day West Virginia).

73) Name 2 of the 3 Canadian provinces known as the "Maritime Provinces."
Answer: New Brunswick, Nova Scotia, and Prince Edward Island.

74) What is the perimeter of a rectangular room 10 feet by 20 feet?
Answer: 60 feet.

75) In which state was the *Brown v. Board of Education* National Historic Site established in Topeka in 1992 to memorialize the 1954 Supreme Court ruling that segregated schools are unconstitutional?
Answer: Kansas.

76) Which weather phenomenon occurs when the sun shines upon falling rain or mist?
Answer: Rainbow.

77) Both Margaret Mitchell and Elvis Presley died on August 16, in 1949 and 1977, respectively. Name the city in which either one of them died.
Answer: Atlanta (Mitchell) or Memphis (Presley).

78) What letter names the notes written on the bass clef in the top space?
Answer: G.

79) Name the "Wizard of Menlo Park," who on October 11, 1868, filed papers for his first invention, an electric vote recorder designed to tabulate Congressional votes.
Answer: Thomas Edison.

80) What name did the ancient world give to March 15, the date on which Julius Caesar was assassinated in 44 B.C.: apex, meridian, equinox, or ides?
Answer: Ides (15th of March, May, July, or Oct., or 13th of other months).

81) Name the American black who became part of Tuskegee Institute's faculty in 1896 and won international fame for agricultural research.
Answer: George Washington Carver.

82) In which Ohio city was the first public weather forecasting started in 1869? This city's Red Stockings became the first professional baseball team in the same year.
Answer: Cincinnati.

83) Name the state whose research triangle is formed by Durham, Chapel Hill, and Raleigh.
Answer: North Carolina.

84) If $x = 5$ and $y = -2$, what is $4x + 3y$?
Answer: 14.

85) Professor William Holtz attributes the authorship of the "Little House" books about prairie life to Rose Wilder Lane, daughter of the author to whom they are credited. Name this author.
Answer: Laura Ingalls Wilder.

86) Which company, incorporated by J.P. Morgan on February 25, 1901, became the first "billion-dollar corporation"? The Bessemer process is important in this industry.
Answer: U.S. Steel Corporation.

87) Which Massachusetts senator is known for his 7th of March Speech pleading for the preservation of the Union? His surname is shared by a famous writer of dictionaries.
Answer: Daniel Webster.

88) In 1846, which religious group led by Brigham Young migrated west from Nauvoo, Illinois, to Utah?
Answer: **Mormons (or Church of Jesus Christ of Latter Day Saints).**

89) If $x = 5$ and $y = -2$, what is $10x - 4y$?
Answer: **58.**

90) Which nation bordering the Pyrenees is headed by King Juan Carlos?
Answer: **Spain.**

CHAPTER TWELVE

1) When it was completed in January 1943 in Virginia, which office building was the world's largest?
Answer: Pentagon.

2) Over which U.S. state was the U.S. flag formally raised on October 18, 1867, following its purchase from Russia by Secretary of State William H. Seward?
Answer: Alaska.

3) Which U.S. state named after an English king has a capital named after an English soldier and explorer?
Answer: North Carolina (Raleigh is the capital).

4) Express the ratio of 12 ounces to one pound as a fraction in lowest terms.
Answer: 3/4.

5) Ross Perot did not carry any states in the 1992 presidential election. Name the former governor of Alabama who in 1968 was the last third-party presidential candidate to win electoral votes.
Answer: George Wallace.

6) Which term beginning with the letter H is used to describe formations with a common structure and origin that may have similar functions, such as the legs of a man and the hindlegs of a horse?
Answer: Homologous.

7) Give the first name of Helen Keller's teacher who is featured in *The Miracle Worker*.
Answer: Anne (Sullivan Macy).

8) Which word is used to designate "a high-temperature oven used to dry, burn, or bake pottery"?
Answer: Kiln.

9) Factor the quantity $x^2 - 6x + 9$.
Answer: $(x - 3)(x - 3)$ or $(x - 3)^2$.

10) Name the Doric temple of Athena built on the Acropolis in Athens.
Answer: Parthenon.

11) What is the primary language spoken in the city of São Paulo?
Answer: Portuguese.

12) Name the 2 English astronomers who with their 1767 survey to settle a land dispute between Maryland and Pennsylvania established the line that came to be the boundary between slave and free states.
Answer: Charles Mason and Jeremiah Dixon (Mason-Dixon Line).

13) In shape, the state of Georgia resembles most closely which of the following states: Wyoming, New Hampshire, Missouri, or Idaho?
Answer: Missouri.

14) If John can walk 6¾ miles in 2¼ hours, how far can he walk in 5 hours at the same speed?
Answer: 15 miles.

15) Identify the country whose soldiers were pitted against stone throwing Palestinians in the Gaza Strip during the 1980s.
Answer: Israel.

16) Which term is used to designate all of the physical parts of a computer system, including printers, monitors, and keyboards?
Answer: Hardware (accept peripherals).

17) Name Hugh Lofting's character who talks to the animals in their own language.
Answer: Dr. Dolittle.

18) What letter names the notes written on the bass clef in the bottom space?
Answer: A.

19) With which of the 5 senses is the olfactory nerve associated?
Answer: Smell.

20) Which 2 countries signed a treaty on December 8, 1987, to eliminate an entire class of nuclear missiles, the 500- to 5,000-kilometer range class?
Answer: U.S. and Soviet Union.

21) Name the 2 states whose combined postal abbreviations spell the word *lane*.
Answer: Louisiana and Nebraska.

22) Which historic document, announced in 1862, did President Lincoln officially issue on January 1, 1863?
Answer: Emancipation Proclamation.

23) The island of Crete in the Mediterranean Sea is located off the Peloponnesus, the southern peninsula of which European country?
Answer: Greece.

24) Find the product of 25 and 42.
Answer: 1050.

25) In 1992, which Southwestern state approved a Martin Luther King Jr. holiday when it became the only state to put the issue to a popular vote? Its capital is Phoenix.
Answer: Arizona.

26) Which yellow, nonmetallic element can be identified by the odor given off when cabbage and turnips are cooked? This element is also found in eggs and dairy products.
Answer: Sulfur.

27) Name the 3 ways in which a pronoun agrees with its antecedent.
Answer: In person, number, and gender.

28) The early Greeks believed that their gods lived on top of the highest mountain in their country. Name it.
Answer: Mount Olympus.

29) 200 is what percent of 40?
Answer: 500 percent.

30) Name the Mongol leader who overran most of Asia and Eastern Europe between the years 1206 and 1227.
Answer: Genghis (Jenghiz) Khan.

31) Which adjective commonly precedes ball, *puss*, *dough*, *cream*, and *grapes*?
Answer: Sour.

32) After Pocahontas, the daughter of Chief Powhatan, married settler John Rolfe in 1614, in which country did she die of smallpox?
Answer: England.

33) In which mountain range, often considered the boundary between Europe and Asia, is Mount Elbrus, Europe's highest point, located?
Answer: Caucasus Mountains.

34) In the equation *4 times the sum of m and 4 equals 32*, what is the value of *m*?
Answer: 4.

35) The former Soviet republics were hit in 1992 by an epidemic of which disease represented by the *D* in the abbreviation DPT for the immunizations routinely given to children in the U.S.?
Answer: Diphtheria.

36) Radiation is one of the 3 basic methods of heat transfer. Name the other two.
Answer: Conduction and convection.

37) Spell the comparative and superlative of the adjective *dry*.
Answer: D-R-I-E-R and D-R-I-E-S-T.

38) Christianity shares early sacred writings and religious heroes with 2 other major world religions. Which of the 2 related religions is older than Christianity?
Answer: Judaism.

39) What is the common term for a computer printout?
Answer: Hard copy.

40) Which Nazi leader served as Adolf Hitler's minister of propaganda: Goebbels, Hess, Rommel, or von Braun?
Answer: Josef Paul Goebbels.

41) Name the tribal stone or adobe dwellings, sometimes as many as 5 stories high, built by Indian tribes in the U.S. Southwest.
Answer: Pueblos.

42) Which 2 explorers sighted the Pacific Ocean for their first time on November 7, 1805, at the mouth of the Columbia River in the Oregon Territory?
Answer: Meriwether Lewis and William Clark.

43) Which U.S. state, the 4th largest in area, entered the Union on November 8, 1889? Its name comes from a Spanish word for "mountainous."
Answer: Montana.

44) Find the average of two-thirds and one-third.
Answer: One half.

45) On which planet with daytime temperatures reaching 800 degrees Fahrenheit did 1992 radar studies indicate the presence of ice? It is the nearest planet to the sun.
Answer: Mercury.

46) For which disease did American-born scientist Jonas Edward Salk develop the first effective vaccine in 1955?
Answer: Poliomyelitis (accept polio).

47) Which forms other than *littler* and *littlest* are used as the comparative and superlative of the adjective *little*?
Answer: Less (or lesser) and least.

48) Which French word identifies a demand made by an audience's applause for a repetition of a performance?
Answer: Encore.

49) What integer does 64 to the two-thirds power equal?
Answer: 16.

50) Hundreds of sculpted bronze body parts, possibly from a vessel that sank sometime between the 3rd century A.D. and the early Middle Ages, were found off the coast of Italy. What term designates such manmade objects that are of historical interest?
Answer: Artifacts.

51) Name the Chinese device that is the world's oldest known mechanical computing aid.
Answer: Abacus (used in China as early as the 6th century B.C.).

52) Name the Italian trader to the court of Kublai Khan whose ancient route has been resurrected using space shuttle photographs and computers.
Answer: Marco Polo.

53) Identify the capital of Liberia. It is named for the U.S. President known for his doctrine opposing European intervention in the Americas.
Answer: Monrovia (James Monroe issued the Monroe Doctrine).

54) If a fair coin is flipped 3 times, what is the probability that the outcome will be exactly two tails and one head?
Answer: 3/8 (three-eighths).

55) Name the "Sagebrush State," where nuclear explosions were banned until June 1993 when nuclear labs were allowed 15 safety tests before a 1996 comprehensive test ban. Carson City is its capital.
Answer: Nevada.

56) Which term designates the piece of computer hardware containing a modulator and a demodulator used in telecommunication of data?
Answer: Modem (*Mo*dulator / *Dem*odulator).

57) Name the Hans Christian Andersen story in which a child in the crowd says, "But he has nothing on!"
Answer: "The Emperor's New Clothes."

58) Identify the daughter of Zeus who sprang forth fully formed and fully armed from his forehead.
Answer: Athena.

59) Identify the word used in biology to designate the series of changes by which a caterpillar becomes a butterfly.
Answer: Metamorphosis.

60) Name the U.S. holiday now celebrated on November 11, which marks the date on which the armistice ending WWI was signed in 1918.
Answer: Veterans Day (formerly called Armistice Day).

61) Which word is defined as "the art and technique of dance notation, especially the art of creating and arranging ballets"?
Answer: Choreography.

62) What is the minimum age requirement for a member of the U.S. House of Representatives?
Answer: 25.

63) In which U.S. state is the Custer Battlefield or Little Bighorn National Monument located?
Answer: Montana.

64) What is the probability of rolling a sum of 7 with a pair of fair dice?
Answer: One out of 6 (or 6 out of 36).

65) In 1992, the nation's first commercial food irradiation plant sought USDA approval to irradiate poultry with gamma rays to kill bacteria. What kind of bacteria that causes food poisoning is found in as many as 40% of chicken carcasses according to the USDA?
Answer: Salmonella.

66) Name the Virginia-born inventor of the first successful mechanical grain reaper.
Answer: Cyrus Hall McCormick.

67) Name the fairyland to which Peter Pan persuades the Darling children to go with him.
Answer: Never-Never Land (or Never Land).

68) Is a xylophone a brass, woodwind, percussion, or stringed musical instrument?
Answer: Percussion.

69) Identify the mathematical term that is defined by the following: the distance from zero to a number on a number line.
Answer: Absolute value.

70) Who was the conqueror of the Aztecs in Mexico in 1521?
Answer: Hernán Cortés (or Hernando Cortéz).

71) Name the 1994 TV show based on Marjorie Kinnan Rawlings's Pulitzer Prize novel about the Baxter family whose love is tested when son Jody adopts an orphaned fawn.
Answer: *The Yearling.*

72) Which state was the site of the infamous Confederate prison at Andersonville, whose commandant Captain Henry Wirz, was executed in 1865 for mistreating prisoners?
Answer: **Georgia.**

73) Identify the island colonized about A.D. 986 by Eric the Red that is now a province of Denmark.
Answer: **Greenland.**

74) If a jet plane travels at an average velocity of 990 kilometers per hour, how much time is required for it to travel a distance of 6,435 kilometers at the same speed?
Answer: **6½ hours.**

75) Name the instrument discovered to be flawed in 1990 after taking its first photograph of Theta Carina, an obscure star cluster.
Answer: **Hubble Telescope (its spherical aberration was corrected in 1983).**

76) Name the chart based on the theory of Russian chemist Dmitri Ivanovich Mendeleev that lists elements in horizontal rows according to their atomic numbers.
Answer: **Periodic Table (of the Elements).**

77) Name the pig who is a loyal friend of Charlotte the spider in E.B. White's *Charlotte's Web.*
Answer: **Wilbur.**

78) Which of the following is not an acceptable pronoun form: himself, ourselves, themselves, theirselves, or itself?
Answer: **Theirselves.**

79) Identify the transparent object that refracts or disperses a beam of light into the spectrum.
Answer: **Prism.**

80) Which country did Germany invade on September 1, 1939, to start WWII?
Answer: **Poland.**

81) What name is given to the small beetle that feeds inside the seed pods of cotton plants?
Answer: **Boll weevil.**

82) Name one of the 2 West Point graduates who completed 2 full terms as President of the U.S.
Answer: Ulysses S. Grant or Dwight Eisenhower.

83) Name 2 of the 3 Latin American countries in which the Yucatán Peninsula lies.
Answer: Mexico, Belize, and Guatemala.

84) Spell the prefix added to the word *circle* to create a word meaning a half-circle.
Answer: S-E-M-I.

85) Which Midwestern state, in preparation for 1992 reunions, marked foundations in cornfields where many German POWs were held during WWII? It is the home of Father Flanagan's Boy's Town, and its capital is Lincoln.
Answer: Nebraska.

86) In a reversal of previous recommendations, CPR experts have said the best way to save someone's life is to call 911, then begin CPR. What do the initials CPR stand for?
Answer: Cardiopulmonary resuscitation.

87) Name the author of *The Red Pony*, a story set in the Salinas Valley of California.
Answer: John Steinbeck.

88) Name the Roman god of agriculture or the planet with 7 thin, flat rings around it.
Answer: Saturn.

89) What is the term for a segment joining 2 points on a circle?
Answer: Chord.

90) In which North African country did the U.S. bomb Tripoli and Benghaze in 1986 in retaliation for the bombing of a West German discotheque? Col. Muammar Gaddafi was this country's leader at the time of the bombing.
Answer: Libya (2 Americans were killed in the bombing).

CHAPTER THIRTEEN

1) Which term designates a person who is holding an office, particularly at the time the officeholder is running for re-election?
   Answer: Incumbent.

2) President Bush is the first incumbent to win less than 40% of the popular vote since which President in 1932? His initials are H.H.
   Answer: Herbert Hoover (Bush, 38%; Clinton, 43%; Perot, 19%).

3) Which city on the Mississippi River was named by French fur traders in honor of King Louis XV and his patron saint, Louis IX?
   Answer: St. Louis.

4) What effect does a bar, or vinculum, over a Roman numeral have?
   Answer: It multiplies the number by 1,000.

5) Name the Ohio Democratic incumbent who was re-elected to the U.S. Senate in 1992 despite his link with convicted savings-and-loan owner Charles Keating. He was the first American to orbit the earth.
   Answer: John Glenn.

6) Muscles may either bend or straighten a limb. What is the term for those that straighten a limb?
   Answer: Extensor.

7) In which story is The Headless Horseman a character?
   Answer: "The Legend of Sleepy Hollow."

8) Gilbert Stuart is famous for his 3 paintings, or portraits, of George Washington. Give the term for a painting of objects, such as books or fruit.
   Answer: Still life.

9) A rectangular floor has an area of 720 square feet. How many square yards of carpeting are needed to cover it?
   Answer: 80.

10) In 1992, Latvia, Lithuania, and Estonia condemned Boris Yeltsin's decision to suspend the withdrawal of Russian

troops from their homelands. On which arm of the North Atlantic Ocean are these nations located?
Answer: Baltic Sea (they are called the Baltic republics).

11) There is a nursery rhyme which says, "I love you a bushel and a peck." How many total pecks is this?
Answer: 5 (four pecks equal one bushel).

12) Which former U.S. President, called the "Great Communicator," said in 1992 about President Bush, "He doesn't seem to stand for anything"?
Answer: Ronald Reagan.

13) In 1994, France enacted a new penal code. Does a penal code establish rules for collecting taxes, punishing criminals, sending messages, or conducting elections?
Answer: Punishing criminals (earlier guidelines were set by Napoleon Bonaparte).

14) What is the perimeter of a square with a side length of 8 centimeters?
Answer: 32 centimeters.

15) Name the arm of the Arabian Sea that a U.S. submarine entered for the first time in 1992 to keep tabs on Iran's first submarine.
Answer: Persian Gulf.

16) Which of the 7 SI base units contains an SI prefix?
Answer: Kilogram.

17) Which literary term designates an interruption of the action in a story to tell about something that happened earlier in time?
Answer: Flashback.

18) What is the name for the star that guided the Magi to the manger for the birth of Jesus as recounted in Matthew 2:1-10?
Answer: Star-of-Bethlehem (accept Star of the Epiphany; accept Star of the East).

19) What is the common name for the colorful display in Arctic skies known as the *aurora borealis*?
Answer: Northern lights.

20) In 1993, which Mideast country was given a 48-hour notice by the U.S. and its allies to either move its missiles out of a no-fly zone south of the 32nd parallel or face military action?
Answer: Iraq.

21) In which state did Franklin Roosevelt lay the cornerstone for the U.S.'s first presidential library, his own, on November 19, 1939, at Hyde Park?
Answer: New York.

22) In which year did 41 Pilgrims aboard a ship off the coast of Massachusetts sign the Mayflower Agreement or Compact that became the basis of government for the colony?
Answer: 1620 (on November 11).

23) When the world's landmasses are divided into just 6 continents, what designation is used for the largest?
Answer: Eurasia.

24) What is the mathematical term for a number whose positive factors excluding itself can be added to produce a sum greater than the given number?
Answer: Abundant number.

25) Which state has the highest average altitude of any U.S. state?
Answer: Colorado.

26) Identify the device invented by Massachusetts-born Eli Whitney for separating the fibers of short-staple cotton from the seeds.
Answer: Cotton gin.

27) Identify one of the 2 youngsters in Katherine Paterson's *Bridge to Terabithia* who create the secret kingdom of Terabithia.
Answer: Jess (Aarons) or Leslie (Burke).

28) Name the Georgia-born author so closely identified with the character he created that he was nicknamed "Uncle Remus" and even received mail addressed to him as such.
Answer: Joel Chandler Harris.

29) Which 2 terms can be used in mathematics to describe lines that are not oblique?
Answer: Horizontal and vertical.

30) In which German city did the U.S. unveil a plaque in 1992 at the future site of its embassy beside the Brandenburg Gate?
Answer: Berlin.

31) Which term derived from the Greek for "great city" is used to designate an extensive, very populated, urban region made up of two or more metropolitan areas?
Answer: Megalopolis (from *megalo* and *polis*).

32) Name the chief justice who swore in Bill Clinton at his 1993 inauguration. He was nominated by President Ronald Reagan to succeed Chief Justice Warren Burger.
Answer: William Rehnquist.

33) In 1992, President Bush won the electoral votes in North Dakota (3) and Texas (32) and all 4 states in a straight line from north to south between the 2. Name 3 of these states.
Answer: South Dakota (3), Nebraska (5), Kansas (6), and Oklahoma (8).

34) If Fred exchanges his U.S. dollars for English pounds and the exchange rate allows 60 pounds for every 100 U.S. dollars, how many pounds does he get if he exchanges $450 U.S. dollars for pounds?
Answer: 270.

35) Name the Virginia home and estate of Thomas Jefferson near Charlottesville.
Answer: Monticello.

36) Name the categories designated by the binomial names of an organism under the system established by Carolus Linnaeus in the 18th century.
Answer: Genus and species, respectively.

37) Spell the word *accommodate*.
Answer: A-C-C-O-M-M-O-D-A-T-E.

38) Which song did Julia Ward Howe write on November 19, 1861, soon after she heard the song "John Brown's Body Lies A-Mouldering in the Grave"?
Answer: "The Battle Hymn of the Republic."

39) Name either of the 2 bones of the forearm.
Answer: Radius or ulna.

40) On which country did the U.S. declare war on April 6, 1917, to enter WWI?
Answer: Germany.

41) What is the religious tradition of Sidwell Friends School, the exclusive private school that Chelsea Clinton began attending in Washington?
Answer: Quaker.

42) Which amendment to the U.S. Constitution reserves to the states any powers not specifically assigned to the federal government?
Answer: Amendment 10.

43) Name the only Canadian province whose name begins and ends in an *A*. Its capital is Edmonton.
Answer: Alberta.

44) How many square millimeters are in 1 square centimeter?
Answer: 100.

45) California has been warned to expect water shortages after 7 years of drought. Spell *drought*.
Answer: D-R-O-U-G-H-T.

46) Give the meaning of the suffix -*meter*.
Answer: Measurement.

47) Which story was Mary Mapes Dodge inspired to write after reading *The Rise of the Dutch Republic*? The subtitle of her work is *The Silver Skates*.
Answer: *Hans Brinker.*

48) Identify the Italian artist whose painting known for its enigmatic smile was stolen from the Louvre in 1911 but was returned on December 10, 1913.
Answer: Leonardo da Vinci.

49) If you are playing "Wheel of Fortune" and there is one "Lose a Turn" section on a wheel divided into 20 equal portions, what is the percent chance of spinning "Lose a Turn"?
Answer: 5%.

50) Name the organization whose headquarters along New York's East River occupy the block of land donated by John D. Rockefeller Jr. in 1946.
Answer: United Nations.

51) What word ending in -*cide* means killing of another person?
Answer: Homicide.

52) In a mock trial famed defense lawyer F. Lee Bailey tried to clear the name of the physician who set the broken leg of John Wilkes Booth, the assassin who killed President Lincoln. Is this doctor named Foxx, Tutt, Mudd, or Liss?
Answer: Dr. Samuel Mudd (after the mock trial, judges said Mudd should never have been tried).

53) Name the only Canadian province whose name begins and ends with the letter *O*. Its capital is Toronto.
Answer: Ontario.

54) 20 is 20% of what number?
Answer: 100.

55) Which group that comprises 1.4 percent of Australia's 16.5 million population did not celebrate the bicentennial because they were in mourning for what they see as a white invasion of their homeland?
Answer: Aborigines.

56) German physician Robert Koch established bacteriology as a separate science and discovered the germ that causes which disease often referred to as TB?
Answer: Tuberculosis (bacillus).

57) Name the Danish author of "The Ugly Duckling," "The Red Shoes," and "The Snow Queen."
Answer: Hans Christian Andersen.

58) Music is usually written on a staff of lines and spaces. How many lines are on a staff?
Answer: 5.

59) Scientists have discovered that the reading on the Fahrenheit and Celsius scales are equal at one and only one point. What is that temperature?
Answer: –40 degrees.

60) Identify the Indian civilization whose Calendar Stone, or Solar Stone, was found beneath Mexico City's Central Plaza on December 17, 1790.
Answer: Aztec.

61) Which Southwestern state, shaped like a sauce pan, was admitted to the Union on November 16, 1907? A Broadway musical tells the story of its cattlemen and farmers.
Answer: Oklahoma.

62) In which year, the last of the Civil War, was slavery and involuntary servitude abolished by the 13th Amendment to the U.S. Constitution?
Answer: 1865.

63) In 1992, Bill Clinton won the electoral votes in Minnesota (10) and Louisiana (7) and all 3 states in a straight line from north to south between the 2. Name 2 of these states.
Answer: Iowa (7), Missouri (10), and Arkansas (6).

64) Subtract the square root of 121 from the square root of 169.
Answer: 2.

65) Name the first person born after WWII to be elected President of the U.S.
Answer: Bill Clinton.

66) What name is given to 0 degrees Kelvin and –273.15 degrees Celsius, theoretically the lowest possible temperature?
Answer: Absolute zero.

67) The word *spending* is used as which part of speech in the following sentence: A Republican set a spending record by a candidate for the U.S. House when he spent more than $4 million in his campaign?
Answer: Adjective.

68) What name is given to any musical note not marked by a sharp or a flat?
Answer: Natural.

69) Of the number: 56,874.12398 (READ: "five, six, eight, seven, four, point, one, two, three, nine, eight"), which number is in the ten-thousandths place?
Answer: 9.

70) Give the full name of NATO, an organization formed on April 4, 1949.
Answer: North Atlantic Treaty Organization.

71) Following the breakup up of the Soviet Union, which country became the world's largest in area?
Answer: Russia.

72) Over which Baltimore fort, today a national monument, did Francis Scott Key see that "our flag was still there"?
Answer: Fort McHenry.

73) Which canal formally opened on November 17, 1869?
Answer: Suez Canal.

74) A hiking team begins at camp and hikes 5 miles north, then 8 miles west, then 6 miles south, then 8 miles east, then 1 mile north. In what direction must they now travel in order to return to camp?
Answer: No direction (they already are at camp).

75) Give the acronym for Strategic Arms Reduction Treaty, the landmark treaty signed in Moscow by President Bush and Russian President Yeltsin.
Answer: START (II).

76) What name is given to the temperature at which a substance changes from a solid to a liquid?
Answer: Melting point.

77) Name the world's first nuclear-powered submarine, launched on January 17, 1955. It shares its name with the vessel in Jules Verne's *20,000 Leagues Under the Sea.*
Answer: *Nautilus* (christened on January 21, 1954).

78) Name the native country of pianist Ignace Jan Paderewski, who abandoned his musical career to help gain his country's freedom in WWI. Located on the Baltic Sea, this country was named for the Polane, a Slavic tribe.
Answer: Poland.

79) Which German physicist introduced the use of mercury in thermometers, improving their accuracy?
Answer: Gabriel Daniel Fahrenheit.

80) Somalis blame Boutros Boutros-Ghali for their country's collapse. What is Boutros-Ghali's title as administrative head of the U.N.?
Answer: Secretary-general.

81) Name the female marksman known as "Little Miss Sure Shot."
Answer: Annie Oakley.

82) Name the first person of Greek descent to serve as governor of an American state or as Vice President of the U.S. He served as Richard Nixon's first Vice President.
Answer: Spiro Agnew.

83) Which term, Greek for "chief sea," is used to designate "a sea with many islands" or "a chain of many islands"?
Answer: Archipelago.

84) How many inches are in a mile?
Answer: 63,360.

85) In which African country did President Bush spend New Year's Eve in 1992, praising the 18,000 American troops deployed there?
Answer: Somalia.

86) Leaves have special cells in which photosynthesis takes place. What is the name for these capsule-like structures?
Answer: Chloroplasts.

87) Which author created the Yellow Brick Road, the ruby slippers, and the Munchkins?
Answer: L. Frank Baum.

88) In four-four time, a half note is tied to a quarter note. For how many beats will the tone be played?
Answer: 3.

89) How many square yards are in one acre?
Answer: 4,840.

90) At which site in the Soviet Union did an explosion occur at a nuclear reactor on April 26, 1986?
Answer: Chernobyl.

CHAPTER FOURTEEN

1) Identify the founder of the University of Virginia, to whom President Roosevelt dedicated a memorial on April 13, 1943, the 200th anniversary of his birth.
   Answer: Thomas Jefferson.

2) According to Article V of the U.S. Constitution, what fraction of the members of both houses of Congress must approve an amendment for its ratification?
   Answer: 2/3.

3) Name the state formally represented by Margaret Chase Smith, who was the first woman to be elected to both houses of the U.S. Congress. Acadia National Park is located in this state.
   Answer: Maine.

4) Using ones and zeroes, express the number two in base two.
   Answer: 10 (one zero).

5) Which country of 15 million people separated into 2 republics at midnight on New Year's Eve 1992? Prague was its capital.
   Answer: Czechoslovakia (now the Czech Republic and Slovakia).

6) Leaves have special cells in which photosynthesis takes place. What is the green colored matter in these capsule-like structures?
   Answer: Chlorophyll.

7) What part of speech is the first word in the sentence, "When did you find that?"
   Answer: Adverb (interrogative adverb).

8) Which Spanish painter, with the initials PP, painted *The Three Musicians*?
   Answer: Pablo Picasso.

9) Give the first 3 positive common multiples for the numbers 2 and 6.
   Answer: 6, 12, 18.

10) In which country on the North Sea did the Germans launch a massive counteroffensive during the Battle of the Bulge on December 16, 1944? Its capital is Brussels.
    Answer: Belgium (the battle took place in the Ardennes Forest).

11) Name the national museum in Washington, D.C., that has displayed heart-wrenching notes and other artifacts left at the Vietnam Veterans' Memorial over the past 10 years.
   Answer: Smithsonian Institution (or Smithsonian; or Smithsonian Institute).

12) According to Article V of the U.S. Constitution, what fraction of the states must approve an amendment through their legislatures for its ratification?
   Answer: 3/4.

13) Name the largest of the 3 states in which Yellowstone National Park is located.
   Answer: Montana (also located in Wyoming and Idaho).

14) If $x = -3$ and $y = (x + 5)(x - 5)$ [READ: y equals the sum of x and five times the quantity of x minus five], then what is the value of y?
   Answer: –16 (negative sixteen).

15) On New Year's Eve in 1992, which President bestowed his 1,000th award in the Points of Light program he initiated for recognition of community service?
   Answer: George Bush.

16) Muscles may either bend or straighten a limb. What is the term for those that bend a limb?
   Answer: Flexor.

17) What part of speech is the last word in the following sentence: "When did you find that?"
   Answer: Pronoun.

18) Identify the Italian artist from Florence who painted the ceiling of the Sistine Chapel.
   Answer: Michelangelo (Buonarroti).

19) In which U.S. state was the world's largest telescope completed in 1992 at an observatory at the summit of the dormant Mauna Kea volcano?
   Answer: Hawaii.

20) Name the French explorer who found Indian settlements at the sites of present-day Quebec City and Montreal in 1535.
   Answer: Jacques Cartier.

21) Identify the Canadian-born inventor of the game of basketball. In 1891, he used 2 peach baskets and a soccer ball to play the first game.
   Answer: James Naismith.

22) Which of the following serves the longest term of office in the U.S.: governor, president, senator, or congressman?
Answer: Senator (a senator serves for 6 years).

23) Name the country whose highest point is Mount Logan. This mountain is located in the Yukon Territory.
Answer: Canada.

24) Express the Roman Numeral IV (READ: "I" "V") in base two.
Answer: 100 (READ: one, zero, zero).

25) Which South American country has the world's largest Roman Catholic population?
Answer: Brazil.

26) Waves are measured in more than one way. What is the measure of distance between a point on one wave and the corresponding point on the next wave?
Answer: Wavelength.

27) What number is included in the title of Jules Verne's *Around the World in _____ Days*?
Answer: *Eighty (80).*

28) Rudolf Nureyev, who defected from Russia in 1961, died at age 54, of cardiac complications resulting from AIDS. Was Nureyev a fashion designer, an artist, a cellist, or a ballet dancer?
Answer: Ballet dancer.

29) In the number set, 1, 4, 5, 5, 6, 6, 6, 9, and 9, which number is the mode?
Answer: 6 (mode is the most frequently occurring number).

30) Which country crushed a U.S.-backed invasion on April 17, 1961, at the Bay of Pigs?
Answer: Cuba.

31) In which city did President Bush throw out the season's first pitch at the Orioles new Camden Yards ballpark in 1992?
Answer: Baltimore.

32) Spell the word which identifies a candidate who currently holds the office for which he is running.
Answer: I-N-C-U-M-B-E-N-T.

33) A 600-ton lead counterweight has been placed to stabilize which Italian monument that experts say could topple at any time?
Answer: (Leaning) Tower of Pisa.

34) Find the product of negative four and negative sixteen.
Answer: 64.

35) In 1993, in which city did the National Civil Rights Museum open an art exhibit to commemorate the 25th anniversary of the assassination of Dr. Martin Luther King Jr.? This museum was built on the site of the Lorraine Motel where Dr. King was killed in 1968.
Answer: Memphis.

36) In science, the strengths of solutions are usually expressed by a combination of number and abbreviation. What does an M in such a designation mean?
Answer: Molar or molarity.

37) How many commas are in the following sentence: "After April 15, 1991, we will live at 414 Robin Lane, Louisville, Kentucky"?
Answer: 4.

38) The Folger Library in Washington, D.C., received a $2.5 million grant to improve the world's largest collection of books and manuscripts by which English playwright born in Stratford-upon-Avon?
Answer: William Shakespeare.

39) What term is used to designate the measure of half the height of a water wave from crest to trough?
Answer: Amplitude.

40) Which U.S. commonwealth in the Caribbean celebrates Discovery Day on November 19, the day Christopher Columbus discovered it on his second voyage in 1493?
Answer: Puerto Rico.

41) What are the two proper nouns in the Pledge of Allegiance?
Answer: United States of America and God.

42) In which year on September 26 was John Jay confirmed as the first chief justice of the U.S. Supreme Court, the same year that George Washington was inaugurated as the first U.S. President?
Answer: 1789.

43) Name the North Carolina cape, nicknamed the "Graveyard of the Atlantic," off which the Union's ironclad ship the *Monitor* sank on December 30, 1862.
Answer: Cape Hatteras.

44) In terms of *pi* and *r*, give the formula for the circumference of a circle.
Answer: 2 *pi r*.

45) An EPA report says secondhand cigarette smoke is a human carcinogen that results in the lung cancer deaths of 3000 nonsmokers a year. What is the full name of the EPA?
Answer: Environmental Protection Agency.

46) Which word beginning with the letter *M* designates "any extinct mammal resembling the elephant and named from the nipple-shaped projections on its molars"?
Answer: Mastodon.

47) In Frances Hodgson Burnett's *The Secret Garden*, who is the young girl who goes to Misselthwaite Manor on the moors?
Answer: Mary Lennox.

48) Give 2 of the 3 letters naming musical tones written between the bass and treble staffs on a score.
Answer: B, C, and D.

49) Imagine that you have been hired to place grass in a small square yard whose perimeter is 20 feet. How many square feet of sod will be needed to cover the yard?
Answer: 25.

50) Which French queen, who allegedly said, "Let them eat cake," was beheaded on October 16, 1793?
Answer: Marie Antoinette.

51) What name is given to the condition in which a person's gums become inflamed and swollen?
Answer: Gingivitis.

52) Which former governor of Tennessee defeated the Mexicans at San Jacinto and later became governor of Texas?
Answer: Sam Houston (only governor to serve 2 states).

53) Which lake, Central America's largest, bears the same name as the nation in which it is located?
Answer: Lake Nicaragua.

54) If a fair coin is tossed, what is the probability of getting "heads" three times in a row?
Answer: 1/8 or 1 out of 8.

55) Name the mountain range in Argentina in whose foothills were discovered the remains of the earliest dinosaur ever found, a dog-sized meat-eater of the species named *Eoraptor*, meaning "dawn stealer."
Answer: Andes Mountains.

56) In science, the strengths of solutions are usually expressed by a combination of number and abbreviation. What does an N in such a designation mean?
Answer: Normal.

57) How many prepositional phrases are in the following quotation from Franklin D. Roosevelt: "I pledge you—I pledge myself—to a new deal for the American people"?
Answer: 2 (*to* and *for*).

58) A clef is a sign in music that is placed at the beginning of a staff to show the exact pitches represented by each line and space. By what more common name do we know the G clef?
Answer: Treble clef.

59) A common minor surgery is referred to as a T & A. What body parts are removed in this procedure?
Answer: Tonsils and adenoids.

60) In which country was political and spiritual leader Mohandas Gandhi assassinated on January 30, 1948, in New Delhi?
Answer: India.

61) *Cro*, a 1993 TV cartoon, features an 11-year-old boy who is an example of which early man inhabiting Europe in the late Paleolithic Era?
Answer: Cro-Magnon.

62) Which U.S. President held his first TV presidential press conference 5 days after his 1961 inauguration?
Answer: John Kennedy.

63) Missouri is bordered by 8 states, including Kentucky and Kansas, both of which start with a *K*. Two more states bordering Missouri have names that start with the same letter. What are these 2 states?
Answer: Illinois and Iowa.

64) Identify a geometric solid whose only base is a polygon and whose faces are triangles.
Answer: Pyramid.

65) Rebels from the breakaway Abkhazia region of the former Soviet Union once reportedly forced Georgia's leader Eduard Shevardnadze to flee his home. On which "colorful" sea is Georgia located?
Answer: Black Sea.

66) If you freeze one liter of pure water, the resulting ice has a volume greater than one liter. What is the difference in mass between the original liter of liquid and the resulting ice?
Answer: None (the mass is the same).

67) Which term is used to designate the internal or external struggle that is the focal point of action in a short story?
Answer: Conflict.

68) In Matthew 2:13 of the King James Bible, who said, "Arise, and take the young child and his mother, and flee into Egypt"?
Answer: An Angel of the Lord.

69) In how many minutes can an automobile travelling at 30 miles per hour make a 30-mile trip without stopping?
Answer: 60 minutes (accept one hour).

70) Which retired battleship, named for the "Show Me State" and nicknamed "Mighty Mo," was the site of Japan's formal surrender in 1945?
Answer: U.S.S. *Missouri*.

71) What's the sum if you add the number of eyes a cyclops has to the number of Hercules' labors?
Answer: 13 (1 + 12).

72) Name the 2 U.S. Presidents who died on July 4, 1826. One's son also served as President, and the other had red hair.
Answer: John Adams and Thomas Jefferson.

73) Name the "Magnolia State" represented by Congressman Mike Espy, who was named the first black secretary of agriculture.
Answer: Mississippi.

74) Is the height of a six-foot tall person closest to 130, 150, 160, or 180 centimeters?
Answer: 180.

75) Name the colorful sea bordering Saudi Arabia from which Tomahawk missiles were fired from U.S. warships into Iraq in 1993.
Answer: Red Sea.

76) Teeth come in various shapes and sizes. How many molars does the typical adult human develop?
Answer: 12.

77) Name the Mark Twain novel that sends a New England fac-
     tory superintendent back to Camelot.
     **Answer: *A Connecticut Yankee in King Arthur's
     Court.***

78) Give the nickname for the most complete skeleton of an
     early ancestor ever found. It was discovered in Ethiopia by
     Don Johanson.
     Answer: Lucy.

79) How many incisors are in a normal set of adult human
     teeth?
     Answer: 8.

80) Which world capital is located on the site where the Aztec
     Indians built the city of Tenochtitlan about A.D. 1325?
     Answer: Mexico City.

81) Which American literary prize was first awarded in 1917 in
     the following categories: biography, history, and journalism?
     Answer: Pulitzer Prize.

82) Lawrence Walsh was the federal prosecutor who investigat-
     ed the Iran-*contra* affair. Spell *prosecutor*.
     Answer: P-R-O-S-E-C-U-T-O-R.

83) Dams on which river flowing into the Pacific generate more
     than a third of the hydroelectric power in the U.S.? This
     river begins in British Columbia.
     Answer: Columbia River.

84) What is the principal square root of six squared?
     Answer: 6.

85) In which Southern state, known as the "Cotton State," was
     Gov. Guy Hunt indicted in 1993 on charges of taking
     $200,000 from an inaugural fund for personal use?
     **Answer: Alabama (5th sitting U.S. governor indicted
     in past 50 years).**

86) What is the product of a sebaceous gland?
     Answer: Oil.

87) Spell the plural form of the noun *analysis*.
     Answer: A-N-A-L-Y-S-E-S.

88) Name the student of Socrates who founded the Academy in
     Athens and wrote the *Republic*.
     Answer: Plato.

89) How much is 1/6 divided by 1/5?
    Answer: 5/6 or five-sixths.

90) According to the Russian who built it, the first Soviet atomic
    bomb was a copy of the U.S.'s A-bomb and was built from
    plans supplied by a spy. In which year did the U.S. drop A-
    bombs on 2 Japanese cities?
    **Answer: 1945 (the Russians exploded their first
    A-bomb in 1949).**

CHAPTER FIFTEEN

1) Which term designates in the U.S. "a period of mild, dry, hazy weather, occurring usually in late October and early November"?
   Answer: Indian summer.

2) Which government post did Luther L. Terry hold in January 1964 when he issued a report describing cigarette smoking as a contributing factor to lung disease?
   Answer: Surgeon General.

3) Which European river, called "the dustless road of the Gypsies," stretches from near Ulm, Germany, to the Black Sea? This is Europe's 2nd longest river.
   Answer: Danube River.

4) Give the first 3 common positive multiples for the numbers 3 and 4.
   Answer: 12, 24, 36.

5) What action did Bill Clinton take at 6 p.m. EST on Sunday, January 17, 1993, to symbolize a message of unity and hope? Thousands of others, including pilots on 3 airlines and astronauts on the space shuttle *Endeavour*, joined him.
   Answer: Rang a bell (Clinton rang a replica of the Liberty Bell).

6) Which 2 words popularized by Carolus Linnaeus designate "the plants and animals of a particular area or time"?
   Answer: Flora and fauna.

7) What type of verb can be used to express both the active and the passive voices?
   Answer: Transitive.

8) Which Greek word, meaning "the throttler," identifies the mythological creature known as a great riddle master with wings, a lion's body, and a woman's head? A sculpture of one still stands guard over the pyramids at Giza.
   Answer: Sphinx.

9) What improper fraction is the square root of 25/9?
   Answer: 5/3.

10) Composer Dimitri Shostakovich dedicated his 1941 *Symphony No.7* to Leningrad, then under siege by the German army. What is Leningrad's current name?
    Answer: St. Petersburg.

11) A nationwide Defense Department computer network was disrupted in November 1988 by a rapidly replicating software program. What is the common name for such attack programs?
Answer: Computer virus (accept virus).

12) Which military fort did Connecticut-born Revolutionary War General Benedict Arnold, with the help of John André, plan to betray to the British?
Answer: West Point.

13) In which U.S. capital is the Lyndon Baines Johnson Library?
Answer: Austin (Texas).

14) What is the result of subtracting 44 from negative 68?
Answer: –112.

15) For his 1993 inauguration, Bill Clinton's bus trip to the White House began at Monticello, home of Thomas Jefferson, father of the Democratic Party, and ended at which memorial to the first Republican President?
Answer: Lincoln Memorial.

16) What did American inventor Thomas Edison say "is one percent inspiration and ninety-nine percent perspiration"?
Answer: Genius.

17) Two types of point of view in fiction are classified as third person. What name is given to the third person type that confines the narration to the thoughts and perspectives of only one character?
Answer: Limited (or limited omniscient).

18) Identify the 19th-century art movement whose style of painting, developed in France in the 1870s, is characterized chiefly by short brush strokes of bright colors to represent the effect of light on objects.
Answer: Impressionism.

19) The rocklike planets closest to the sun are called inner planets, and the farther gaseous planets are called outer planets. What is the outermost inner planet?
Answer: Mars.

20) Name the French palace where a peace conference formally opened on January 18, 1919, following WWI.
Answer: Versailles (known as the Versailles Peace Conference).

21) Which SEC university team, nicknamed the "Crimson Tide," was crowned the 1992 national football champion after defeating the Miami Hurricanes 34-13 in the Sugar Bowl?
Answer: University of Alabama.

22) In 1807, Vice President Aaron Burr was acquitted of which crime specified by the U.S. Constitution as "levying war against the U.S. or giving aid and comfort to its enemies"?
Answer: Treason (he was charged with a scheme to colonize the Southwest).

23) Identify the national park in Colorado whose Spanish name means "green table."
Answer: Mesa Verde (known for its cliff dwellings).

24) Give the mathematical term for a polynomial with one term.
Answer: Monomial.

25) Identify the "Mile High City" in which a Columbus Day parade was canceled in 1992 to avoid a clash with American Indian activists.
Answer: Denver.

26) Radioactive materials give off different types of radiation, named with letters of the Greek alphabet. Which letter names the negatively charged electrons emitted?
Answer: Beta (beta particles).

27) Comparisons are often used in figurative language. What is the term for a direct comparison using words such a "like," "as," or "as if"?
Answer: Simile.

28) The house in a neighborhood that inspired a Dr. Seuss book was demolished despite its listing on the National Register of Historic Places. Complete the title of this book, *And to Think I Saw It on* _____.
Answer: *Mulberry Street.*

29) Find the product of 9.06 and .045.
Answer: .4077.

30) Name the most populous nation with a democratic parliamentary form of government.
Answer: India.

31) Give President Clinton's middle name, a name that also identifies the surname of the 3rd U.S. President.
Answer: Jefferson (William Jefferson Clinton).

32) When Robert Weaver was sworn in as secretary of HUD on January 18, 1966, he became the first black U.S. Cabinet member. Which department is known as HUD?
Answer: Department of Housing and Urban Development.

33) Thousands lined the banks of which river in 1992 to watch the 40th re-enactment of George Washington's Christmas Day crossing into New Jersey during the Revolutionary War?
Answer: Delaware River (to wage a surprise attack on Trenton on December 26, 1776).

34) Solve for x: $x - 4 + 4 = 6 + 4$.
Answer: $x = 10$.

35) Which former Democratic President expressed concern over the $28 million price tag on Clinton's 1993 inaugural, 7 times more than the $4 million spent on his 1977 inaugural celebration? With inflation, the $4 million would be $10 million today.
Answer: Jimmy Carter.

36) Radioactive materials give off different types of radiation, named with letters of the Greek alphabet. Which letter names the positively charged helium nuclei emitted?
Answer: Alpha (alpha particles).

37) In which U.S. state is Julie alone and lost on its North Slope in Jean Craighead George's *Julie of the Wolves*?
Answer: Alaska.

38) Christianity shares early sacred writings and religious heroes with 2 other major world religions. Which of the 2 related religions is younger than Christianity?
Answer: Islam (accept also "the Muslim religion").

39) What is the complementary color of yellow?
Answer: Violet, or purple.

40) Name the small Central American country from which the U.S. is scheduled to remove all of its troops by 1999 when it relinquishes control of a major waterway.
Answer: Panama (the Panama Canal reverts to Panama on 12/31/1999).

41) Broccoli is a garden vegetable with loose, green, leafy, edible flower clusters. Spell *broccoli*.
Answer: B-R-O-C-C-O-L-I.

42) Which senator from which state was chosen as George Bush's Vice President in 1988?
Answer: Dan Quayle from Indiana.

43) Usually lasting only 12 to 18 months, the warming of waters resulting from the onset of El Niño in 1991 was the longest on record. El Niño affects waters in which ocean?
Answer: Pacific (1993's Midwest floods were attributed to El Niño).

44) Of *complementary*, *congruent*, and *supplementary*, which one describes the corresponding angles formed when 2 parallel lines are cut by a transversal?
Answer: Congruent.

45) What kind of animal was Ling-Ling, who died in 1992 at the National Zoo in Washington? She was survived by her mate Hsing-Hsing, who arrived with her as a gift from the People's Republic of China after President Nixon's visit in 1972.
Answer: Giant Panda (accept Panda).

46) Elements are identified not only by names and symbols but also by numbers. What is the term for the number of protons in the nucleus of one atom of an element?
Answer: Atomic number.

47) Edward Bellamy presents his ideas for a perfect society in his 1888 novel *Looking Backward*. What word derived from the Greek for "no place" is used to designate a "perfect place" such as the one he describes?
Answer: Utopia.

48) Name the village in Galilee where according to the Gospel of John Jesus performed his first miracle of changing water into wine. Its name begins with the letter *C*.
Answer: Cana.

49) What is the volume of a cube 3 feet high, 3 feet wide, and 3 feet deep?
Answer: 27 cubic feet.

50) A New York library exhibit in 1994 documenting the impact of the first half-century of the printed word featured the inventor of the printing press. Name him.
Answer: Johannes Gutenberg.

51) Hillary Clinton held the Bible as her husband took the oath for President. In 1965, which First Lady from Texas initiated this practice?
Answer: Lady Bird Johnson (Supreme Court clerks traditionally held the Bible).

52) Bill Clinton's inaugural speech reflected the themes of personal responsibility and service also emphasized in the inaugural address by which President whom Clinton met in 1963 in the Rose Garden?
Answer: John F. Kennedy.

53) Which term beginning with the letter *W* designates a row of trees planted between fields of crops to prevent erosion?
Answer: Windbreak.

54) Consider the arithmetic sequence 3, 6, 9, 12, and so on. What would the tenth term in the sequence be?
Answer: 30.

55) Which U.S. President, known for the motto "the buck stops here," issued an executive order to integrate the military in 1948?
Answer: Harry S Truman.

56) What is the term for the sum of the numbers of neutrons and protons in the nucleus of one atom of an element?
Answer: Mass number (accept mass).

57) Alexander Dumas wrote *The Man in the Iron Mask*, and Edward Everett Hale wrote *The Man Without A Country*. Which American humorist wrote "The Man That Corrupted Hadleyburg"?
Answer: Mark Twain or Samuel Clemens.

58) What literary term is illustrated by the following words: babbling, buzz, creak, hiss, groan, and thud?
Answer: Onomatopoeia.

59) What does a person have too many of if he or she is polydactyl?
Answer: Toes or fingers.

60) Fulfilling a 1988 agreement, from which country did Soviet troops pull out in 1989 to end their occupation? This country's capital is Kabul.
Answer: Afghanistan.

61) Name the Durham, North Carolina, university that has won the men's NCAA basketball championship.
Answer: Duke.

62) Name the White House room in which the President's desk is located.
Answer: Oval Office.

63) In which Southern state was a monument honoring black soldiers in the Civil War erected at Petersburg National Battlefield Park just south of Richmond?
Answer: Virginia.

64) Bill and Tom had a yardsale to get rid of some of their unused belongings. If the profits totalled $200 and they split the profits using a 40:60 ratio, how much money did each get?
Answer: $80 and $120 (must have both).

65) In 1989, in which city did Israeli police units clash with stone-throwing Palestinians at the Dome of the Rock mosque, one of Israel's holiest places?
Answer: Jerusalem.

66) On the summer solstice, the sun can be seen for 24 hours in the northern part of the earth extending to 66 degrees, 33 minutes north latitude. What is the common name for this line demarcating the polar region?
Answer: Arctic Circle.

67) What word is used to designate the pattern of stressed and unstressed sounds in poetry?
Answer: Rhythm, or meter.

68) Name the composer and band conductor often called the "March King," whose most famous composition is "The Stars and Stripes Forever."
Answer: John Philip Sousa.

69) Using 3.14 as an approximation for *pi*, find the circumference of a wheel with a spoke 21 inches long.
Answer: 131.88 inches.

70) Which war officially ended when the Treaty of Guadalupe Hidalgo was signed on February 2, 1848?
Answer: Mexican War.

71) Following his 1993 inaugural, down which street did President Clinton travel from the Capitol to the White House?
Answer: Pennsylvania Avenue.

72) After ratifying the 14th amendment, which state became the first of the 11 defeated Southern states to be readmitted to the Union? Its capital is Nashville.
Answer: Tennessee.

73) Which peninsula is bordered on the east by the South China Sea and the Gulf of Thailand and on the west by the Strait of Malacca and the Andaman Sea of the Indian Ocean? It forms parts of Thailand and Malaysia.
Answer: Malay Peninsula.

74) If a rectangular garden is 8 feet wide and 11 feet long, what is its area?
Answer: 88 square feet.

75) What 2-word greeting completes these lines at the end of Maya Angelou's inaugural poem: "And say simply / Very simply / With hope / _____ _____"?
Answer: Good morning.

76) What is the most common element by mass in protoplasm?
Answer: Oxygen.

77) What is the term for an actor's thinking aloud to himself while he is alone on the stage, or a speech made by an actor to himself?
Answer: Soliloquy.

78) In the *Odyssey*, the seamen of Odysseus were almost home when they curiously but foolishly opened a bag given them by Aeolus. What came out of the bag?
Answer: Winds (all the winds but the west wind).

79) A solution is sometimes described with the abbreviation *PPM*. For what does this abbreviation stand?
Answer: Parts per million.

80) What city lay at the northern end of the ancient road called The Appian Way?
Answer: Rome.

81) Name the small mountainous European country whose citizens had at one time the world's highest average income. Its flag has a white cross on a red background, and its capital is Bern.
Answer: Switzerland.

82) As a result of the 20th or "Lame Duck" Amendment to the U.S. Constitution, who was the first President to be sworn in on January 20? The year was 1937.
Answer: Franklin Roosevelt.

83) Name the city and state where President Clinton was born.
Answer: Hope, Arkansas.

84) Find the product of .236 and 12.13.
    Answer: 2.86268.

85) Which instrument did Bill Clinton play at the Arkansas Ball
    on inaugural night in 1993 to the tune of "Your Mama Don't
    Dance and Your Daddy Don't Rock 'n' Roll"?
    Answer: Saxophone.

86) Pepsin is one of the common enzymes in the digestive juices
    of the stomach. What type of food is broken down by pepsin?
    Answer: Protein.

87) In drama, not all actors' speeches are addressed to the other
    actors on the stage. What is the term for an actor's direct
    address to the audience?
    Answer: Aside.

88) In the fairy tale, how does Hansel destroy the witch to save
    himself and his sister Gretel?
    Answer: Shoves the witch into an oven.

89) What geometric term denotes the intersection of two differ-
    ent lines?
    Answer: Point.

90) In 1901, in which island, the "Pearl of the Antilles," did
    Major William C. Gorgas of the U.S. Army begin a campaign
    to eradicate yellow fever?
    Answer: Cuba.

CHAPTER SIXTEEN

1) Name the president of Princeton University whose name was proposed for President of the U.S. in a dinner given in his honor on February 3, 1906. This man, whose initials are W.W., later became President of the U.S.
   Answer: Woodrow Wilson.

2) To which of the 3 branches of the U.S. government does the Speaker of the House belong?
   Answer: Legislative.

3) Name the city in which Georgetown University, the Catholic school from which President Clinton graduated, is located.
   Answer: Washington, D.C.

4) If 6 posts are set at 15-foot intervals at the edge of a field, how many feet is the first post from the last?
   Answer: 75 (feet).

5) In 1993, which Williamsburg, Virginia, college marked its founding with a convocation address by Prince Charles, whose ancestors granted the college its charter in 1693?
   Answer: William and Mary (chartered by King William III and Queen Mary II).

6) Nuclear reactions are of 2 types. Which term is used to designate the reaction in which nuclei combine to produce a larger nucleus?
   Answer: Fusion.

7) In reading a play we see 2 kinds of writing: that which is spoken by the actors and that which tells the directors and actors what to do or how to feel when certain lines are spoken. What is the term for the lines spoken by the actors?
   Answer: Dialogue.

8) Name the Boston-born author of "The Pit and the Pendulum" and other tales of terror.
   Answer: Edgar Allan Poe.

9) What is the absolute value of the result of the following calculation: $6 - 342 - 23$?
   Answer: 359 (or + 359).

10) Which war ended with the Treaty of Paris in 1763, twenty years before another Treaty of Paris ended the American Revolutionary War?
Answer: French and Indian War (signed on February 10, 1763).

11) Peanuts and popcorn are still the preferred fare at baseball parks, but small cakes of cold rice garnished with raw or cooked fish can also be bought now at some parks. Give the Japanese word for this food item.
Answer: Sushi.

12) Which American frontiersman, adopted by the Shawnee Indians after having been captured, blazed the Wilderness Road through the Appalachian mountains?
Answer: Daniel Boone.

13) Which capital city has implemented a plan to become the first major western European city to banish all non-vital traffic from its streets? Its museums hold many paintings by natives Rembrandt and Van Gogh.
Answer: Amsterdam (The Netherlands).

14) Twelve is 25% of what number?
Answer: 48.

15) In which country did Jean Chrétien's Liberal Party soundly defeat Prime Minister Kim Campbell's Conservative Party in national elections in 1993?
Answer: Canada (Conservatives won 2 seats, compared with 154 before the election).

16) Nuclear reactions are of 2 types. Which term is used to designate the reaction in which a nucleus breaks into 2 nuclei?
Answer: Fission.

17) What 2-word term is used to designate the instructions from the playwright included in the script of the play?
Answer: Stage directions.

18) Which Austrian musician, who began performing at age 3 and writing music at age 5, composed *The Marriage of Figaro*?
Answer: Wolfgang Amadeus Mozart.

19) Which chemical element contributes more to the weight of the human body than any other?
Answer: Oxygen.

20) The 1929 Lateran Treaty signed by Cardinal Gasparri and Benito Mussolini on February 11 guaranteed an independent state for the Catholic Church headquarters. Name this independent state.
Answer: The Vatican.

21) Identify the system of writing for the blind which uses raised dots to represent letters and numerals and is named after a Frenchman who developed it.
Answer: Braille.

22) Which of the following states does not include any part of the territory acquired by the Louisiana Purchase of December 20, 1803: Indiana, Iowa, Missouri, or Montana?
Answer: Indiana (purchase from France cost about $20 per square mile).

23) Which U.S. city has the longest subway line with 493 miles?
Answer: New York (2nd is Chicago; 3rd is Washington, D.C.).

24) What number increased by 25% of itself equals 120?
Answer: 96.

25) Name the country of Brian Mulroney, President Clinton's first visiting foreign leader. He was the prime minister of the U.S.'s largest trading partner and the world's second largest country in land size.
Answer: Canada.

26) The rocklike planets closest to the sun are called inner planets, and the farther gaseous planets are called outer planets. What is the innermost outer planet?
Answer: Jupiter.

27) Of the 2 types of point of view in fiction classified as third person, which type offers the thoughts and the perspectives of multiple characters?
Answer: Omniscient.

28) Name the New York City-born artist and illustrator known for his many cover paintings for the *Saturday Evening Post*.
Answer: Norman Rockwell.

29) What is three to the fifth power divided by three cubed?
Answer: 9 (accept 3 squared).

30) According to an old legend, animals of the class Aves choose their mates on Valentine's Day, February 14. Which animals make up this class?
Answer: Birds.

31) In which Japanese form of wrestling did a 455-pound American become the first foreigner to win the highest award?
    Answer: Sumo (wrestling; Chad Rowan, the titlist, is Hawaiian).

32) Name the Virginia-born 9th U.S. President, who was the last President born before the American Revolution and the first President to die in office.
    Answer: William Henry Harrison.

33) Which Alabama city is called the "Queen City of the Gulf"?
    Answer: Mobile.

34) What is 2 squared times 2 cubed?
    Answer: 32 (accept two to the fifth power).

35) Citing potential uses in agriculture, rescue missions, and other projects, which country experimented with lighting the night on Earth by shining a reflected solar spotlight from space in the early 1990s? It launched Sputnik in the 1950s.
    Answer: Russia.

36) Give the term for any of the many very small planets that revolve around the sun and are also called planetoids or minor planets.
    Answer: Asteroids.

37) When finally overcome by the Knight of the White Moon, which fictional hero abandoned the life of knight-errantry and returned home? Spanish author Cervantes created this hero.
    Answer: Don Quixote.

38) Which Biblical country was known as the "land of bondage"?
    Answer: Egypt.

39) What element is used to coat steel to make it galvanized? Its symbol is Zn.
    Answer: Zinc.

40) Of the U.S. battleships destroyed at Pearl Harbor, which one now serves as a memorial for those who died in the attack?
    Answer: U.S.S. *Arizona*.

41) Which word rhymes with *fog*, spelled backward is slang for "a sailor," and is used as a verb with the word *down*?
    Answer: Bog.

42) Which department, headed by Bruce Babbitt in the Clinton administration, oversees the National Park Service?
    Answer: Department of Interior.

43) Name the U.S. state capital that at 7,000 feet is the highest state capital in the U.S. Its name is Spanish for "holy faith," and it is the oldest seat of government in the U.S.
Answer: Santa Fe (founded in 1610).

44) What is the greatest common divisor of the numbers 32, 48, and 80?
Answer: 16.

45) Which country, whose monarch is Queen Sonja, hosted the 1994 Winter Games, in the city of Lillehammer north of Oslo?
Answer: Norway.

46) Water ecosystems in a freshwater biome are of several different types. Which water ecosystem beginning with the letter *M* is characterized by thick growths of grasses, reeds, and other water plants?
Answer: Marsh.

47) Comparisons are often used in figurative language. What is the term for an indirect comparison that does not make use of the words *like* or *as*?
Answer: Metaphor.

48) Which biblical person is known as the "woman who looked back"?
Answer: Lot's wife.

49) For what does the mathematical abbreviation l.c.m. stand?
Answer: Lowest common multiple (accept least common multiple).

50) In 1956, which Russian leader called for "peaceful coexistence" between East and West?
Answer: Nikita Khrushchev.

51) Which word rhymes with gnaw, spelled backward means "skin blemishes," and completes the saying "that's the last _____"?
Answer: straw.

52) Name the Charleston, South Carolina, fort that was returned to Union control on February 17, 1865.
Answer: Fort Sumter.

53) Name the river that runs through New Mexico from north to south, virtually bisecting the state.
Answer: Rio Grande.

54) How many sheets of metal 1/2 inch thick are there in a pile 25½ inches high?
Answer: 51.

55) Name the 16th century Italian astronomer who discovered the first practical use of the telescope.
Answer: Galileo.

56) Which water ecosystem is characterized by a permanently waterlogged area of overgrown vegetation and stands of trees?
Answer: Swamp (bog or fen).

57) Edward L. Stratemeyer created 2 series of mystery books intended for young readers. Identify his series of books designed for young female readers.
Answer: Nancy Drew mysteries.

58) From which book of the Bible did John Steinbeck take the title for his novel *East of Eden*?
Answer: Genesis.

59) The most powerfully contracting chamber of the heart forces blood into the aorta. Which chamber is this?
Answer: Left ventricle.

60) Name the author of *Birds of America*, the 1839 book that in 1993 brought $4 million at an auction in New York.
Answer: John James Audubon.

61) Spell the word *hygiene*.
Answer: H-Y-G-I-E-N-E.

62) In 1993, the government of Pakistan promised to track down and extradite a suspect accused of murdering 2 employees of which federal agency with headquarters in Virginia? It gathers information about foreign countries.
Answer: CIA (Central Intelligence Agency).

63) A historian made a mid-1993 expedition from Senegal following the route he says was traveled as early as 800 B.C. by explorers crossing the Atlantic Ocean. On which continent is Senegal located?
Answer: Africa (these early explorers allegedly landed in Mexico).

64) If 20 men assemble 8 cars in a day, how many men working at the same rate are needed to assemble 12 cars in a day?
Answer: 30.

65) Name the novel about a New England woman who answers a Midwest farmer's ad for a wife to help him with his children.
Answer: *Sarah, Plain and Tall* (by Patricia Mac-Lachlan).

66) Buckminsterfullerene is only the 3rd form of pure carbon known to exist. Name the other two.
Answer: Graphite and diamond.

67) Name the Mark Twain short story in which an amphibian with athletic ambitions is weighted down by a heavy stomach.
Answer: "The Celebrated Jumping Frog of Calaveras County."

68) What word is used to describe singing slightly lower than the proper pitch?
Answer: Flat.

69) In a proportion, the first and last terms are called extremes; what name is given to the second and third terms?
Answer: Means.

70) In 1993, Russian President Boris Yeltsin marked the 50th anniversary of the WWII battle that claimed the lives of more than 1 million Soviet soldiers and civilians in which city renamed Volgograd after the death of Joseph Stalin?
Answer: Stalingrad.

71) Which sport, because of its popularity in the U.S., is often called the "national pastime"?
Answer: Baseball.

72) President Bush broke a record for a string of successful vetoes. Name the President who previously had the record with an unbroken string of 30 successful vetoes from late 1963 to 1968.
Answer: Lyndon Johnson.

73) Name the building in Philadelphia where the Continental Congress and the Federal Constitutional Convention met. It is now part of a national historical park.
Answer: Independence Hall (in Independence National Historical Park).

74) Sixteen percent of a number is 128. What is the number?
Answer: 800.

75) Presidential candidate Steve Forbes favored a single-rate tax of 17% to replace the federal graduated income tax. What synonym for *fixed* or *unvarying* is used to name a single-rate tax?
Answer: Flat (tax).

76) What name is given to a substance obtained from one or more other substances as a result of a chemical reaction?
Answer: Product.

77) Which part of speech is a word most likely to be if it ends in the suffix -*ment*?
Answer: Noun.

78) From which book of the Bible did Thornton Wilder take the title for his play *The Skin of Our Teeth*? This book with a 3-letter title bears the name of the man whose faith is tested by Satan.
Answer: Job (19:20).

79) What percent of 2/3 is 1/2?
Answer: 75%.

80) Which country has restored the double-headed eagle as its official emblem after ousting the famed hammer and sickle as the symbol of peasants and workers?
Answer: Russia.

81) Is Julia Child best known for her culinary, oratorical, musical, or dramatic skills?
Answer: Culinary (meaning "pertaining to cooking").

82) Name the ex-slave whose statue in Boston Common is dedicated to the memory of those who died in the Boston Massacre. He was supposedly the first to die in the American Revolution.
Answer: Crispus Attucks.

83) In which state does the flooding Gila River sometimes damage rich farm land near the Painted Rock Dam, 90 miles east of Yuma?
Answer: Arizona.

84) What is the result of multiplying negative 4 times negative 6 times 3?
Answer: 72.

85) In 1995, President Clinton turned down Japan's request for an apology from the U.S. for dropping the atomic bomb on which 2 cities 50 years ago?
Answer: Hiroshima and Nagasaki.

86) Resistance is a term used to designate the measure of how difficult it is for electrons to flow through a conductor. In what units is this measurement expressed?
Answer: Ohms.

87) When baseball players use the phrase "to pull a Casey" to describe a player's action, what has the player done? The phrase alludes to Ernest Lawrence Thayer's poem about a baseball game in Mudville.
Answer: Struck out.

88) Name either the Boston-born artist known for his seascapes such as *The Gulf Stream* or the author of the *Iliad*.
Answer: Winslow Homer, or Homer.

89) What is the absolute value of the result of the following calculation: 405 + 17 − 231?
Answer: 191.

90) Name the Communist country that withdrew from the Nuclear Non-Proliferation Treaty in protest of forced inspections of suspected secret nuclear sites. Its capital is Pyongyang.
Answer: North Korea.

CHAPTER SEVENTEEN

1) Name the small box connected by cable to a computer and used to select items on the screen by clicking one or more button style switches.
   Answer: Mouse.

2) Name the state bordering Alabama, Tennessee, Louisiana, and Arkansas for which Hiram Revels began serving the unexpired Senate term of Jefferson Davis in 1870, thus becoming the first black in the U.S. Senate.
   Answer: Mississippi (Revels began his term on February 25, 1870).

3) Identify the Arizona national park established on February 26, 1919.
   Answer: Grand Canyon National Park.

4) Which 2 prime numbers sum to 13?
   Answer: 11 and 2.

5) Which U.S. President did 2 Puerto Rican terrorists try to assassinate in Blair House on November 1, 1950? He followed a President with the initials FDR and preceded one with the initials DDE.
   Answer: Harry S Truman.

6) Different objects affect light in different ways. What is the term for the return of light from a surface?
   Answer: Reflection.

7) Which one of the following words does not have a double consonant immediately preceding its suffix: *biggest, baggage, occurrence, offering*?
   Answer: Offering.

8) If someone is singing slightly lower than the proper pitch, the singing is flat. What adjective is used to describe singing that is slightly higher than proper pitch?
   Answer: Sharp.

9) What is the result when 6.1 is divided into 43.31?
   Answer: 7.1.

10) Egyptian President Mubarak once threatened an immediate military strike if Iran based warships at a port in which country, the largest in Africa?
    Answer: Sudan (at Port Sudan).

11) It is easier to pay someone a compliment than to pay one's own bill. Spell compliment.
   Answer: C-O-M-P-L-I-M-E-N-T.

12) Which U.S. political party held the office of President for 20 years from 1933 to 1953?
   Answer: Democratic Party.

13) An Old West theme park built in Japan includes a replica of which 60-foot-tall granite monument in South Dakota honoring 4 U.S. presidents?
   Answer: Mount Rushmore.

14) Express 3/8 as a decimal.
   Answer: .375.

15) Which federal act of 1973 is credited with helping bring back by 1993 the Arctic peregrine falcon from near extinction after pesticides contaminated their eggs?
   Answer: Endangered Species Act.

16) Different objects affect light in different ways. What is the term for the bending of light as it passes from one substance to another?
   Answer: Refraction.

17) Name the young Jewish girl whom the late Jan Gies and his wife helped hide during WWII. They were mentioned in this girl's diary that was first published in 1947.
   Answer: Anne Frank.

18) Identify the French impressionist known for his *On the Stage* and other ballet scenes.
   Answer: Edgar Degas.

19) What are the two standard products when an acid and a base counteract each other?
   Answer: A salt and water.

20) At the 1st international conference of Communists since the Soviet Union's collapse, delegates reaffirmed their faith in the beliefs of communism's founder. Name him.
   Answer: Karl Marx.

21) During the Stone Age, what type of rock was most often used for cutting tools?
   Answer: Flint.

22) Name the U.S. senator who was assassinated in Los Angeles while campaigning for the Democratic presidential nomination in 1968.
   Answer: Robert Kennedy.

23) When a boat enters the Mississippi River from the Gulf of Mexico and travels north, what is the first state capital this boat will pass?
Answer: Baton Rouge (Louisiana).

24) What is the supplement of an 80 degree angle?
Answer: 100 degrees.

25) In which Alabama city was the first Civil Rights Memorial dedicated in 1989? This memorial recognizes the 40 people who died during the civil rights struggle of the 1950s and 60s.
Answer: Montgomery.

26) At what angle must the sun, earth, and moon be for a neap tide to occur?
Answer: Right angle or 90 degrees.

27) Name the 3 principal parts of a verb from which all the tenses of the verb can be formed.
Answer: Present infinitive (infinitive), past, and past participle.

28) The Roman Catholic feast of the Annunciation, celebrated on March 25, commemorates the day an angel told Mary that she was to be the Mother of Christ. Name this messenger angel.
Answer: Gabriel.

29) Divide 3/4 by 1/8, and express the result as an integer.
Answer: 6.

30) Name the Pope who issued on February 24, 1582, a calendar to correct the Julian Calendar, then 10 days in error.
Answer: Pope Gregory (XIII; the Gregorian Calendar became effective in most countries on 10/4/1582, with the following day set as 10/15).

31) Which amendment grants 18-year-olds the right to vote in U.S. elections? It is the 16th amendment following the Bill of Rights.
Answer: 26th Amendment (proposed by Congress on March 23, 1971).

32) Against which U.S. President did the House of Representatives vote articles of impeachment in a proceeding that began on February 24, 1868?
Answer: Andrew Johnson.

33) When a boat enters the Mississippi River from its source at Lake Itasca and travels south, what is the first state capital this boat will pass?
Answer: St. Paul (Minnesota).

34) Over the set of reals, completely factor the following: $21x^2y^2 - 7x^3y^3$ (READ: twenty-one x squared y squared minus seven x cubed y cubed).
Answer: $7x^2y^2$ (3 − xy).

35) Neo-fascist candidate Alessandra Mussolini lost a mayoral race in Naples, Italy. Does *neo-* in *neo-fascist* mean "old," "new," "against," or "false"?
Answer: New (she is Benito Mussolini's grand-daughter).

36) An organism may have either matched or unmatched genes for a particular trait. What is the term for an organism having matched genes for a given trait?
Answer: Homozygous or purebred.

37) Name the author of the following lines, "If you can keep your head when all about you / Are losing theirs and blaming it on you, . . ." He is an India-born British author.
Answer: Rudyard Kipling.

38) Identify the carnivorous mammal of the genus *Vulpes* whose name has come to mean "a sly, cunning, deceitful person."
Answer: Fox.

39) An organism may have either matched or unmatched genes for a particular trait. What is the term for one carrying unlike genes for a trait?
Answer: Heterozygous or hybrid.

40) What is the term for "submission of an issue to the people for a direct vote": *caucus, gerrymander, primary,* or *referendum*?
Answer: Referendum.

41) Which word, Japanese for "empty orchestra," is used to designate a stereo and video machine that provides words and music to sing to?
Answer: Karaoke.

42) Name the only other President besides John F. Kennedy to be buried in Virginia's Arlington National Cemetery. Before his death in 1930, he also served as chief justice of the U.S.
Answer: William Howard Taft.

43) Name the highest mountain system in the world, which extends from Pakistan, the world's first Islamic republic, into India, Tibet, and Nepal.
   Answer: Himalayas.

44) In computer programming, what name is given to the repetition of some function within a program until a terminating condition is reached?
   Answer: Loop.

45) Identify the capital of India where 100,000 police prevented a planned anti-government rally by Hindu extremists in 1992.
   Answer: New Delhi.

46) Which carbohydrate is the chief substance in plant cell walls?
   Answer: Cellulose.

47) In which U.S. state did Paul Bunyan and his blue ox Babe allegedly create ten thousand lakes when their footprints filled with water?
   Answer: Minnesota.

48) Identify the 11th-century English woman who allegedly rode naked through Coventry to protest her husband's imposition of taxes on the people.
   Answer: Lady Godiva.

49) Completely factor the following: $x^3 - 8x^2$.
   Answer: $x^2 (x - 8)$.

50) In which Canadian province did President Clinton hold a summit with Boris Yeltsin in the city of Vancouver?
   Answer: British Columbia.

51) Name the alleged assassin who was killed by Jack Ruby before he could be tried. Ruby was convicted of the murder on March 14, 1964.
   Answer: Lee Harvey Oswald (he killed President John Kennedy).

52) Which Ohio-born President was assassinated at a Washington, D.C., railway station in 1881?
   Answer: James A. Garfield.

53) Which South American country is the first one due south of Miami, Florida, at 80 degrees West longitude?
   Answer: Ecuador.

54) An 18-wheeler loaded with birdseed weighs 20,000 pounds. If the truck represents 20% of the weight, how much does the birdseed weigh?
   Answer: 16,000 pounds.

55) In which country, whose name comes from the Latin word for "southern," did Prime Minister Paul Keating call for Britain's Queen Elizabeth to be replaced as head of state?
Answer: **Australia (the Latin word *australis* means "southern").**

56) What is the term for the end of a nerve cell that triggers a nerve impulse when stimulated?
Answer: **Dendrite (accept dendron).**

57) Which character in a Lewis Carroll work repeatedly shouts "Off with his head!" when she is crossed during a croquet match?
Answer: **Queen of Hearts (in *Alice's Adventures in Wonderland*).**

58) Name 2 of the 3 German composers known as the "3 B's" of the musical world.
Answer: **Johann Sebastian Bach, Ludwig van Beethoven, and Johannes Brahms.**

59) By genus and species, man is a *Homo sapiens*. What is his family?
Answer: **Hominidae.**

60) In which city was a prison-fortress called the Bastille stormed by a revolutionary mob on July 14, 1789? This prison stood as a hated symbol of the monarchy's oppression of the people.
Answer: **Paris.**

61) In which year did all of the following take place: the creation of the Dewey Decimal System, the Battle of Little Big Horn, the awarding of the first U.S. patent for the telephone to Alexander Graham Bell, and the U.S. Centennial Exposition?
Answer: **1876.**

62) Which patriot in 1775 spoke these words in favor of arming the militia: "I know not what course others may take, but as for me, give me liberty or give me death"?
Answer: **Patrick Henry.**

63) As western European floods claimed 29 lives in 1995, up to a quarter of a million people fled their homes in the Netherlands. On which sea does this small low-lying country lie?
Answer: **North Sea.**

64) What is the product of the 5 smallest positive integers?
Answer: **120 (1 times 2 times 3 times 4 times 5).**

65) In which rain forest extending across much of Northern Brazil was a brand-new species of monkey found in 1992?
Answer: Amazon rain forest (the new species is named the Maues marmoset).

66) The term *Homo sapiens* designates man's genus and species. What is his order?
Answer: Primates.

67) Give the tense and voice of the verb, "He was throwing the ball too hard."
Answer: Past tense (or past progressive tense), active voice.

68) A judge upheld a city's barring of 19 suspected gang members from entering a neighborhood, a decision that lawyers say may violate freedom-of-assembly rights guaranteed under the 1st Amendment. Spell *guaranteed*.
Answer: G-U-A-R-A-N-T-E-E-D.

69) What is the square root of 1,225?
Answer: 35.

70) In 1993, the tiny principality of Andorra voted to end 7 centuries of feudal rule by the French head of state and the bishop of Urgel in Spain. In which mountains between France and Spain is Andorra located?
Answer: Pyrenees.

71) In 1993, nuns left their convent at Auschwitz in Poland in order to preserve it as a memorial to the more than 2-million Jews executed there. What word including the Greek root for "burnt" designates this attempted genocide of the Jewish people?
Answer: Holocaust (*holo-* means "whole"; *caust* means "burnt").

72) In which year did Delaware become the first to ratify the proposed U.S. Constitution on December 7?
Answer: 1787 (Delaware is known as the "First State of the Union").

73) Identify the state whose governor Walter Hickel once supported the killing of 100 wolves in order to help boost the delta caribou herd. This state is known as "The Last Frontier."
Answer: Alaska.

74) Find the slope of the line with equation $y = 4$.
Answer: Zero (do NOT accept "undefined" or "no slope").

75) Name the world's second-tallest building, site of a 1993 bomb explosion that killed 5 people, injured 600, and forced thousands to flee down dark, smoke-filled stairs.
Answer: World Trade Center.

76) Which term is used to designate a layer of permanently frozen subsoil?
Answer: Permafrost.

77) In which century was playwright and actor William Shakespeare born?
Answer: 16th (Shakespeare was born in 1564 and died in 1616).

78) In which spacecraft, named for the Greek god of the sun, did Frank Borman circle the moon 10 times on Christmas Eve and Christmas Day, 1968?
Answer: *Apollo* (8).

79) Name the Austrian biologist and monk who discovered the laws of heredity by experimenting with pea plants.
Answer: Gregor Mendel.

80) In the aftermath of which 1962 crisis did President Kennedy and Nikita Khrushchev exchange the letters later released by the U.S. and Russian governments?
Answer: Cuban Missile Crisis.

81) Monitors are members of the taxonomic family of the world's largest lizards. Identify the largest of these monitors, one that grows up to ten feet long and has the word "dragon" as part of its name.
Answer: Komodo dragon.

82) Which future U.S. President began his first political race on March 9, 1832, when he announced his candidacy for the Illinois legislature?
Answer: Abraham Lincoln.

83) Name the world's tallest building, a 1,454-foot tower in Chicago.
Answer: Sears Tower.

84) How much barbed wire is needed to cross diagonally over a rectangular field that is 66 feet wide and 88 feet long?
Answer: 110 feet.

85) Which vast Russian region covered by ice and snow about 6 months a year was used by the Communist regime as a place of exile for political prisoners?
Answer: Siberia.

86) Four molars, two on the upper jaw and two on the lower jaw, are the last teeth to emerge in the mouth. What is the name for these teeth that appear during the late teens or early twenties?
Answer: Wisdom teeth.

87) Identify the sentence structure error that occurs when a comma, instead of a period, a semicolon, or a coordinating conjunction, is used between 2 complete sentences.
Answer: Comma fault or comma splice (accept run-on sentence).

88) In 1993, an estimated 15,000 people died before rebels seized Angola's second most populous city, Huambo. Spell *seized*.
Answer: S-E-I-Z-E-D.

89) What is the result of the following calculation: negative 2 times negative 2 times negative 2 divided by negative 2?
Answer: 4.

90) Which country came into formal existence on September 21, 1949, when the 3 Western zones were officially combined?
Answer: West Germany (or the Federal Republic of Germany).

CHAPTER EIGHTEEN

1) Name the electronic device surgically implanted into a person's body to regulate the heartbeat.
   Answer: Pacemaker (or a sinoatrial node).

2) On August 2, 1776, 50 of the 56 delegates officially signed which important U.S. document?
   Answer: Declaration of Independence.

3) Name the national park along the border between North Carolina and Tennessee.
   Answer: Great Smoky Mountains (accept Smoky Mountains).

4) What is the square root of .09?
   Answer: .3.

5) According to an EPA survey, a number of U.S. schools have unacceptably high levels of which gas that is the second leading cause of lung cancer?
   Answer: Radon.

6) Which word identifies the roof of the mouth that separates the mouth from the nasal cavity?
   Answer: Palate.

7) English playwright William Shakespeare was baptized on April 26, 1564, in the parish church at Stratford-on-Avon. Spell *playwright*.
   Answer: P-L-A-Y-W-R-I-G-H-T.

8) What name is given to the period of artistic and intellectual achievement during which Michelangelo served as the architect of St. Peter's in Rome and sculpted *David* and *The Pietà*?
   Answer: Renaissance.

9) Find the area of a trapezoid whose bases are 20 inches and 30 inches in length and whose height is 15 inches.
   Answer: 375 square inches.

10) In which country was the RAF founded on April 1, 1918?
    Answer: Great Britain (the RAF is the Royal Air Force).

11) What name is given to scientists who study seismic waves produced by earthquakes or explosions?
Answer: Seismologists.

12) How many votes are required to break a filibuster in the U.S. Senate, a count that equals 3/5 of the membership?
Answer: 60 votes.

13) President Clinton's special emissary for POW-MIA affairs visited Vietnam to assess the country's help in accounting for Americans missing since the war. What is Vietnam's capital?
Answer: Hanoi.

14) Find the slope of the line with equation $x = 5$.
Answer: No slope (accept "undefined" but do NOT accept "zero").

15) Around which South American cape must ships sail to break a sailing record when making a voyage from San Francisco to Boston?
Answer: Cape Horn.

16) Which part of the human body consists of a bowl-shaped group of bones connecting the trunk of the body to the legs and supporting the spine? It includes the hip bones and the lower part of the backbone.
Answer: Pelvis.

17) Which "colorful" term is used to describe "professional or office wage earners whose work generally does not involve manual labor"?
Answer: White collar.

18) Spell the word *larynx*.
Answer: L-A-R-Y-N-X.

19) What name is given to the 24 bones that enclose the heart and lungs?
Answer: Ribs (or rib cage).

20) Name the 2 houses of the British Parliament.
Answer: House of Commons and House of Lords.

21) Give the full name of the NAACP. It is the nation's oldest and largest civil rights group.
Answer: National Association for the Advancement of Colored People.

22) Before a joint session of Congress on April 2, 1917, what did President Wilson say "must be made safe for democracy"?
Answer: "The world."

23) Name the grassy strip of land between the Washington Monument and the Capitol near which the new U.S. Holocaust Memorial Museum is located.
Answer: The Mall (or The Washington Mall; the museum honors those who perished under Nazism).

24) Identify the type of equation defined by the following: two ratios equal to each other, for example, a is to c as b is to d.
Answer: Proportion.

25) A Florida doctor charged with killing his terminally ill wife with a drug overdose was found not guilty. Which word from the Greek for "good death" means "mercy killing"?
Answer: Euthanasia.

26) What name is given to the ringlike bones that makeup the spinal column?
Answer: Vertebrae (vertebra is the singular).

27) Identify the city in which the Stuart Little family lives in E.B. White's children's novel *Stuart Little*.
Answer: New York City.

28) American teacher and journalist Noah Webster published his first dictionary in 1806. Is a maker of dictionaries a *cartographer, lexicographer, graphologist,* or *pathologist*?
Answer: Lexicographer.

29) Give all values of x satisfying the following equation: absolute value of x equals 2.
Answer: 2 and –2 (two and negative two; both answers are required).

30) Which South American country celebrates April 2 as a national holiday to commemorate its attempt to recover what it calls the Malvinas Islands, known also as the Falkland Islands? It is the second largest country in South America.
Answer: Argentina (it engaged in a fight with Britain from April 2 to June 14, 1982).

31) Name the Russian space station that celebrated its seventh anniversary in orbit in 1993. Its name means "peace."
Answer: *Mir* (it is expected to continue operating through 1996).

32) Name the English engineer who in 1856 patented his process for making steel from molten pig iron.
Answer: Henry Bessemer.

33) Which building celebrated its 60th anniversary in 1991? Faye Wray and King Kong who helped immortalize this building in the 1933 movie *King. Kong* showed up at the 1991 festivities.
Answer: Empire State Building.

34) Its surface area is found by squaring the length of one edge and multiplying by six. Its volume is found by cubing the length of one edge. Name this geometric solid.
Answer: Cube.

35) What word beginning and ending with the letter *A* designates "the schedule of issues to be discussed at a peace talk or any other meeting"?
Answer: Agenda.

36) Which Georgia city derives its name from the term for tropical or subtropical grasslands?
Answer: Savannah.

37) In Katherine Paterson's *Bridge to Terabithia*, in which activity does newcomer Leslie Burke beat all the boys in Mrs. Myers' fifth grade class, thereby ending the competition?
Answer: Running (or racing).

38) Name King Arthur's sister who, according to one legend, threw his sword Excalibur into the lake and tried to murder him by means of a poisoned robe.
Answer: Morgan(a) le Fay (or Margan la Fée).

39) Which name is Greek for "naked seed" and identifies a seed plant with seeds not enclosed in an ovary? The conifers are the most familiar group of this type.
Answer: Gymnosperm.

40) Give the English meaning of the Russian word *glasnost*.
Answer: Openness ("forthrightness" in publicizing problems and weaknesses of the former Soviet society).

41) Name Caesar's adoptive son who, by the time of his death in A.D. 14, had totally transformed the physical appearance of Rome through an impressive building program. A summer month is named for him.
Answer: Augustus (Octavian).

42) Which U.S. President is known for saying, "Speak softly and carry a big stick"?
Answer: Theodore Roosevelt.

43) Which 2 U.S. capitals beginning with the letter *S* are located in states bordering the Pacific Ocean?
Answer: Sacramento (California) and Salem (Oregon).

44) The following formula would find the volume of which geometric solid: 4/3 *pi* times the radius cubed?
Answer: Sphere.

45) Identify the 2 Indian groups of Mexico and Central America that developed advanced civilizations with written languages and large cities.
Answer: Aztecs and Mayas.

46) Which term designates both the reproductive structure of a conifer and a type of light-sensitive neuron in the retina of a vertebrate?
Answer: Cone.

47) Six years after he was taken to Ireland by pirates and sold into slavery, who escaped, became a monk in France, and later returned to Ireland as a missionary? March 17 commemorates his feast day.
Answer: Saint Patrick.

48) Which name designates both the Jewish Feast of Weeks and the Christian feast celebrating the coming of the Holy Spirit upon Jesus disciples? This term is derived from the Greek word for "fiftieth."
Answer: Pentecost (the 7th Sunday, or 50th day, after Easter).

49) Simplify the following expression: $66y/3 - 34y$ = (READ: 66y divided by 3 minus 34y).
Answer: –12y.

50) Saints Peter and Paul were allegedly executed in 64 A.D. after which emperor blamed the Christians for the fire that destroyed most of Rome?
Answer: Nero.

51) Which name for the second period of the Mesozoic Era, during which dinosaurs dominated and flying reptiles and birds appeared, completes the title of Michael Crichton's novel _____ *Park*?
Answer: *Jurassic*.

52) Name the town where Captain John Parker rallied the militia on April 19, 1775, by saying, "Don't fire unless fired upon, but if they mean to have a war, let it begin here!"
Answer: Lexington (Massachusetts).

53) How many independent countries are there on the South American continent? The number is the same as the number of signs of the zodiac.
Answer: 12.

54) Give the next number in the following sequence: 810, 270, 90, 30,....
Answer: 10.

55) Name the U.S. state whose House of Representatives voted in 1988 to impeach Republican Governor Evan Mecham. Tucson is its second largest city.
Answer: Arizona.

56) What name is given to the process in science involving the loss of two hydrogen atoms for every oxygen atom, or "the removal of water"?
Answer: Dehydration.

57) Lt. William L. Calley Jr. was the only military man court-martialed and convicted for the 1968 My Lai massacre of over 100 unarmed civilians in Viet Nam. Spell *massacre*.
Answer: M-A-S-S-A-C-R-E.

58) Name Tibet's spiritual ruler who fled from his country following a revolt by natives against Communist Chinese troops on March 13, 1959. He was awarded the 1989 Nobel Peace Prize.
Answer: Dalai Lama.

59) Emphysema affects the lungs. What part of the body does glaucoma affect?
Answer: Eyes.

60) Name the country of Prince Rainier, whom Grace Kelly married in 1956.
Answer: Monaco.

61) In which U.S. city was the Space Needle opened at the 1962 World's Fair?
Answer: Seattle (Washington).

62) Name one of the following 2 U.S. presidents: the one who left office in 1869 or the one who left office in 1969.
Answer: Andrew Johnson or Lyndon Johnson.

63) Which state bordering the province of Quebec was admitted as the 23rd state on March 15, 1820? Its capital shares its name with the Georgia city that hosts the Masters golf tournament.
Answer: Maine (Maine's capital is Augusta).

64) A student must answer exactly 12 questions on a test in order to receive the lowest passing grade of 75%. How many questions were on the examination?
Answer: 16.

65) What term designating a kind of meat also describes government funds acquired by a legislator for special local projects as a kind of political favor?
Answer: Pork.

66) Which endocrine gland releases 2 important hormones, insulin and glucagon?
Answer: Pancreas (or isles of Langerhans).

67) Name the Civil War nurse who wrote *Little Men* and *Little Women*.
Answer: Louisa May Alcott.

68) "The Star-Spangled Banner" was officially adopted as the national anthem on March 3, 1931. Complete the question that ends this song: "Oh! say, does that star-spangled banner yet wave / O'er the ...?"
Answer: "land of the free and the home of the brave?"

69) If 5 factorial is multiplies by the multiplicative inverse of 4 factorial, what is the answer?
Answer: 5.

70) In which decade of the 19th century did the Spanish-American War begin?
Answer: 1890s (on April 21, 1898).

71) Traditionally, how many colors are said to be in a rainbow?
Answer: 7.

72) Name the 2 U.S. Presidents born in Massachusetts in the 20th century.
Answer: John Kennedy and George Bush.

73) Name 3 of the 4 U.S. capitals whose names begin with the letter *H*.
Answer: Hartford (Connecticut), Honolulu (Hawaii), Helena (Montana), and Harrisburg (Pennsylvania).

74) How many square yards are there in a rectangular floor that is 6 feet by 6 feet?
Answer: 4 square yards.

75) The world's longest and toughest auto race, an 8,000-mile grind from Paris to Dakar, generates its share of protest from conservationists and others. On which 2 continents is this race run?
Answer: Europe and Africa.

76) What name is given to the process by which oxygen and iron form rust? This same process occurs when apples or potatoes turn brown as a result of combining with oxygen.
Answer: Oxidation.

77) How many ghosts visit Ebenezer Scrooge on Christmas Eve in Charles Dickens' *A Christmas Carol*?
Answer: Four (Ghost of Christmas Past / Ghost of Christmas Present / Ghost of Christmas Future / Jacob Marley).

78) What name is give to the primitive method of clearing land by cutting vegetation, letting it dry, and then setting it on fire prior to cultivating the soil and planting crops?
Answer: Slash-and-burn.

79) Which Greek formulated the principle that an object immersed in a fluid is buoyed up by a force equal to the weight of the fluid it displaces?
Answer: Archimedes (Archimedes' principle).

80) Give the current name for the Latin American nation called British Honduras until it gained independence from Britain on September 21, 1981.
Answer: Belize.

81) On which day in medieval times did villagers dance around a pole while holding ribbons streaming from its top? This day is now celebrated as Labor Day in socialist countries.
Answer: May Day, or May 1.

82) Which U.S. President shocked the country by announcing on March 31, 1968, that he would not run for reelection? At the same time, he announced a reduction in the bombing attacks on North Vietnam.
Answer: Lyndon Johnson.

83) Yellowstone National Park was established by Congress on March 1, 1872, as the nation's first national park. In which rectangularly shaped state is it primarily located?
Answer: Wyoming.

84) Give the next number in the following sequence: 2, 6, 14, 30, 62,....
Answer: 126.

85) Name the former Texas congresswoman, later a professor at the University of Texas in Austin, who was inducted into the African-American Hall of Fame. Her surname also designates a river of Biblical fame.
Answer: Barbara Jordan (she died at age 59 in 1996).

86) To which of the 3 classes of rock does obsidian belong?
Answer: Igneous.

87) Identify the New England poet who wrote "The Road Not Taken" and "Mending Wall."
Answer: Robert Frost.

88) Which word beginning with the letters *Pr* designates "a piece of music that introduces a suite or fugue"?
Answer: Prelude.

89) Are geometric figures that have the same shape but not the same size said to be *congruent, isosceles, parallel,* or *similar*?
Answer: Similar.

90) Name the founder of the Russian Communist Party, who was born Vladimir I. Ulyanov. He died on January 21, 1924.
Answer: V.I. Lenin.

CHAPTER NINETEEN

1) In which U.S. state did the Calvert family serve as the lords proprietor?
   Answer: Maryland.

2) Which Virginia-born U.S. President moved into the Octagon House after the British burned the White House in 1814?
   Answer: James Madison.

3) In which state did Congress establish Hot Springs National Park?
   Answer: Arkansas.

4) If a woman earns $2,000 simple interest over four years on an investment of $5,000, what is the annual interest rate she receives?
   Answer: 10%.

5) Nearly 7 years after it was introduced, which bill requiring a 5-day waiting period for handgun purchases was passed by Congress and signed by President Clinton?
   Answer: Brady bill (introduced in 1986; named for James Brady, who was injured in an assassination attempt on President Reagan in 1981).

6) To which of the 3 classes of rock does marble belong?
   Answer: Metamorphic.

7) Name the British author whose tales about Peter Rabbit and friends have been animated for TV although in 1935 she refused Walt Disney's request to animate her works.
   Answer: Beatrix Potter.

8) Identify the German nun whose drawings inspired the world-famous cherub-like figurines named for her. These drawings are now displayed in a new Texas museum housing her work.
   Answer: Sister M.I. Hummel (the museum is in New Braunfels).

9) How many different 3-letter arrangements are there for the letters A, B, and C?
   Answer: 6.

10) Identify any one of the 3 centuries in which the Crusades, the military expeditions Christians undertook to recapture the Holy Land, took place.
Answer: 11th, 12th, or 13th.

11) Name the baseball player whose 1919 sales agreement was sold in 1992 for $99,000, only $1,000 less than the actual price the New York Yankees paid the Boston Red Sox for the rights to this player sometimes called "Bambino."
Answer: Babe Ruth.

12) Which North American Indians, renowned as great fighters, formed a League or Confederacy of Five Nations about 1570? They controlled both boat travel on the Great Lakes and the fur trade in their area.
Answer: Iroquois.

13) Identify the U.S. territory whose Spanish name means "rich port."
Answer: Puerto Rico.

14) Solve for x in the following equation: $x^2 + 1 = 10$.
Answer: $x = 3$ and $x = -3$ (both answers required).

15) On March 8, 1993, which celestial body was 17,326 miles closer to Earth than average in its elliptical orbit, teaming up with the Earth and sun in a rare alignment that created surging tides throughout the U.S. as it did the last time the 3 lined up 31 years earlier?
Answer: Moon.

16) Name the useful material made up of about 72% silica or sand, 15% sodium oxide or soda, and 9% calcium oxide or lime.
Answer: Glass (and 4% minor ingredients).

17) In which Robert Louis Stevenson novel are the hero and villain the same person?
Answer: *Dr. Jekyll and Mr. Hyde.*

18) In which religion, established in India in the 6th century B.C., do adherents seek to follow the Noble Eightfold Path?
Answer: Buddhism.

19) Which color is produced when yellow and blue pigments are mixed?
Answer: Green.

20) In which year was D-Day's 50th anniversary marked by ceremonies on the beaches in Normandy?
Answer: 1994 (in commemorating D-Day, June 6, 1944).

21) Congress passed the Standard Time Act in March 1918, authorizing the ICC to establish standard time zones. Name the 4 time zones in the continental U.S.
Answer: Eastern, Central, Mountain, and Pacific.

22) In which year did the U.S. declare war on Germany on April 6 to enter WWI?
Answer: 1917.

23) One of the steps on the capitol building of which U.S. state capital is exactly 5,280 feet above sea level?
Answer: Denver.

24) What is the mean for the following set of 6 numbers: −3, −1, 0, 2, 2, 3?
Answer: .5 (or 1/2).

25) Scientists have identified a gene that apparently causes the progressively paralyzing disease ALS. For which New York Yankees star who died of the illness in 1941 is this disease popularly named?
Answer: Lou Gehrig (the disease is amyotrophic lateral sclerosis).

26) Which word, Latin for "crown," is used in astronomy to designate a ring of light seen around the sun, moon, or other luminous bodies?
Answer: Corona.

27) Name the school teacher frightened by the headless horseman in Washington Irving's *The Legend of Sleepy Hollow*.
Answer: Ichabod Crane.

28) Which island 2,200 miles off the coast of Chile is known for its gigantic prehistoric statues? It is named for a religious holiday.
Answer: Easter Island.

29) In the division problem x divided by y, what name beginning with the letter D is given to x?
Answer: Dividend.

30) At a commemoration of Thomas Jefferson's 250th birthday, President Clinton compared his run-in with Congress on a stalled jobs bill to the opposition Jefferson faced with which 1803 transaction to buy 828,000 square miles for about $15 million?
Answer: Louisiana Purchase.

31) Which term designates either of the 2 times during the year when day and night are of equal length? One of these occurs about March 20, marking the first day of spring in the Northern Hemisphere.
Answer: Equinox (March equinox is the vernal, or spring, equinox).

32) Name the black trail blazer who, along with Robert Peary and 4 Eskimos, reached the North Pole on April 6, 1909.
Answer: Matthew Henson.

33) In which state have archaeologists found evidence of a camp dating back 11,700 years, making it possibly the oldest inhabited site in North America? This archaeological site is about 225 miles south of Barrow.
Answer: Alaska.

34) In which quadrant is the point with coordinates (−.4,−.4) located?
Answer: Three or Third.

35) According to the Supreme Court, which amendment was violated when Cincinnati officials prohibited the distribution of magazines from sidewalk vending machines while allowing about 2,000 newspaper dispensers?
Answer: First Amendment (guaranteeing right of free speech or free press).

36) Which 3 planets, unknown to the ancient Greeks, were discovered after the invention of the telescope?
Answer: Uranus, Neptune, and Pluto.

37) Colonel Juan Perón became the absolute dictator in Argentina in 1945. Which of the following is a synonym for dictator: *monarch, charlatan, pedagogue,* or *despot*?
Answer: Despot.

38) According to scientists, wall paintings in the Vatican's Sistine Chapel in Rome have been damaged by perspiring visitors who exude 220 pounds of moisture a day. What are pictures painted directly on a wall called?
Answer: Murals (accept frescoes).

39) In its white form, which element, whose name is derived from the Greek for "light bearer," glows in the dark when exposed to air?
Answer: Phosphorus.

40) From which island nation of the Western Hemisphere did 14,000 children migrate to the U.S. without their parents between 1961 and 1963 because of the fear that children would be sent to the Soviet Union for Communist indoctrination?
   Answer: Cuba (the project was called "Operation Peter Pan").

41) The Ayatollah Khomeini, the invasion of Panama, the movie *Tootsie*, and the eruption of Mt. St. Helens are all included in a photo essay book about which decade?
   Answer: 1980s (the book is *The Eighties: Images of America*).

42) Name the controversial FBI director who died on May 2, 1972, after 48 years of service. He shares his surname with a former U.S. President for whom a large dam on the Colorado River is named.
   Answer: J. Edgar Hoover.

43) Which Confederate general is famous for his "charge" against the center of a dug-in Union line at Gettysburg in July 1863?
   Answer: George Pickett.

44) If you have a collection of 28 coins of quarters and nickels totaling $4.00, how many coins of each are there?
   Answer: 15 nickels, and 13 quarters.

45) A NASA spacecraft revealed that a planet may have harbored life in oceans up to 75 feet deep that once covered its surface. Name this planet that has been called Earth's twin.
   Answer: Venus (the spacecraft is *Pioneer Venus*).

46) Which disease, sometimes called consumption, primarily affects the lungs?
   Answer: Tuberculosis.

47) Identify the author whose young adult novels *The Winter Room*, *Hatchet*, and *Dogsong* have all been named Newbery Honor books.
   Answer: Gary Paulsen.

48) On the steps of which Washington, D.C., memorial did Marian Anderson sing on Easter Sunday in 1939 after having been denied use of the DAR's Constitution Hall?
   Answer: Lincoln Memorial.

49) Evaluate the algebraic expression $ab + c$ if $a = 5$, $b = 4$, and $c = 3$.
   Answer: 23.

50) Name the Soviet dictator, born Joseph Dzhugashvili, who died on March 5, 1953, after ruling for 24 years.
Answer: Joseph Stalin.

51) Identify the movie star whose name on the booster rockets of a Conestoga missile promoted the movie *Last Action Hero* in the first ad in space.
Answer: Arnold Schwarzenegger (the ad was bought by Columbia Pictures).

52) Name the first female U.S. attorney general, confirmed in 1993 by a 98-0 Senate vote. Her surname identifies a city in Nevada.
Answer: Janet Reno.

53) Spell the name of the state, the third smallest, in which Yale University was founded in Branford in 1701. The school was moved to New Haven in 1716.
Answer: C-O-N-N-E-C-T-I-C-U-T.

54) What name is given to a numerical superscript that expresses the power to which a quantity is to be raised?
Answer: Exponent.

55) Astronomers are studying at least 20 comet fragments that are now orbiting which large planet, fueling the possibility that similar debris may have bombarded Earth and wiped out dinosaurs 65 million years ago? Io and Europa are among this planet's 16 known satellites.
Answer: Jupiter.

56) Which term designates any substance dispensed from a container as a liquid spray by a propellant under pressure?
Answer: Aerosol.

57) Mildred Wirt Benson has been publicly recognized as the original Carolyn Keene, the pen name used for books about which teen sleuth?
Answer: Nancy Drew.

58) An *album* is a recording of different musical pieces. What word beginning with *A* designates a collection of writings?
Answer: Anthology.

59) Identify the natural component of the atmosphere that absorbs solar ultraviolet radiation. The atmospheric layer it forms is being destroyed by CFCs, or chlorofluorocarbons, used as propellants in aerosol containers.
Answer: Ozone.

60) On September 14, 1812, which Russian city was set on fire by its residents after Napoleon and his French troops invaded it? Hunger and cold later defeated Napoleon's Grand Army.
Answer: Moscow.

61) Which journalism award did the *Miami Herald* win in public service in reporting on Hurricane Andrew's devastation?
Answer: Pulitzer Prize (it also won a Pulitzer for commentary).

62) Following President Franklin Roosevelt's death at the Little White House in Warm Springs, Georgia, on April 12, 1945, who was sworn in as President in the White House in Washington, D.C.?
Answer: Harry S Truman.

63) On which strait between the city of Vancouver and Vancouver Island did President Clinton take a boat ride? A U.S. state and a former Soviet republic share its name.
Answer: Strait of Georgia.

64) Evaluate the following algebraic expression: $2x^2 + 3y + 6$ if $x = 2$ and $y = 9$.
Answer: 41.

65) Which European ruler was the subject of a $9.1 million exhibit in Memphis that included uniforms he wore? He was nicknamed the "Little Corporal."
Answer: Napoleon Bonaparte (accept Napoleon).

66) Which word is used in science to designate the chief means by which nutrients dissolved in fluids pass in and out of plant and animal cells?
Answer: Osmosis.

67) Which of the following names the pirate marooned by Captain Flint in Robert Louis Stevenson's *Treasure Island*: Pistol, Gunn, Rifle, or Cannon?
Answer: Ben Gunn.

68) Identify the art form in which small pieces of colored glass, stone, or tile are set into mortar to make pictures or designs.
Answer: Mosaic.

69) Add the following: the number of degrees in a right angle plus the number of degrees in a circle.
Answer: 450.

70) Name the former president of Panama who was convicted in a U.S. federal court on April 9, 1992, of cocaine trafficking and money laundering.
Answer: General Manuel Antonio Noriega.

71) In which 2 states does major league baseball spring training take place?
Answer: Florida and Arizona.

72) In which decade did Congress pass a major civil rights act on April 11, one week after the assassination of Dr. Martin Luther King Jr.?
Answer: 1960s (Civil Rights Act of 1968 prohibiting discrimination in housing sales).

73) In which state was the highest velocity natural wind in the U.S. recorded at Mount Washington in 1934? It joins Vermont to make a somewhat irregular rectangle.
Answer: New Hampshire.

74) What is the measure of an angle that is a complement of an angle measuring 17 degrees?
Answer: 73 degrees.

75) Identify Donald Trump's $1 billion casino resort in Atlantic City that opened in 1990. It shares the name of an Indian tomb built by a ruler for his favorite wife.
Answer: Taj Mahal.

76) Which astronomer and mathematician predicted that the great comet he observed in 1682 would reappear 76 years later? This comet is now named for him.
Answer: Edmund Halley.

77) Name the "Lady with the Lamp" who worked night and day during the Crimean War and is considered the founder of modern nursing.
Answer: Florence Nightingale.

78) Which word beginning with the letters *Ov* designates the orchestral introduction to an opera, Broadway musical, or other extended musical work?
Answer: Overture.

79) What have you injured if you have hurt your proboscis?
Answer: Nose.

80) On February 12, 1839, which U.S. state became involved in a border dispute with the Canadian province of New Brunswick in what is known as the Aroostook War? The name of its capital begins and ends with the same vowel.
Answer: Maine (its capital is Augusta).

81) Name either of the 2 spring training leagues in major league baseball. One bears the name of a citrus fruit, and the other, a desert plant.
Answer: Grapefruit League (Florida) or Cactus League (Arizona).

82) Identify the system of escape stations used to help runaway slaves reach Canada during the 1850s and 1860s.
Answer: Underground railroad.

83) Which of the following designates a valley in the ocean: reef, trench, atoll, or nadir?
Answer: Trench.

84) What is the mode for the following set of 6 numbers: −3, −1, 0, 2, 2, 3?
Answer: 2.

85) What is the popular name for the metropolitan police force founded in London on September 29, 1829, a name derived from the site of its first headquarters near Charing Cross?
Answer: (New) Scotland Yard.

86) Identify the legendary huge, ape-like creature said to live in the Pacific Northwest. The Canadians call this creature Sasquatch.
Answer: Bigfoot.

87) In which country does Hugh Lofting's Dr. Dolittle make his home at Puddleby-on-the-Marsh?
Answer: England.

88) Which German composer wrote an orchestral overture for *A Midsummer Night's Dream* in 1826 when he was 17 years old? Seventeen years later he wrote the "Wedding March" for the same play.
Answer: Felix Mendelssohn.

89) Solve for x in the following equation: $x^2 - 16 = 0$.
Answer: $x = 4$ and $x = -4$ (both answers required).

90) Name the king of Egypt who at age 9 or 10 ascended the throne about 1348 B.C. and served until he died in 1339 B.C.
Answer: Tutankhamen (or Tutankhaton).

CHAPTER TWENTY

1) Identify the California-born U.S. Supreme Court chief justice who headed the investigation of John Kennedy's death. His surname identifies the commission report resulting from this investigation.
   Answer: (Earl) Warren (the Warren Commission Report).

2) Identify the 17th U.S. President. He took office upon the death of his predecessor.
   Answer: Andrew Johnson.

3) According to a conservation group, which 1,885-mile river that flows from Colorado to the Gulf of Mexico is one of the most endangered rivers in North America?
   Answer: Rio Grande.

4) The square of the perimeter of a square is 3,600. What is the area of the square?
   Answer: 225.

5) After 30 years of war that ended in 1991, citizens of Eritrea voted in a worldwide 3-day referendum in 1993 to declare independence from which African country bordering Sudan, Somalia, and Kenya?
   Answer: Ethiopia.

6) Give the formula for table salt, or sodium chloride.
   Answer: $NaCl$.

7) Give the word for "a corpse that becomes reanimated at night and leaves its grave to suck the blood of sleeping persons."
   Answer: Vampire.

8) Which Asian country has the largest Hindu population?
   Answer: India.

9) What percent is equal to 1/8?
   Answer: 12½% (12.5%).

10) Identify the 2 countries that signed an accord on September 17, 1978, at Camp David, Maryland, after President Jimmy Carter oversaw the negotiations.
    Answer: Israel and Egypt.

11) Name the 1992 NBA rookie who in his first 3½ months with the Orlando Magic had $30 million in ad deals with Reebok, Pepsi Cola, Spalding, and Scoreboard trading cards.
Answer: Shaquille O'Neal.

12) On which mountain did the Civil War "Battle of the Clouds" begin in Tennessee on November 23, 1863? Its name designates a person who keeps watch.
Answer: Lookout Mountain.

13) In which state do avalanches sometime result in extreme hazard ratings for the mountains near Aspen and Crested Butte?
Answer: Colorado.

14) If the hands on the clock indicate 8:00, how many degrees are in the smaller angle formed by the hands?
Answer: 120.

15) GATT is a 123-nation world trade agreement signed in 1994. What words represented by the 2 *T*'s complete GATT's full name, General Agreement on _____ and _____?
Answer: Tariffs and Trade (developed over a period of 7 years).

16) Give the common name for sodium bicarbonate.
Answer: Baking soda.

17) What is the grammatical function of the pronoun *him* in the following sentence: "I brought him with me."
Answer: Direct object.

18) Which of the following French impressionists is known for his paintings of his garden at Giverny and at Argenteuil: Manet, Morisot, Monet, or Renoir?
Answer: Claude Monet.

19) Of hydrogen, helium, nitrogen, or magnesium, which one comprises about 70 per cent of the chemical makeup of the sun?
Answer: Hydrogen.

20) What is the capital of the Jutland Peninsula country in which Queen Margrethe's birthday, April 16, is a national holiday?
Answer: Copenhagen (Denmark).

21) Pitcairn Island, 1,100 miles west of Easter Island, is inhabited by descendants of the mutineers who set commander William Bligh adrift in 1789 from which British ship?
Answer: H.M.S. *Bounty*.

22) Which island, now incorporated as part of New York City, did Dutch colonizer Peter Minuit buy from the Indians sometime after landing there on May 4, 1626?
Answer: Manhattan Island.

23) Name the 3 contiguous U.S. states bordering the Pacific Ocean.
Answer: California, Oregon, and Washington.

24) Solve the following equation: $2y - 17 = -29$.
Answer: $y = -6$ (y equals negative six).

25) Name the fruit targeted in a nationwide boycott in the 1960s by California farm labor organizer Cesar Chavez.
Answer: Grapes.

26) In computer hardware, what does the term CPU stand for?
Answer: Central Processing Unit.

27) Name the poet whose books, particularly *I Know Why The Caged Bird Sings* and a poetry collection, increased in sales 300-600% following her 1993 inaugural appearance.
Answer: Maya Angelou.

28) Which major league pitcher on May 5, 1904, threw baseball's first perfect game in the 20th century? The annual award for the outstanding major league pitchers is named for him.
Answer: Denton T. "Cy" Young.

29) A pair of $70 shoes has been discounted 15%. What is the sale price?
Answer: $59.50.

30) Which Englishman, who died on his ship off the coast of Panama on January 28, 1596, was the first from his country to circumnavigate the world?
Answer: Sir Francis Drake.

31) Which day is Labor Day in the U.S.?
Answer: First Monday in September.

32) Give the beginning and ending years of the U.S. Civil War.
Answer: 1861-1865.

33) Name the largest lake in North America.
Answer: Lake Superior.

34) In lowest terms, what is the ratio of cashew nuts to peanuts in a mixture that contains 3 pounds of cashew nuts to 3 ounces of peanuts?
Answer: 16 to 1.

35) In which U.S. state did former Philippine leader Ferdinand Marcos die in 1989?
Answer: Hawaii.

36) Which of the following words designates the yellowing of the skin and other tissues that accompanies hepatitis: *edema, jaundice, pallor,* or *ruddiness?*
Answer: Jaundice.

37) What is the present participle of the verb *rise?*
Answer: Rising.

38) Several scholars questioned why the FBI did not take more seriously David Koresh's reflections on images of "fire mixed with blood" in the last book of the Bible. Name this book, also known as The Apocalypse.
Answer: Revelation.

39) Which word beginning with the letter *W* designates "the moon between the new moon and the full moon"?
Answer: Waxing moon.

40) In which region now controlled by China is the 1,000-room palace called the Potala located in the capital city of Lhasa?
Answer: Tibet.

41) On which monument in South Dakota did Casimir Ziolkowski begin working in 1948? When the carving is completed, this Indian chief on horseback will be 9 times taller than Mount Rushmore.
Answer: Crazy Horse (on Crazy Horse Mountain).

42) Which U.S. President was called the "Colossus of Debate"? This President, born in Massachusetts, was also the father of a U.S. President.
Answer: John Adams.

43) Near which Massachusetts city did Henry David Thoreau accidentally set fire to the woods on April 30, 1844, burning 100 acres? Its name means "harmony or agreement."
Answer: Concord.

44) If one angle of an isosceles triangle is 120 degrees, what is the measure of each of the other 2 angles?
Answer: 30 degrees.

45) In 1990, which international police agency located in Paris did the Soviet Union join?
Answer: Interpol.

46) Which Italian physicist and astronomer allegedly said, "But it [i.e., the earth] does move"? This remark was made after he was forced to recant his belief that the earth moves around the sun.
Answer: Galileo.

47) In the sentence "Speak up," what part of speech is the word "up"?
Answer: Adverb.

48) Identify a trombone as either a brass, woodwind, percussion, or stringed musical instrument.
Answer: Brass.

49) A rectangle is 45 feet long and 5 feet wide. What is the length of a side of a square that has the same area?
Answer: 15 feet.

50) Which African country fell to the Italians in May 1936 with the capture of the capital of Addis Ababa?
Answer: Ethiopia.

51) Name the "City of Brotherly Love," where the first U.S. mint was established by Congress on April 2, 1792.
Answer: Philadelphia.

52) Which Latin word is translated in English as "I forbid" and designates the "constitutional right or vested right of a ruler to reject bills passed by a government branch"?
Answer: Veto.

53) Of Central America, the Central U.S., Central Europe, Central Australia, or Central Asia, which one is the least populated?
Answer: Central Australia.

54) What integer is two-seventeenths of 51?
Answer: 6.

55) While serving a prison sentence for giving medical aid to John Wilkes Booth, Dr. Samuel Mudd saved many prisoners and guards during an epidemic of which infectious disease with a color in its name? President Johnson pardoned Mudd in 1869.
Answer: Yellow fever.

56) On which scale is the intensity of an earthquake measured—Richter, Mohs, Celsius, or Boyle scale?
Answer: Richter scale.

57) In which language was the story of Pinocchio originally written?
Answer: Italian.

58) Name the mythological giant cyclops who was defeated by Odysseus.
Answer: Polyphemus.

59) Which term designates the amount of heat required to raise the temperature of one lb. of water one degree Fahrenheit?
Answer: British Thermal Unit (accept BTU).

60) Give the year in which the German surrender was ratified in Berlin on May 7, a date now known as VE Day, or Victory in Europe Day.
Answer: 1945 (also announced by Truman on this date).

61) All or nothing: give the Pledge of Allegiance.
Answer: "I pledge allegiance to the flag of the United States of America and to the Republic for which it stands, one Nation under God, indivisible, with liberty and justice for all."

62) Who was commissioned as commander of all the Union armies on March 9, 1864?
Answer: Ulysses S. Grant.

63) In which modern-day Asian country is the ancient land of Mesopotamia primarily located?
Answer: Iraq.

64) Give the sum of the 4 interior angles of a quadrilateral.
Answer: 360 degrees.

65) Which amendment to the U.S. Constitution did former Housing Secretary Samuel Pierce invoke in refusing to answer questions during the investigation of influence-peddling in his department in 1989?
Answer: Fifth Amendment.

66) Which 2 minerals make up about 60% of the weight in the bones of the human body and give them hardness?
Answer: Calcium and phosphate.

67) Which of the following words means "fear of foreigners": claustrophobia, hydrophobia, xenophobia, or agoraphobia?
Answer: Xenophobia.

68) Name 2 of the 4 religions in India with the greatest percent of followers.
Answer: Hinduism, Islam (or Moslem), Christianity, and Sikhism.

69) Name the quadrilateral with only one pair of sides parallel.
Answer: Trapezoid.

70) Who was the king of England when the American Revolutionary War began?
Answer: George III.

71) Which once popular military vehicle has the U.S. replaced with the odd-looking "humvee"?
Answer: The jeep.

72) Identify the 26th U.S. President, who was the 5th cousin of the 32nd U.S. President.
Answer: Theodore Roosevelt.

73) In which continental U.S. state is the only living coral reef? This reef is threatened by pollution and human contact.
Answer: Florida.

74) If 1,500 people voted in a local election, and one woman received 80% of the vote, how many votes did she get?
Answer: 1,200.

75) Of North, East, South, or West, which one names a member of President Reagan's administration involved in the Iran-*Contra* affair?
Answer: (Oliver) North.

76) Which biological term designates any living thing?
Answer: Organism.

77) Which fictional character visited a fantastic land with her dog Toto?
Answer: Dorothy.

78) From which religious group were Christians attempting to recover the Holy Land during the Crusades from the 11th to the 13th century?
Answer: Muslims.

79) With which animals did Russian physiologist Ivan Pavlov conduct experiments involving a conditioned response?
Answer: Dogs.

80) After it seized millions of dollars' worth of American property, with which nearby country did the U.S. end diplomatic relations in January 1961?
Answer: Cuba.

81) Which sport is played on a gridiron?
Answer: Football.

82) Which U.S. President served the shortest time in office?
Answer: William Henry Harrison.

83) Which U.S. state is at the center of the New Madrid Fault zone, the most earthquake-prone area east of the Rocky Mountains? This state is known as the "Show-Me State."
Answer: Missouri.

84) What is the numerical value of 4 factorial?
Answer: 24.

85) Identify the British prime minister who led her country to victory over Argentina during the Falklands War in 1982.
Answer: Margaret Thatcher.

86) Of linear, square, or cubic units of measure, which one describes a measurement of .09 meters?
Answer: Linear.

87) Identify the literary character whose name today designates "an excessively optimistic person." The little girl in the novel by Eleanor Porter finds good in everything.
Answer: Pollyanna.

88) Which Italian 2-word term beginning with the letter *T* designates earthenware?
Answer: Terra cotta.

89) By what special name do we know a parallelogram with all sides congruent and all angles congruent?
Answer: Square (do NOT accept rectangle).

90) Who was queen of England from 1558 until her death in 1603?
Answer: Elizabeth I.

CHAPTER TWENTY-ONE

1) In the 1990s, customers could for the first time fax their ticket orders for a production in which New York City center of professional theater nicknamed "The Great White Way"?
Answer: Broadway.

2) Samuel Pierce was the first former Cabinet-level official to claim protection against self-incrimination under congressional questioning since the Teapot Dome scandal rocked the administration of which Republican President in the 1920s?
Answer: Warren Harding.

3) Lapland is a region that extends across parts of 4 countries. Name 2 of them.
Answer: Russia, Finland, Sweden, and Norway.

4) If each step in a staircase is 12 inches high, how many steps are in a staircase 15 feet high?
Answer: 15.

5) Which 2 cities were linked together again in 1989 when the Bay Bridge reopened a month after a section of it collapsed in the California earthquake?
Answer: San Francisco and Oakland.

6) Of the following, which one is NOT a compound: water, sugar, air, or nitrogen?
Answer: Nitrogen.

7) Which literary work features the Brobdinagians as characters?
Answer: *Gulliver's Travels.*

8) Which word beginning with the letter *G* describes the application of a thin layer of gold on the outer surface of pottery?
Answer: Gilding.

9) A box contains 100 pennies, 60 nickels, and 40 dimes. If one coin is taken from the box at random, what is the probability that it will be a dime?
Answer: 1/5 (accept 1 out of 5 and 40 out of 200).

10) On which continent was the ancient civilization of the Incas found?
Answer: South America.

11) Name the first woman to be pictured on a U.S. coin in general circulation.
Answer: Susan B. Anthony (she appeared on the dollar in 1979).

12) In 1989, L. Douglas Wilder made history by becoming the first black elected governor in the U.S. In which state, known as "The Old Dominion," was he elected?
Answer: Virginia.

13) Between which 2 states is the lake that Samuel de Champlain named after himself located?
Answer: New York and Vermont.

14) What is the area of a rectangle with a length of 9 feet and a width of 7.2 feet?
Answer: 64.8 square feet.

15) In which year, one year before the countries were reunified, did East Germany symbolically tear down the Berlin Wall by opening its borders with West Germany?
Answer: (November 9) 1989.

16) What term is used to describe fish and any other animal whose body temperature varies with the external environment?
Answer: Cold-blooded (also poikilothermous, poikilothermic, or ectothermic).

17) Name the great English poet who died on October 25, 1400, and was the first poet to be honored by burial in Westminster Abbey. He wrote *The Canterbury Tales*.
Answer: Geoffrey Chaucer.

18) Which word for "a clear, transparent quartz" completes the following line from Langston Hughes's poem "Mother to Son": "Life for me ain't been no _____ stair"?
Answer: "crystal."

19) What term designates scientists who study the physical history and structure of the earth and the physical changes which it has undergone and is still undergoing, especially as recorded in rock formations?
Answer: Geologists (accept geophysicists).

20) Who became the leader of the Soviet Union in 1985?
Answer: Mikhail Gorbachev.

21) Which terrorist group, with the initials IRA, had been responsible for huge bombs that shattered London's financial district?
Answer: Irish Republican Army.

22) To help save the nation's faltering banking system, which President closed the banks on March 5, 1933, for a period referred to as a "bank holiday"?
Answer: Franklin Roosevelt.

23) Name the highest mountain in Africa.
Answer: Mount Kilimanjaro.

24) What fraction is the reciprocal of the mixed number 4¾?
Answer: 4/19.

25) Name the Texan whose book *United We Stand: How We Can Take Back Our Country* was released 5 weeks after he gave up his bid for the presidency in 1992.
Answer: H. Ross Perot.

26) 6,000 grams equals how many kilograms?
Answer: 6.

27) Fishermen sometimes tend to exaggerate the size of the fish that got away. Spell the word *exaggerate*.
Answer: E-X-A-G-G-E-R-A-T-E.

28) Give the Italian word for "tail" that in music designates "a more or less independent passage at the end of a composition to bring it to a satisfactory close."
Answer: *Coda.*

29) Solve the following equation for x: *x over 7 minus 4x over 9 equals 1.*
Answer: $x = -63/19$ (accept $-3\frac{6}{19}$).

30) The Berlin Wall may have fallen, but on which island in the Mediterranean Sea does the so-called green line separate the Greek and Turkish sectors? Its capital is Nicosia.
Answer: Cyprus.

31) Identify the Eskimo canoe made of animal skins stretched over a wooden frame and designed to seat one person.
Answer: Kayak (or kaiak).

32) In which century did the U.S. gain its independence?
Answer: 18th.

33) Which 2 rivers flowed through ancient Mesopotamia?
Answer: Tigris and Euphrates.

34) If two lines intersect in right angles, what are the two lines said to be?
Answer: Perpendicular.

35) In which tiny European country did Prince Franz Josef II die in 1989 after a 51-year reign? This country is bordered by Switzerland and Austria, and its capital is Vaduz.
Answer: Liechtenstein.

36) What term is used to group and identify all animals with backbones?
Answer: Vertebrates.

37) What is the past participle of the verb *to go*?
Answer: Gone.

38) Identify a tuba as a brass, woodwind, percussion, or stringed musical instrument.
Answer: Brass.

39) Which 2 planets have the most moons, one with 23 and the other with 16.
Answer: Saturn (23) and Jupiter (16).

40) With which war is the cry "Remember the Maine" associated?
Answer: Spanish-American War.

41) Which unit of length used by ancient people designated the distance from a man's elbow to the tip of his middle finger?
Answer: Cubit.

42) In which war was Mathew Brady a famous photographer?
Answer: American Civil War.

43) Which country is the site of Mount Kilimanjaro, Africa's highest peak?
Answer: Tanzania.

44) Give the area of a square which is circumscribed about a circle that has an area of 16 *pi*.
Answer: 64.

45) In 1988, which French leader won a stunning victory when he became the first president reelected in the 30 years of the French Republic?
Answer: François Mitterrand.

46) Between the orbits of which 2 planets do asteroids primarily travel?
Answer: Mars and Jupiter.

47) A famous Uncle Remus story involves Br'er Rabbit, Br'er Bear, and what kind of "baby"?
Answer: Tar Baby.

48) Which color is proverbially associated with envy?
Answer: Green.

49) How big is an angle whose measure is 1/2 that of its supplement?
Answer: 60 degrees.

50) Which treaty signed on September 3, 1783, ended the American Revolution, with British recognition of American independence?
Answer: Treaty of Paris.

51) In which U.S. city is the Superdome?
Answer: New Orleans.

52) Where in Pennsylvania did the Continental Army camp for the winter in 1777?
Answer: Valley Forge.

53) In which Asian mountain range is The Abominable Snowman, or "Yeti," allegedly found?
Answer: Himalayas.

54) What integer does the fifth root of negative 32 equal?
Answer: Negative 2.

55) In which Midwest state did 200 diplomats from 9 countries meet in 1995 with the presidents of Bosnia, Serbia, and Croatia for peace talks at Wright-Patterson Air Force Base? The names of its 3 largest cities begin with C.
Answer: Ohio (the base is located near Dayton).

56) Of the 3 basic methods of heat transfer, in which one must an object have direct contact with another object?
Answer: Conduction.

57) Which 19th-century poet wrote the lines "Hang a lantern aloft in the belfry arch / Of the North Church tower as a signal light" in his poem "Paul Revere's Ride"?
Answer: Henry Wadsworth Longfellow.

58) In which country was the temple of Apollo located at Delphi?
Answer: Greece.

59) The term light-year is given to the distance traveled by light in a year's time. About how many trillion of miles is this distance?
Answer: 6 trillion.

60) Give the nationality of Juan Ponce de León, the explorer who searched for the Fountain of Youth in 1513.
Answer: Spanish.

61) Name the spirited gray mare Robert E. Lee rode during the Civil War.
Answer: Traveller.

62) Which U.S. document contains the following statement: "We hold these truths to be self-evident: that all men are created equal, that they are endowed by their Creator with certain unalienable rights"?
Answer: Declaration of Independence.

63) A man who bought Alex Haley's Pulitzer Prize for *Roots* at an auction turned the award over to the official museum of which state where Haley grew up in the town of Henning? It extends westward from North Carolina to Arkansas.
Answer: Tennessee (the museum is in Nashville).

64) The area of a rectangular garden plot is 100 square feet. If the width of this garden is 5 feet, what is its length?
Answer: 20 feet.

65) Name the first black U.S. Supreme Court justice, who died in 1993 at age 84.
Answer: Thurgood Marshall.

66) Which of the 3 main classes of foods essential to the body is the primary source of energy for animals and plants?
Answer: Carbohydrates.

67) What punctuation mark other than a period can end an imperative sentence?
Answer: Exclamation point.

68) Which literary character's beauty caused the Trojan War?
Answer: Helen (of Troy).

69) Give the area in square units of a right triangle whose sides are of lengths 3, 4, and 5.
Answer: 6 square units.

70) Identify the European capital city founded on 7 hills, including Palentine and Esquiline. The Pantheon and the Arch of Constantine are located in this city.
Answer: Rome.

71) Traditionally, how many more weeks of winter will ensue if the groundhog sees his shadow on February 2?
Answer: 6 weeks.

72) Name Dwight Eisenhower's Vice President who gave the "Checkers" speech in 1952 to protect his candidacy.
Answer: Richard Nixon.

73) Mount Kilimanjaro is in Tanzania. Which neighboring country is nearest to this mountain?
Answer: Kenya.

74) What is the product of 1/4 and 3/4?
Answer: 3/16.

75) The nation's oldest environmental group has money problems. Identify this 600,000-member club that bears part of the name of a rugged mountain range in California.
Answer: Sierra Club (the Sierra Nevada are in California).

76) By what name do we know a scientist who studies the remains of early people?
Answer: Archaeologist (or Anthropologist).

77) What is the subject of the following sentence: "Please write to me"?
Answer: You (understood).

78) Name the only one of the 12 Apostles who was a tax collector. The others were of the laboring class.
Answer: Matthew.

79) Give the term used in botany for the female part of the flower.
Answer: Pistil.

80) In which harbor in which country was the American battleship the *Maine* blown up while at anchor on February 15, 1898, with the loss of 260 crew members?
Answer: Havana, Cuba.

81) Give the full name of SDI, better known as Star Wars in the Reagan administration.
Answer: Strategic Defense Initiative.

82) On March 4, 1893, which President was inaugurated for a second, but nonconsecutive, term of office? His surname also identifies Ohio's second largest city.
Answer: Grover Cleveland.

83) Identify the great depression extending from Syria to Mozambique that is an area of intense geologic activity where the African continent appears to be splitting apart.
Answer: Great Rift Valley.

84) Find the quotient when .23 is divided into 10.81.
Answer: 47.

85) "Green" begins the name of a worldwide organization that has attempted to stop the test-firing of the Navy's Trident 2 missiles. Name this organization.
Answer: Greenpeace.

86) What have you injured if you have hurt your scapula?
Answer: Shoulder blade.

87) Give the word for a book of synonyms, antonyms, and related words.
Answer: Thesaurus.

88) Identify either the Greek or Roman god known for having wings on his ankles.
Answer: Hermes or Mercury.

89) What is the larger of two numbers whose average is 8 and whose product is 48?
Answer: 12.

90) Identify the war whose cease-fire was signed at Paris on January 27, 1973, effective the next day at 8:00 a.m. Saigon time.
Answer: Vietnam War.

CHAPTER TWENTY-TWO

1) Which almanac's 199th annual edition in 1990 predicted a winter "cold as the dickens"?
   Answer: *The Old Farmer's Almanac* (accept *Farmer's Almanac*).

2) Name the state in which Nellie T. Ross was inaugurated as the first woman governor in the U.S., on January 5, 1925. It's known for its Frontier Days rodeo in Cheyenne.
   Answer: Wyoming.

3) Which island country inhabited by the Arawak Indians did Christopher Columbus discover in the Caribbean Sea on May 4, 1494? Its capital is Kingston.
   Answer: Jamaica.

4) Give the numerical value of the square of the expression $3y$ when $y = -3$?
   Answer: 81.

5) In 1993, a survey showed the U.S. had become the third most populous nation. Which countries have larger populations?
   Answer: China, 1st, and India, 2nd (Russia is 4th).

6) Of the following, which term designates a substance's capability of being deformed permanently by externally applied forces: resilience, plasticity, density, or buoyancy?
   Answer: Plasticity.

7) Which 19th century American author wrote the classic horror story "The Tell-Tale Heart"?
   Answer: Edgar Allan Poe.

8) Identify Hera's husband, the most important of the Greek gods.
   Answer: Zeus.

9) If you ate one ounce of a 3-pound cake, what fraction of that cake did you eat?
   Answer: 1/48.

10) The Mozambique National Resistance, or Renamo, killed more than 100,000 people in the 1980s. On which continent is Mozambique?
    Answer: Africa.

11) On January 13, 1888, which organization was created to gather and disseminate geographic knowledge?
     Answer: National Geographic Society.

12) General Burnside, who was defeated by Gen. Lee's forces in Virginia on December 13, 1862, is better known for his side whiskers than for his career as a military leader. What word for "side whiskers" comes from his name?
     Answer: Sideburns.

13) Identify the U.S. state capital with a 2-word name, each of which begins with the letter *C*. It is the capital of Nevada.
     Answer: Carson City.

14) What is the product of 20 and 36?
     Answer: 720.

15) A 1996 book by Christopher Matthews details the friendship between which 2 men who were elected to the House in 1946 and faced each other in presidential debates in 1960?
     Answer: John Kennedy and Richard Nixon (the book is entitled *Kennedy and Nixon*).

16) From which vegetable often called yams did George Washington Carver make about 300 products?
     Answer: Sweet potatoes.

17) Name the fictional Washington Irving character who slept for twenty years.
     Answer: Rip Van Winkle.

18) Name the New York Yankee ballplayer who hit in a record 56 straight games.
     Answer: Joe DiMaggio.

19) Name the Swedish inventor who founded an international award program in 6 different fields.
     Answer: Alfred Nobel.

20) Identify the basic document in English constitutional law accepted by the king in the 13th century in a meadow alongside the River Thames west of London.
     Answer: Magna Carta (or Great Charter).

21) Which U.S. state flag has a Union Jack in the upper left corner?
     Answer: Hawaii.

22) What did Joseph Glidden patent in 1874 that ended the open range for grazing cattle and made possible the development of the Great Plains for farming?
     Answer: Barbed wire.

23) Name the lengthy group of islands extending from the Alaska Peninsula. A chain of active volcanoes is located on these islands.
Answer: Aleutian Islands.

24) What is the average of 90, 77, 70, 50, and 63?
Answer: 70.

25) In which country did a Harvard- and Oxford-educated woman join the world's oldest surviving royal family when she wed the heir to the Chrysanthemum Throne?
Answer: Japan (Prince Naruhito wed Masako Owada).

26) Name 3 of the 5 most common types of scientific measurements.
Answer: Length, volume, mass, pressure, and temperature.

27) What word does the famous raven in an Edgar Allan Poe poem repeat continually?
Answer: "Nevermore."

28) If you are "tickling the ivories," which musical instrument are you playing?
Answer: Piano.

29) An ace has been drawn from a 52-card deck and not replaced. If another card is drawn randomly, what is the chance that it will also be an ace?
Answer: 1/17 (accept 3/51).

30) Name the prime minister of Great Britain during WWII who popularized the phrase "The Iron Curtain."
Answer: Winston Churchill.

31) How many decades are there in a century?
Answer: 10.

32) Which U.S. President reappointed Republican Charles Evans Hughes to the Supreme Court 14 years after Hughes had resigned from the court to run against Woodrow Wilson in the 1916 presidential race?
Answer: Herbert Hoover.

33) Which mountain in Colorado was sighted on November 15, 1806, by an explorer whose first name was Zebulon?
Answer: Pikes Peak.

34) If each room can sleep 6 people, how many rooms are needed to sleep 26 people?
Answer: 5.

35) According to *Money* magazine in 1996, the Clintons were close to bankruptcy from mounting legal bills. What is a U.S. President's annual salary?
Answer: $200,000 (plus a $50,000 expense account).

36) What is the term for the solid outer layer of the earth, the hard outer shell of an animal, and a piece of stale bread?
Answer: Crust.

37) Edward L. Stratemeyer created 2 series of mystery books intended for young readers. Identify his series of books designed for young male readers.
Answer: Hardy Boys mysteries.

38) Give the collective name for the biblical Melchior, Balthasar, and Gaspar. They are traditionally considered to be the bearers of 3 important gifts.
Answer: The Magi, or the Three Wise Men.

39) Which planet has been the farthest from the sun since 1979 and will remain the farthest until 1999?
Answer: Neptune.

40) In which country was Portuguese navigator Ferdinand Magellan killed on April 27, 1521, a year and a half after he set sail from Spain with 5 ships on the first round-the-world voyage? This island country is located in the southwest Pacific Ocean.
Answer: Philippines.

41) What name is given to a person who foretells the future by studying the stars?
Answer: Astrologer.

42) Which Virginian is known as "The Father of the Declaration of Independence"?
Answer: Thomas Jefferson.

43) Name the arm of the Mediterranean Sea between Italy, the former Yugoslavia, and Albania.
Answer: Adriatic Sea.

44) What power is 10 raised to in the scientific notation form for 1,123,654?
Answer: Sixth.

45) In 1995, President Alberto Fujimori was elected to a second 5-year term in the first peaceful elections since 1980 in which South American country on the Pacific? Its capital is Lima.
Answer: Peru.

46) What is a break in the earth's crust along which earthquakes occur called?
Answer: Fault.

47) In which capital city was Anne Frank in hiding when she kept her famous diary during WWII?
Answer: Amsterdam (in The Netherlands).

48) Which adjective beginning with the letter *O* describes a surface that does not let light pass through?
Answer: Opaque.

49) Find the height of the trapezoid whose bases are of lengths 8 cm. and 10 cm. and whose area is 36 sq. cm.
Answer: 4 cm.

50) Which U.S. President was the first American awarded the Nobel Peace Prize? Before becoming President, he organized the cavalry volunteers known as Rough Riders.
Answer: Theodore Roosevelt (he was awarded the prize on December 10, 1906).

51) What name was given to Cape Canaveral between 1963 and 1973?
Answer: Cape Kennedy.

52) Name either the 6th or 8th U.S. Presidents. One preceded Andrew Jackson in office and the other followed him.
Answer: John Quincy Adams or Martin van Buren.

53) Which U.S. city, often called the "Pittsburgh of the South," was named after a large, steel-producing English city?
Answer: Birmingham (Alabama).

54) Which term in mathematics designates a counting number greater than one that has more than 2 factors?
Answer: Composite number.

55) Name the company whose ship, the *Valdez*, ran aground in Alaska's Prince William Sound and spilled 11 million gallons of oil on March 24, 1989.
Answer: Exxon.

56) Except for the Precambrian Era, into which smaller divisions is each era divided?
Answer: Periods.

57) Identify the nationality of Hans Christian Andersen, the author best remembered for his more than 150 fairy tales.
Answer: Danish.

58) On which day does Lent begin?
   Answer: Ash Wednesday.

59) Which word, meaning "earth pig" in Afrikaans, is defined as "a large, burrowing, nocturnal African mammal with an extensive tongue, powerful claws, and large ears"? It feeds on termites and ants.
   Answer: Aardvark.

60) At which Virginia site has a key to a French prison been hanging since it was presented to George Washington in 1798 as a tribute by a Frenchman who served as his aide de camp? The key was returned briefly to France for display during its bicentennial in 1989.
   Answer: Mount Vernon.

61) If two dry gallons equal one peck, how many gallons of love are in the nursery rhyme line, "I love you a bushel and a peck"?
   Answer: 10.

62) If both the U.S. President and the Vice President should die or become disqualified, which official is next in the line of succession?
   Answer: Speaker of the House (accept the name of the current speaker).

63) Which mountain range, whose name begins with the letter *U*, is considered to form the border between Europe and Asia?
   Answer: Ural Mountains.

64) What positive number has the same cube and cube root?
   Answer: 1.

65) Which U.S. territory set a popular election in 1993 to decide if it wanted to become the 51st state, remain a U.S. Commonwealth, or establish its independence? This territory is between the Dominican Republic and Guadeloupe.
   Answer: Puerto Rico (the vote was non-binding and it remained a commonwealth).

66) Which physician announced a "safe and effective" polio vaccine on April 12, 1955? His surname rhymes with a word for "an illegal, misleading move by a baseball pitcher."
   Answer: Dr. Jonas E. Salk (a *balk* is a pitcher's illegal move).

67) Give 2 of the 3 words in the English language that end in *-ceed* (C-E-E-D).
   Answer: Exceed, proceed, and succeed (accept emceed).

68) Give the Latin name of the Chinese philosopher whose title *K'ung Fu-tzu* means "Great Master K'ung."
Answer: Confucius.

69) Subtract negative 1 from negative 8.
Answer: Negative 7.

70) Which Chinese Nationalist leader, driven by Communists from the mainland of China in 1949, became president of Nationalist China, or Taiwan, in 1950?
Answer: Chiang Kai-shek (or Chiang Chung-cheng).

71) Gloria Estefan's album *Mi Tierra* debuted on Billboard's Top 200 at No. 41, the highest debut ever for an album in Spanish. What is the English translation for *Mi Terra*?
Answer: "My Land."

72) Give the first words of both the U.S. Constitution's Preamble and the Declaration of Independence.
Answer: "We" and "When."

73) What is the highest mountain on the continent of South America?
Answer: Mount Aconcagua.

74) How many 2-digit numbers can be formed from the digits 5, 6, 7, and 8 if the digits cannot be repeated?
Answer: 12.

75) In which Western Hemisphere country with a battered economy did stocks rise in early 1995 after the U.S. offered $40 billion in loan guarantees?
Answer: Mexico.

76) Identify the scale of hardness on which diamond is the hardest?
Answer: Moh's scale.

77) When you see the word "a" or "an," you know that it precedes a particular part of speech. Name that part of speech.
Answer: Noun.

78) The CIA Director once told Congress that the Third World was making gains in developing ballistic missiles. Spell the word *ballistic*.
Answer: B-A-L-L-I-S-T-I-C.

79) In the 5-kingdom classification system of organisms used today by many scientists, which kingdom's name means "first," or "earliest"?
Answer: Protista.

80) Which President on December 2, 1823, in his annual message to Congress set forth a doctrine that warned European countries not to interfere with the free nations of the Western Hemisphere?
Answer: James Monroe (Monroe Doctrine).

81) Which 3 words complete the following quotation: "That all men are created equal, that they are endowed by their Creator with certain unalienable rights, that among these are _____, _____, and the pursuit of _____"?
Answer: "life" / "liberty" / "happiness."

82) In which decade did James Marshall discover gold while building a California sawmill for John Augustus Sutter?
Answer: 1840s (on January 24, 1848).

83) In which state is the Three Mile Island nuclear power plant located? It is the site of the U.S.'s worst nuclear accident.
Answer: Pennsylvania.

84) What addition property is illustrated by the following $a + b = b + a$?
Answer: Commutative.

85) In 1995, French commandos stormed a jetliner at the Marseilles airport to free the 170 passengers being held hostage by hijackers from which African country once under French control?
Answer: Algeria (the commandos killed the 4 hijackers).

86) What is the abbreviation of Trinitrotoluene, a high explosive?
Answer: TNT.

87) Zlata Filipovic gave the name Mimmy to her diary published in 1994 as *Zlata's Diary: A Child's Life in Sarajevo*. What name for a feline did Anne Frank give to her diary?
Answer: Kitty.

88) The word *occurrence* is generally a difficult word to spell. So spell it.
Answer: O-C-C-U-R-R-E-N-C-E.

89) Which geometric term identifies a line drawn from any vertex of a triangle to the midpoint of the opposite side?
Answer: Median.

90) What word meaning "protection from" completes the phrase *diplomatic* _____, which some embassies claim exempts them from U.S. laws, including paying parking fines?
Answer: Immunity.

CHAPTER TWENTY-THREE

1) Which color is used to describe the kind of journalism that focuses on sensational and exaggerated news stories? The same color is used to describe cowardice.
   Answer: Yellow (*yellow journalism* was coined to describe the style of newspaper editor William Randolph Hearst).

2) On August 10, 1993, who was sworn in as the second woman ever to serve on the U.S. Supreme Court?
   Answer: Ruth Bader Ginsburg (the court's other female is Sandra Day O'Connor).

3) On which ocean is Mogadishu, the capital city of an African country?
   Answer: Indian Ocean (Mogadishu is the capital of Somalia).

4) Solve the following proportion: 6 is to 10 as 18 is to what number?
   Answer: 30.

5) On which popular summer resort off the southern coast of Cape Cod did President Clinton and his family spend much of their August 1993 vacation? Part of its name designates a place where grapes are grown.
   Answer: Martha's Vineyard.

6) Identify the planet whose name completes the 2-word phrase _____ *effect* used to designate the sometimes feared planetary alignment that occurred on March 10, 1982, without causing any of the predicted disasters. This planet is known for its Great Red Spot.
   Answer: Jupiter (effect).

7) Which of the following is NOT a synonym for "to scold": *admonish*, *reprove*, *reprimand*, or *revere*?
   Answer: Revere.

8) Which Parisian museum celebrated its 200th birthday by inaugurating a new wing in 1993?
   Answer: The Louvre.

9) If *y* to the one-third power equals 3, what does *y* equal?
   Answer: 27.

10) When Congress approved the Gulf of Tonkin Resolution on August 7, 1964, which U.S. President was given complete authority to use whatever force was necessary in Vietnam?
Answer: Lyndon Johnson.

11) Because of advanced technology, the Coast Guard has ended the use of which emergency transmission system employing dots and dashes?
Answer: The Morse code.

12) Which amendment, with a prime number, extended the right to vote to women in 1920?
Answer: 19th amendment (ratified on August 18, 1920).

13) Identify the volcano that erupted in A.D. 79 in southern Italy, destroying the cities of Pompeii, Stabiae, and Herculaneum.
Answer: Mount Vesuvius.

14) Which geometric term identifies figures that have both the same size and the same shape?
Answer: Congruent figures.

15) Which Canadian city was the first permanent French settlement in North America?
Answer: Quebec.

16) Identify the stable form of carbon that has a density of about 2 grams cm^{-3} and is very soft and black.
Answer: Graphite.

17) Identify Sir Lancelot's legendary son whose name is used today to identify any young man with a pure heart.
Answer: Sir Galahad.

18) At least one meteor was visible every 4 minutes in the U.S. and Europe in August 1993 during a meteor shower named for which constellation? It allegedly represents the son of Zeus who cut off the head of Medusa.
Answer: Perseus (known as the Perseid meteor shower).

19) Identify the form of carbon that has a density of 3.5 grams cm^{-3} and is the hardest known natural substance.
Answer: Diamond.

20) Identify the person known as the "Father of India," the one called the *Mahatma* or "Great Soul."
Answer: Mohandas (Karamchand) Gandhi.

21) Which palace with a Green Drawing Room, a White Drawing Room, and a Throne Room was opened to the public in 1993 for the first time for $12 per person to help raise money to repair fire-damaged Windsor Castle?
Answer: Buckingham Palace (in London).

22) Name the American statesman who received the 1994 $50,000 J. William Fulbright Prize for International Understanding for his humanitarian work, especially as a negotiator in Haiti.
Answer: Jimmy Carter.

23) The date of August 21, 1993, was eliminated on Kwajalein, the largest islet in the Marshall Islands, when it jumped from one side of the International Date Line to the other. In which ocean is Kwajalein located?
Answer: Pacific Ocean.

24) What is the greatest common factor of the numbers 12 and 16?
Answer: 4.

25) In 1993, which Mideastern country did the U.S. strike with Tomahawk missiles in retaliation for a plot to assassinate former President Bush while he was visiting Kuwait?
Answer: Iraq.

26) NASA lost contact with a spacecraft on a $980 million mission 3 days before it was to photograph which planet, the one whose moons are named Deimos and Phobos?
Answer: Mars.

27) In Katherine Paterson's *Bridge to Terabithia*, what does Leslie Burke not have at home to use for a class assignment because her writer parents are "reassessing their value structure"?
Answer: A T.V. (in order to watch a Jacques Cousteau special).

28) Which 2 months of the year are named for Roman emperors?
Answer: July and August (for Julius Caesar and Augustus Caesar, respectively).

29) What is the least common multiple of the numbers 12 and 16?
Answer: 48.

30) From which country did Texas declare its independence in March 1836?
Answer: Mexico.

31) Give the full name of NAFTA, the trade agreement passed by Congress in 1993.
Answer: North American Free Trade Agreement.

32) Give the name for Northerners in the South who profited from the unsettled social and political conditions during the Reconstruction Period following the U.S. Civil War.
Answer: Carpetbaggers.

33) In which country consisting of more than 13,600 islands along the equator did the volcanic island of Krakatoa erupt on August 26, 1883? Its capital is Jakarta.
Answer: Indonesia.

34) What is the surface area of a cube measuring 3 centimeters on each edge?
Answer: 54 cm^2.

35) In 1995, which West Bank city, described in the Bible as the city whose walls fell down when the Israelites marched around it and blew their trumpets, was turned over to the Palestinians?
Answer: Jericho.

36) Of the 4 compass points, North, East, South, or West, which one's abbreviation does not identify the symbol of a chemical element?
Answer: East.

37) Which of the following means "to force by pressure or threat": *condone, coerce, comply,* or *curtail*?
Answer: Coerce.

38) Which day of the week was named for Odin, the ruler of the gods in Norse mythology?
Answer: Wednesday (Odin's Anglo-Saxon name was Woden).

39) Name the fatty substance in animal tissue that forms gall stones within concentrated bile. This same fatty substance often clogs the arteries and leads to heart attacks.
Answer: Cholesterol (or cholesterin).

40) In which capital on the Thames River did a great fire burn for 4 days in 1666?
Answer: London.

41) In which U.S. state did surveyors discover a rich source of iron-ore on the Mesabi Range near Lake Superior on September 19, 1844? Its capital is named for a saint.
Answer: Minnesota (its capital is St. Paul).

42) In which city, subject of a famous Carl Sandburg poem, did social reformer Jane Addams open Hull House, one of the first settlement houses in America, in 1889?
Answer: Chicago (on September 18, 1889).

43) In 1993, only 4 teams were allowed to climb which mountain, the world's tallest, in an effort to protect its fragile ecology?
Answer: Mount Everest.

44) If 4 congruent squares are placed side by side to form a rectangle with an outside perimeter of 120 cm, what is the area of each one of the squares?
Answer: 144 cm².

45) In 1989, a Vice President of the Philippines visited former leader Ferdinand Marcos in Hawaii as a "humanitarian" gesture. Spell the word *humanitarian*.
Answer: H-U-M-A-N-I-T-A-R-I-A-N.

46) Identify the pear-shaped sac under the liver where bile is stored.
Answer: Gall bladder (or cholecyst).

47) Which American author of children's books, who died in 1991, was awarded a special Pulitzer Prize in 1984? He wrote *The Cat in the Hat*.
Answer: Theodor Seuss Geisel (or Dr. Seuss).

48) What word designates a Muslim house of worship?
Answer: Mosque.

49) What is the total pay for an 8-hour day at the hourly minimum wage of $4.25?
Answer: $34.00.

50) Name the husband of Marie Antoinette, whose beheading in 1793 was commemorated 200 years later by about 5,000 people gathered in Paris.
Answer: Louis XVI.

51) What is the official language of Egypt, Lebanon, Jordan, and Sudan, all of which have predominately Muslim populations?
Answer: Arabic.

52) Give the nationality of explorer Juan Cabrillo, who sailed into San Diego's harbor in September 1542, qualifying him as the European discoverer of California.
Answer: Portuguese.

53) What name is given to the almost continuous barrier of sandbars along the North Carolina coast frequently damaged by hurricanes?
Answer: Outer Banks.

54) What fraction is the positive square root of 1/25?
Answer: 1/5.

55) To promote the Administration's health-care reform plan, Hillary Rodham Clinton held a town meeting at the Mayo Clinic in Rochester. In which state known for its twin cities is this city located?
Answer: Minnesota (the twin cities are St. Paul and Minneapolis).

56) The Smithsonian's Museum of Natural History reopened in 1993 its only exhibit with living subjects. Name the animals it features, all of which have 6 legs.
Answer: Insects (it is called the O. Orkin Insect Zoo).

57) Of the following, which is a synonym for *reprimand*: rebuke, repress, relinquish or revert?
Answer: Rebuke.

58) The Tennessee Department of Education once sent to high schools materials that misspelled *Scarlet* in *The Scarlet Letter* and *Gaul*, an earlier name for France. Spell *Scarlet*.
Answer: S-C-A-R-L-E-T (misspelled as S-C-A-R-L-E-T-T and G-U-A-L).

59) What name is given to the effect caused by the thick blanket of carbon dioxide surrounding Venus, resulting in surface temperatures near 460 degrees Centigrade?
Answer: Greenhouse effect.

60) Identify the North American Indian people who ruled a powerful Mexico during the 1400s and early 1500s. They used a slash-and-burn method of agriculture in the densely forested lowlands.
Answer: Aztecs.

61) According to legend, which twins founded the city of Rome?
Answer: Romulus and Remus.

62) Replicas of which document signed on September 17, 1787, were signed at 96 national parks, 5 presidential libraries, and 3 regional archives on September 17, 1993?
Answer: U.S. Constitution.

63) Identify the national airline of Spain, whose name is the same as the name of the peninsula on which Spain is located.
Answer: Iberia.

64) What fraction is the square of 1/25?
Answer: 1/625.

65) On March 20, 1951, in which country, known for its *pampas*, or grassy plains, did dictator Juan Perón seize control of *La Prensa*, the opposition newspaper?
Answer: Argentina.

66) Give the 5-letter word beginning with *A* that identifies a homogeneous mixture of 2 or more metals such as bronze.
Answer: Alloy.

67) On September 17, 1787, delegates from 12 states unanimously approved the U.S. Constitution in Philadelphia. Spell *unanimously*.
Answer: U-N-A-N-I-M-O-U-S-L-Y (Rhode Island did not send delegates).

68) Is the sousaphone a woodwind, brass, stringed, or percussion instrument?
Answer: Brass.

69) What is the exact value of the simplified form of the square root of 72?
Answer: 6 times the square root of 2.

70) Which Central American country, whose name means "The Savior," gained its independence from Spain in 1821 along with Costa Rica, Guatemala, Honduras, and Nicaragua?
Answer: El Salvador.

71) Which U.S. city, nicknamed the "City by the Bay," was once named the world's best destination in a *Conde Nast Traveler* poll? It is known for its Fisherman's Wharf and Golden Gate Bridge.
Answer: San Francisco.

72) Name the leader of the Nez Perce Indians who after a 1,700-mile retreat surrendered to U.S. troops in Montana in 1877. He is remembered for saying, "From where the sun now stands, I will fight no more forever."
Answer: Chief Joseph.

73) Identify the U.S. President after whom the National Expansion Memorial in St. Louis, Missouri, is named. The Gateway Arch, the U.S.'s tallest man-made monument, is part of this memorial.
Answer: Thomas Jefferson.

74) What is the l.c.m., or least common multiple, of 6 and 4?
Answer: 12.

75) A Washington, D.C., park was dedicated to which lawyer and amateur verse writer on the anniversary of the day in 1814 when he wrote the words of our national anthem?
Answer: Francis Scott Key.

76) Give the 5-letter word that identifies a section of the large intestine. This name also identifies a punctuation mark used before a list or after the salutation of a business letter.
Answer: Colon.

77) The Internal Security Act providing for the registration of Communists and for their internment in times of an emergency was adopted by Congress in 1950. Does *internment* mean "burial," "deportation," "confinement," or "execution"?
Answer: Confinement (restriction to a specified space).

78) The Jewish Feast of Tabernacles is the commemoration of the Jews' years of wandering in the desert. How many years did the Jews wander?
Answer: 40 years (the 9-day festival is also known as Sukkot, or Succoth).

79) To which of the 3 classes of rock does sandstone belong?
Answer: Sedimentary.

80) On September 19, 1945, to which Asian country did the British prime minister pledge to grant self-government following local elections that winter? One of its largest cities is Bombay.
Answer: India (Clement Attlee was Britain's prime minister at the time).

81) In which world capital city is the famous St. Basil's Cathedral located on Red Square?
Answer: Moscow.

82) Name the American admiral, the "Hero of the Spanish-American War," who returned from Manila to a huge welcome in New York in September 1899. His surname also identifies a system for cataloguing library books.
Answer: George Dewey (Melvil Dewey developed the Dewey decimal system).

83) Identify one of the 2 U.S. states that joined the Union in 1912.
Answer: New Mexico or Arizona.

84) Expressed as a Roman numeral, what is the square root of the Roman numeral CXXI?
Answer: XI.

85) Three rare Civil War photographs taken at the Battle of Antietam in 1862 have been made public. In which state did this battle take place?
Answer: Maryland.

86) According to a report in *Science* magazine, the crater left by a huge meteor that fell on the Yucatan Peninsula is 186 miles across, nearly twice as big as previously believed, strengthening the theory that the impact wiped out the dinosaurs. On which body of water is the Yucatan Peninsula located?
Answer: Gulf of Mexico (it is called the Chicxulub crater).

87) Harvard College held its first commencement, or graduation, exercises in 1642. By derivation, what does the word *commencement* mean?
Answer: A beginning (commencement signals the *beginning* of a new stage of life).

88) St. Jerome, the patron saint of scholars and librarians, compiled the *Vulgate*, a complete translation of the Bible from Hebrew into which language?
Answer: Latin.

89) Solve the following equation for x: $3(x - 4) = 5(x - 6)$ [READ: three times the quantity of x minus four equals five times the quantity of x minus six].
Answer: 9.

90) On the eve of a 1996 visit by Pope John Paul II, President Alvaro Arzu escaped injury in an assassination attempt in which country bordering Mexico?
Answer: Guatemala.

CHAPTER TWENTY-FOUR

1) What is the meaning of the Latin word *Pisces*, the name given to the sign of the Zodiac for February 19 to March 20, the 12th period in the astrological chart?
Answer: Fish.

2) Identify the notorious Apache warrior of the 1880s who was featured in the first show in TNT's series about native Americans.
Answer: Geronimo.

3) According to the 1990 Census, Mesa was the U.S.'s fastest-growing large city in the 1980s. In which state is Mesa?
Answer: Arizona (It was up 89% to 288,091).

4) Using 3.14 as an approximation for *pi*, what is the area of a circle with a radius of 10 cm.?
Answer: 314 cm².

5) By a 45-43 vote over Beijing, which city was awarded the year 2000 Summer Olympics, returning the Games to Australia for the first time since 1956?
Answer: Sydney.

6) Name the element that British physicist and chemist Henry Cavendish identified and called "inflammable air." It is the lightest element.
Answer: Hydrogen.

7) Name the author and illustrator whose 1993 book, his first in more than 10 years, focuses on homeless children. He is known for his books *Chicken Soup With Rice* and *Where The Wild Things Are*.
Answer: Maurice Sendak (new book is *We Are All in the Dumps With Jack and Guy*).

8) Which Spanish word, derived from Arabic, is used to designate a Spanish-speaking neighborhood in a U.S. city?
Answer: Barrio.

9) Using 3.14 as an approximation for *pi*, what is the circumference of a circle with a radius of 10 cm.?
Answer: 62.8 cm.

10) At which battle in 1066 did Norman leader William the Conqueror defeat Harold to become king of England?
Answer: Hastings.

11) Which French phrase for "good-bye" literally means "until we meet again"?
Answer: Au revoir.

12) Hillary Rodham Clinton was only the 3rd first lady to testify before Congress and the first to be the top advocate for a huge legislative program when she spoke about the Administration's health-reform plan. Name either of the other 2 first ladies who spoke before Congress in the 1940s and 1970s, respectively.
Answer: Eleanor Roosevelt or Rosalyn Carter.

13) Name the 4th largest continent, one located in the Western Hemisphere.
Answer: South America.

14) In how many ways can 2 standard, fair dice be tossed to give a sum of six?
Answer: 5.

15) President Boris Yeltsin once dissolved Russia's parliament. Spell *parliament*.
Answer: P-A-R-L-I-A-M-E-N-T.

16) Identify the radioactive element ending in *-ium* that is named for the Polish-born French scientist who was the first person to be awarded a 2nd Nobel Prize.
Answer: Curium (for Marie Curie).

17) Senator Kay Hutchison, the first woman senator elected in Texas, was indicted on charges of misconduct during her 2½ years as state treasurer. Spell *indicted*.
Answer: I-N-D-I-C-T-E-D.

18) Which movie, based on a children's book by Francis H. Burnett, tells the story of Mary Lennox, who leaves India to live with her British uncle, Archibald Craven?
Answer: *The Secret Garden.*

19) Give the name for soft coal, or coal with a lower carbon content than anthracite.
Answer: Bituminous coal.

20) In September 1961, which country withdrew from the United Arab Republic, leaving Egypt as the only member? Its capital is Damascus.
Answer: Syria.

21) At which Washington, D.C., building does the public now have access to almost 300 intelligence reports written by the CIA between 1947 and 1961? This building also houses the Declaration of Independence and the U.S. Constitution.
Answer: National Archives.

22) Identify one of the 2 Whig U.S. Presidents who died in office.
Answer: William Henry Harrison or Zachary Taylor.

23) Name the British explorer who in 1609 claimed for Holland the land along a New York river now named for him.
Answer: Henry Hudson.

24) If a salesperson's commission is 8%, how many dollars' worth of goods must he sell in order to earn $1200 in commissions?
Answer: $15,000.

25) In which state did preservationists buy a 56-acre parcel of land adjacent to Harpers Ferry National Park to stop future development on the site where Confederate Gen. Stonewall Jackson's forces captured 12,500 Union soldiers in 1862?
Answer: West Virginia.

26) Name the 3.15-acre mini-world in Arizona from which 4 men and 4 women emerged in 1993 after spending 2 years separated from the rest of the world in an effort to understand the world's ecology.
Answer: Biosphere 2.

27) Is a person who studies birds an aviator, graphologist, ophthalmologist, or ornithologist?
Answer: Ornithologist.

28) Which of the following correctly completes the phrase "gave the book to John and _____": she, I, me, we?
Answer: Me.

29) If one player has lost 25% of his or her total chess pieces, and there are 32 playing pieces required on the board at the beginning of a game, how many pieces has this player lost?
Answer: 4 (NOTE: each player has 16 pieces).

30) Two months after a summit with President Kennedy, which Soviet leader built the Berlin Wall as a barrier to the West during the first year of Kennedy's presidency?
Answer: Nikita Khrushchev.

31) What 2-word term expressing an affirmative response in radio operators' lingo is the basis for designating October 4 as a day of recognition for radio operators?
Answer: Ten-Four.

32) Which name was used by New York-born Isabella Baumfree, one of the best-known Abolitionists and the first black woman orator to speak out against slavery?
Answer: Sojourner Truth.

33) Which lake, 9 times as salty as the ocean, is the world's saltiest body of water? This body of water is shared by Jordan and Israel.
Answer: Dead Sea.

34) What is the term for an integer greater than 1 whose only positive factors are 1 and itself?
Answer: Prime number (accept prime).

35) Name the country whose National Party is imitating the Irish Republican Army in conducting fundraising in the U.S. to help with its plan to secede from England. This country was the home of poet Robert Burns.
Answer: Scotland (about 17 million Americans of Scottish descent reside in U.S.).

36) Give the scientific name for the human kneecap.
Answer: Patella.

37) The 1994 young adult novel *Troubling A Star*, a story of intrigue set in the Antarctic, is by which author who also wrote *A Wrinkle in Time*?
Answer: Madeleine L'Engle.

38) Stock shares of Nike fell as much as 2½ points in 1993 after its chief pitchman announced his retirement from the NBA's Chicago Bulls. Name him.
Answer: Michael Jordan.

39) Name the process that accounts for a lowering of the water level in a container of water left open to the air for 24 hours.
Answer: Evaporation.

40) Mayor Raymond Flynn of Boston resigned his position to accept the nomination as ambassador to the world's smallest independent state. Name this state.
Answer: Vatican City (accept Vatican or The Holy See).

41) Mrs. O'Leary's cow allegedly caused the October 8, 1871, fire that destroyed a large part of Chicago. Spell *allegedly*.
Answer: A-L-L-E-G-E-D-L-Y.

42) What name is given to the period of economic hardship that began on October 24, 1929, Black Tuesday, when investors began panic selling of stocks, dumping more than 13 million shares?
Answer: (Great) Depression.

43) Which Middle Eastern country is the only one rich in both oil and water? The Tigris and Euphrates rivers run through it into the Persian Gulf.
Answer: Iraq.

44) What is the length of the radius of a circle with a diameter of 1?
Answer: 1/2.

45) In 1996, oceanographers urged congressional lawmakers to give the same support to the study of the oceans as they have to the study of outer space. What percent of the Earth is covered by the oceans: 40%, 50%, 60%, or 70%?
Answer: 70%.

46) For every increase of one on the Richter scale, for example from 5.5 to 6.5, how much greater is the ground motion?
Answer: 10 times greater.

47) Identify the structure of the following sentence as *simple*, *complex*, or *compound*: "A runaway barge's collision with a bridge was blamed for causing the train wreck in Alabama in which 47 people were killed."
Answer: Complex.

48) Name the first black American ever to win the Nobel Prize in literature and only the second American woman so honored. She wrote *Song of Solomon*, *Beloved*, and *Jazz*.
Answer: Toni Morrison (1st U.S. woman was Pearl Buck for *The Good Earth* in 1938).

49) What is the next highest consecutive cube after 64?
Answer: 125.

50) What is Helmut Kohl's title as head of Germany's government?
Answer: Chancellor.

51) Jesse Leroy Brown was the first black American naval aviator and the first black naval officer to die in combat. During which war was he shot down in 1950?
Answer: Korean War.

52) Which former U.S. President, nicknamed Teddy, delivered a speech before seeking medical care for the gun-shot wound inflicted by a would-be assassin in 1912?
Answer: Theodore Roosevelt.

53) Pulitzer Prize-winning author John Hersey chronicled the dropping of the first atomic bomb in a book named for the Japanese city on which it fell on August 6, 1945. Identify this city.
Answer: Hiroshima.

54) If on a blueprint scale 1/4 inch represents 3 feet, how long is a pipe that is 3 inches long on the blueprint?
Answer: 36 feet.

55) In which state, the most populous, did legislators pass a bill to move its presidential primary from one of the last in June to one of the first in March? This state has more electoral votes than any other state.
Answer: California.

56) In October 1855, English engineer Henry Bessemer patented his process for making steel from which substance known by the symbol Fe?
Answer: Iron (pig iron).

57) On December 2, 1982, Dr. Barney Clark, a dentist, became the 1st recipient of a permanent artificial heart. Spell *recipient.*
Answer: R-E-C-I-P-I-E-N-T.

58) Dancer and choreographer Agnes DeMille made her breakthrough in which Rodgers and Hammerstein musical? It shares its name with a Midwest state.
Answer: *Oklahoma!*

59) Beatle Paul McCartney once told a sold-out concert crowd in Norway that killing which large sea animals is as wrong as slavery?
Answer: Whales.

60) The U.S. flag was formally raised over Alaska on October 18, 1867, following its purchase from Russia by William H. Seward. Spell *formally.*
Answer: F-O-R-M-A-L-L-Y.

61) Complete the name of Haiti's capital Port-au-_____ by giving the name of the pop star who began using a symbol as his moniker.
Answer: Prince (Port-au-Prince).

62) Based on a 1767 survey, the Mason-Dixon Line was set as the boundary between which 2 states settled by Charles Calvert and William Penn, respectively?
Answer: Maryland and Pennsylvania.

63) In its worst flooding in nearly 70 years, Europe's main north-south commercial waterway overflowed in 1993, causing the evacuation of thousands. Identify this river for which an artificial diamond-like gem is named.
Answer: Rhine River (rhinestones were first made at Strasbourg on the Rhine).

64) Express one millisecond as a decimal fraction of one second.
Answer: 0.001 second (one one-thousandth of a second).

65) When President Clinton signed the National Service Act, he did so with the same two pens used to create the Civilian Conservation Corps and the Peace Corps. Which 2 U.S. Presidents, often referred to by the initials FDR and JFK, signed papers enacting these earlier programs?
Answer: Franklin D. Roosevelt and John F. Kennedy.

66) Complete the word beginning with the prefix *bio-* that means "capable of being decomposed by living organisms, such as bacteria."
Answer: Biodegradable.

67) Name the author of *All God's Children Need Traveling Shoes*, who joined about 600 writers across the U.S. in a simultaneous series of readings to help raise money to fight hunger. She read a poem at President Clinton's inauguration.
Answer: Maya Angelou.

68) A photograph of the hands of which American artist known for her desert scenes brought $398,500, the most money ever paid at an auction for a photograph? Her first name designates the "Peach State."
Answer: Georgia O'Keeffe.

69) What is the measure in degrees of one exterior angle of an equilateral triangle?
Answer: 120 (degrees).

70) To distance himself from the Communist past, President Boris Yeltsin halted in 1993 the changing of the guard at the tomb of which leader who founded the Soviet Union?
Answer: Vladimir Lenin.

71) Name the architect honored by the following epitaph in St. Paul's Cathedral in London: "If you would see his monument, look about you." His surname identifies a small, active songbird with dull brown or gray feathers.
Answer: Sir Christopher Wren.

72) President Clinton's health care reform plan was the biggest social initiative since the New Deal issued by which President to pull the U.S. out of the Great Depression? He was elected to 4 consecutive terms.
Answer: Franklin D. Roosevelt.

73) Children around the world helped select the new name for the animated cartoon mascot chosen for the 1996 Summer Olympics in Atlanta. Identify this mascot.
Answer: "Izzy."

74) If $2m - 7 = 5$, what is the value of m?
Answer: 6.

75) In 1993, to honor Indian contributions to the state, the Georgia Supreme Court convened at New Echota, the last capital of which Indian tribe that was forced west on the Trail of Tears in the 1830s?
Answer: Cherokee.

76) Identify the chemical element whose symbol is a one-letter pronoun.
Answer: Iodine (I).

77) How many hats are worn by Bartholomew Cubbins in a work by Dr. Seuss?
Answer: 500.

78) Which orchestral work by Sergei Prokofiev is subtitled *Symphonic Tale for Children?*
Answer: *Peter and the Wolf.*

79) Identify the chemical element whose symbol is a two-letter pronoun.
Answer: Helium (He).

80) Spell the name of the Caribbean island nation to which the first 600 U.S. troops were deployed in 1993 as part of a 6-month U.N. mission to help restore democracy.
Answer: H-A-I-T-I.

81) In which state does Punxsutawney Phil venture out of his burrow on Groundhog Day?
Answer: Pennsylvania.

82) Name the French sculptor of the Statue of Liberty, or *Liberty Enlightening the World.* It was dedicated on October 28, 1886, on Bedloe's Island, or Liberty Island.
Answer: Frédéric Auguste Bartholdi (Liberty Island is in New York Harbor).

83) What name did an area in South Dakota acquire when early explorers found the land bumpy, difficult to travel across, and unfit for cultivation?
Answer: Badlands (French explorers called it *les mauvaises terres*).

84) If $2m - 7 = 3$, what is the value of m^2?
Answer: 25.

85) In 1993, President Yeltsin's forces stopped anti-government protestors and ended what has been called Moscow's worst political violence since the Bolshevik Revolution occurred in which of these years: 1865, 1917, 1939, or 1962?
Answer: 1917.

86) Which drugs used by some athletes in the late 20th century for body-building are prohibited by the regulations of high school, college, and professional athletic programs?
Answer: Steroids.

87) Of the following, which means "to clear from blame": *exonerate*, *expedite*, *explicate*, or *extradite*?
Answer: Exonerate.

88) According to researchers, students who listened to Mozart's *Sonata for Two Pianos in D. Major, K.448*, scored higher on IQ tests than those hearing a relaxation tape or no music at all. What does the abbreviation IQ stand for?
Answer: Intelligence quotient.

89) If a rectangular-shaped floor measures 9 feet by 13 feet, how many square yards of carpet will be needed to cover the floor?
Answer: 13 (square yards).

90) In 1993, the U.N. formally ended 3 decades of sanctions against which nation that formed a new, freely elected government on April 27, 1994, to end the era of apartheid?
Answer: South Africa.

CHAPTER TWENTY-FIVE

1) Which of the following words means "with the support of members from both parties, without regard for political allegiance": *bicuspid, biennial, binary,* or *bipartisan?*
   Answer: Bipartisan.

2) House Minority Leader Robert Michel, a Republican from Illinois, retired from Congress at the end of his 19th term in January 1995. How many years did he serve?
   Answer: 38 years (House term is 2 years).

3) In fulfillment of a pledge made 40 years before and as the result of the 1991 parliamentary vote, Germany agreed in 1993 to complete the move of its capital to which city by the end of the year 2000?
   Answer: Berlin (Bonn continued as seat of government in the unified country).

4) If the sum of 2 consecutive whole numbers is the cube root of 125, what are the numbers?
   Answer: 2 and 3.

5) Hamar Olympic Hall, the world's largest indoor ice skating hall and venue for speedskating during the 1994 Winter Olympic Games, is shaped like an inverted ship used by which daring Scandinavian explorers?
   Answer: Vikings.

6) January through June, 1992, was the fifth warmest period on record because of a Pacific Ocean warming. What name, meaning "the child" in Spanish, is given to such a warming of the Pacific near the equator?
   Answer: El Niño.

7) Who is the real murderer of young Dr. Robinson in *The Adventures of Tom Sawyer?*
   Answer: Injun Joe.

8) According to Greek myth, which giants provided the lightning bolts that helped Zeus defeat Cronus? These giants had but one eye.
   Answer: Cyclops.

9) What is the absolute value of the difference between .05 and .005?
   Answer: .045.

10) Secretary of State Warren Christopher ended a 1993 trip to former Soviet republics by calling for the complete withdrawal of Russian troops from the 3 Baltic nations. Name the 2 whose names begin with *L*.
    Answer: Lithuania and Latvia (Estonia is the third Baltic nation).

11) To offset 1993 losses, a 300-year-old English-based insurance society revamped the way it did business. Name this company known for insuring almost any risk.
    Answer: Lloyd's of London.

12) Identify the famous American female speed skater whose surname also identifies the presidential guest house near the White House. President Harry S Truman was there when 2 Puerto Ricans tried to assassinate him in 1950.
    Answer: Bonnie Blair (Blair House is the presidential guest house).

13) Composer Aaron Copland won the 1945 Pulitzer Prize for his music for Martha Graham's ballet *Appalachian Spring*. Spell *Appalachian*.
    Answer: A-P-P-A-L-A-C-H-I-A-N.

14) Randy's best high jump was 4¾ feet. Expressed as a mixed fraction in simplest terms, how many feet below the meet record of 6$\frac{7}{12}$ feet was Randy's jump?
    Answer: 1⅚ feet.

15) In 1995, Democrats kept control in the legislature of which Southern state that has never had a GOP-controlled legislature even though it elected Republican George Allen as its governor two years earlier? Its capital was once the capital of the Confederacy.
    Answer: Virginia (Confederate capital was moved from Montgomery, Alabama, to Richmond on May 29, 1861).

16) Name the simplest hydrocarbon, CH_4, which is found in small amounts in the atmosphere of Titan, the only satellite in the solar system with a substantial atmosphere.
    Answer: Methane (nitrogen is the largest component of Titan's atmosphere).

17) Who is wrongly accused of murdering Dr. Robinson in *The Adventures of Tom Sawyer*?
    Answer: Muff Potter.

18) What Greek tragic figure has a name meaning "swollen-foot"? He killed his father and unknowingly married his mother.
    Answer: Oedipus.

19) The U.S.'s $11 billion supercollider project was officially ended in 1993 when Congress refused to approve further expenditures. What is the more common name for a supercollider?
Answer: Atom smasher ($2 billion had already been spent on the project in Texas).

20) Name the instrument used in the 1793 execution of Marie Antoinette at Place de la Concorde in Paris during the French Revolution.
Answer: Guillotine.

21) Under a measure adopted at their 1993 national convention, which word in the Girl Scout motto may now be replaced by one that meets the individual's beliefs?
Answer: God.

22) Which former U.S. Vice President attended the 1993 dedication of his museum? One of his books includes a chapter entitled "Murphy and Me" about his rift with TV character Murphy Brown.
Answer: Dan Quayle (the museum is located in Huntington, Indiana).

23) Which Middle Eastern country, because of its total lack of rivers and its sparse rainfall, is considered to be the world's driest among large nations? It is located on the Arabian Peninsula.
Answer: Saudi Arabia (with desalination equipment and wells, water is plentiful, however).

24) If 3 angles X, Y, Z have measures 35 degrees, 145 degrees, and 55 degrees respectively, what geometric term describes the relationship between angles X and Y?
Answer: Supplementary.

25) In 1994, a 2.6 percent cost-of-living increase, the second smallest in nearly 20 years, was given to 45 million Americans receiving what type of federal benefits?
Answer: Social Security.

26) According to environmentalists, which chemical, used widely to purify water, should be banned in the Great Lakes because of the pollution it is causing?
Answer: Chlorine.

27) Spell *personnel*, meaning "a group of people employed by an organization or business."
Answer: P-E-R-S-O-N-N-E-L.

28) In 1930, William Taft became the first U.S. President to be buried in Arlington National Cemetery. Which synonym for *buried* contains the Latin root for "land"?
Answer: Interred (Kennedy is the only other President buried there).

29) Combine the following 2 fractions into a single fraction in lowest terms: $x/3 - (2x - 1)/6$ (READ: x over three minus the quantity two x minus one over six).
Answer: 1/6.

30) Which Caribbean island did the U.S. invade in 1983 to prevent a Soviet-Cuban takeover? Its name is similar to that of the Spanish site of the Alhambra palace.
Answer: Grenada (the Alhambra is in Granada in southeastern Spain).

31) Name the unofficial "national anthem" of the Confederate States of America allegedly written by Daniel Decatur Emmett.
Answer: "Dixie."

32) In which state did the Stars and Stripes first fly in a land battle on August 16, 1777, when troops fought in the Battle of Bennington? This state borders New York.
Answer: Vermont.

33) In which California town, site of the J. Paul Getty Museum and home to many stars, did fires fanned by Santa Ana winds in 1993 do extensive damage?
Answer: Malibu (accept Los Angeles).

34) If you are given the diameter of a circle, by what constant do you multiply to find the exact circumference?
Answer: *Pi* [$C = pi$ times d].

35) Despite previous safety concerns, Ukrainian lawmakers voted in 1993 to keep open which nuclear power station, site of the world's worst nuclear power accident?
Answer: Chernobyl (the accident occurred in 1986).

36) According to health officials, polio, sometimes called infantile paralysis, could be eradicated within in the Western Hemisphere in the 1990s. Spell *paralysis*.
Answer: P-A-R-A-L-Y-S-I-S.

37) Each year, a stranger leaves 3 white roses and a bottle of cognac on the Baltimore grave of which author on the anniversary of his birth, January 19, 1809? He wrote such tales as "The Fall of the House of Usher."
Answer: Edgar Allan Poe.

38) In the 18th century, publisher John Peter Zenger was arrested and imprisoned for defaming colonial governor William Cosby. What word designates written material that attacks a person with false or malicious statements?
Answer: Libel.

39) According to Harvard researchers, which weed, once imported to prevent erosion, may contain extracts that can help treat alcoholism? These weeds often choke trees in the South.
Answer: Kudzu.

40) Which word completes the title of Alfred, Lord Tennyson's poem "The Charge of the Light _____" about the 1854 Battle of Balaklava during the Crimean War?
Answer: "Brigade."

41) Which 2-word term is used to describe the condition of a stamp or block of stamps that is in the same condition as when it was first printed?
Answer: Mint condition.

42) The first stamps issued in the United States bore the portraits of George Washington and which printer and scientist who was the postmaster general of the American colonies?
Answer: Benjamin Franklin.

43) In 1993, the U.S. Capitol celebrated its bicentennial with the return of which 130-year-old, newly restored bronze statue to the top of its dome?
Answer: *Freedom* (or *Statue of Freedom*).

44) What is the maximum area of a rectangle whose perimeter is 36 inches?
Answer: 81 square inches.

45) A federal court ordered an investigation into allegations that White House officials in the Bush administration unlawfully influenced the Endangered Species Committee to permit logging on federal land in Oregon inhabited by the northern spotted variety of which nocturnal bird?
Answer: Owl (it was the 2nd exemption to the 1973 Endangered Species Act).

46) Doctors at George Washington University Medical Center developed a technique to produce identical twins, triplets, or more siblings from a single organism in its early stages of development. Name this prefetal organism.
Answer: Embryo.

47) What term beginning with the letter *F* is the general name for a crime more serious than a misdemeanor?
Answer: Felony.

48) Richard Nixon held what he called at the time his "last" press conference on November 7, 1962, after his defeat in the California gubernatorial race. Spell *gubernatorial*.
Answer: G-U-B-E-R-N-A-T-O-R-I-A-L.

49) Of 2/6, 12/36, and 11/30, which fraction is not equal to 1/3?
Answer: 11/30.

50) Which country was once headed by Josip Broz, better known as Tito? This country's capital is Belgrade.
Answer: Yugoslavia.

51) What hobby is designated by the word *philately*? It has been called "the hobby of kings and the king of hobbies."
Answer: Stamp collecting.

52) On November 4, 1979, in which country were 66 Americans taken hostage, 52 of whom were held for 444 days until they were released on Inauguration Day, January 20, 1981?
Answer: Iran (they were taken in Teheran).

53) Spell the name of the Caribbean island that celebrated its 500th birthday with street festivals, art shows, and the Central American Games, which opened in San Juan on November 19, 1993?
Answer: P-U-E-R-T-O R-I-C-O.

54) If Walter hiked 21 miles in 3 hours and 30 minutes, how long would it take him to hike 28 miles at the same pace?
Answer: 4 hours, 40 minutes (accept 4⅔ hours).

55) In which state did Edwin Edwards defeat David Duke by a 60-40% margin in the gubernatorial race in 1991? It's known as the "Pelican State."
Answer: Louisiana.

56) 1993 guidelines for science literacy state that 8th graders should know that the moon circles the Earth in about how many days?
Answer: 28 (accept 27 as *World Book* states 27 1/3 days; from the American Academy for the Advancement of Science Literacy).

57) What is the English title of the Spanish children's book entitled *Los Tres Osos*?
Answer: *The Three Bears.*

58) The cornerstone of the White House, designed by architect James Hoban, was laid on October 12, 1792. Spell *architect*.
Answer: **A-R-C-H-I-T-E-C-T (it was first called the "presidential palace").**

59) To combat the problem of time inconsistencies created by the different dates on which countries change from daylight saving to standard time, airlines with international routes fly on Zulu Time, based on which time referred to as GMT?
Answer: **Greenwich Mean Time (Zulu comes from the old Army code word for zero).**

60) Which 2 European countries were connected by a 31-mile Channel Tunnel in 1994? The highway, nicknamed the "Chunnel," links the cities of Folkestone and Calais.
Answer: **England and France.**

61) Being PC is the subtext of Kermit the Frog's first book for adults, *One Frog Can Make a Difference: Kermit's Guide to Life in the '90s*. Give the meaning of PC.
Answer: **Politically correct.**

62) In 1993, the Associated Press became the first U.S. news organization to return on a full-time basis to Vietnam since the end of the war involving the U.S. Did that war end in 1955, 1965, 1975, or 1985?
Answer: **1975.**

63) China launches satellites from which desert, the world's coldest and most northern?
Answer: **Gobi Desert.**

64) Frank had $40.00, and he bought a book for $23.75 and a pair of socks for $8.25. What percentage of his money did he have left after making these purchases?
Answer: **20%.**

65) In 1994, Canada's Prime Minister repeated his opposition to NAFTA. Of the following, which means "to repeat": *renege, reiterate, renovate*, or *rescind*?
Answer: **Reiterate.**

66) According to the CDC, which disease, with the medical name *rubeola*, has virtually disappeared in the U.S.? In 1993, only 175 cases were reported, the lowest number in the 50 years that records have been kept.
Answer: **Measles.**

67) Arizona's Governor Symington, elected on a platform to apply his business sense to state government, filed for bankruptcy. Spell *bankruptcy*.
Answer: **B-A-N-K-R-U-P-T-C-Y.**

68) The film *The Last Emperor* was awarded the 1987 Academy Award as Best Picture. Of which country was Pu Yi the last emperor?
Answer: China.

69) What is the least number of faces a polyhedron can have?
Answer: 4.

70) On November 4, 1931, which international body created in 1920 condemned Japan for its willful aggression in Manchuria?
Answer: League of Nations.

71) Gov. William Donald Schaefer of Maryland pushed for legislation to eliminate the gas chamber as a means of execution. What is the legal term for a death sentence?
Answer: Capital punishment.

72) Which tomb did President Harding dedicate on November 11, 1921? The tomb bears the inscription, "Here rests in honored glory an American soldier known but to God."
Answer: Tomb of the Unknown Soldier (in Virginia's Arlington National Cemetery).

73) Identify the Union leader during the Civil War who began his 300-mile march of destruction across Georgia to the sea in 1864.
Answer: General William T. Sherman.

74) What is the least number of faces a prism can have?
Answer: 5.

75) A copyright suit against a rap group for recording a humorous imitation of "Oh, Pretty Woman" reached the U.S. Supreme Court. What word beginning with the letter *P* designates "a humorous imitation of a literary or artistic work"?
Answer: Parody.

76) A Cincinnati mayoral candidate in the 1990s was the son of the man who invented a technique for ejecting an object from the trachea of a choking person. Name this maneuver.
Answer: Heimlich maneuver.

77) Name the boy who finds a treasure map in Robert Louis Stevenson's *Treasure Island*.
Answer: Jim Hawkins.

78) Which word designates an extreme shortage of food?
Answer: Famine.

79) Does osteoporosis affect the arteries, bones, blood cells, or liver?
Answer: Bones.

80) In what year was the Berlin Wall erected? It was "opened" on November 9, 1989, after 28 years as a closed border.
Answer: 1961.

81) The Vietnam Women's Memorial in Washington, D.C., located 300 feet from the Vietnam Veterans Memorial, was officially dedicated in 1993. On which date is this holiday observed?
Answer: November 11 (Veterans Day).

82) On November 14, 1961, which U.S. President decided to increase the number of American advisers in Vietnam from 1,000 to 16,000 over the next 2 years?
Answer: John F. Kennedy.

83) Which of the following composers wrote "God Bless America," the song Kate Smith first sang on the radio in 1938: Berlin, Paris, Roma, or Bernstein?
Answer: Berlin (Irving Berlin).

84) How many representatives did not vote when the House rejected a bill to let the District of Columbia become a state by a vote of 277-153?
Answer: 5 (the House has 435 members).

85) In which southern state did Jim Folsom Jr. become governor in 1993 after the former governor was convicted of illegally taking $200,000 from an inaugural fund? Its list of famous residents includes Rosa Parks, Harper Lee, and Booker T. Washington.
Answer: Alabama (Guy Hunt was the governor).

86) What is the Louisiana French word for the slow-moving marshy inlets in the area of southern Louisiana where the Cajuns, or French Acadians, settled?
Answer: Bayous.

87) Identify the Henry Wadsworth Longfellow poem that describes the journey of the Acadians who were driven out of Canada during the 1750s.
**Answer: *Evangeline.*

88) In a major art robbery in 1993, $52 million worth of uninsured art work was stolen from Sweden's Museum of Modern Art, including 5 framed paintings by which Spanish artist whose first personal style is called the *Blue Period?*
Answer: Pablo Picasso.

89) If a kilometer is approximately equivalent to .62 miles, what is the approximate measure in kilometers of a 26-mile course: 16, 32, 42, or 52?
Answer: 42 (kilometers).

90) In which year did the Versailles or Paris Peace Conference open in France on January 18, following the end of World War I?
Answer: 1919.

CHAPTER TWENTY-SIX

1) Who wrote "The Battle Hymn of the Republic" in 1861, the day after she heard the song "John Brown's Body Lies A-Mouldering in the Grave"?
Answer: Julia Ward Howe.

2) Aboard which ship was Peregrine White born on November 20, 1620, in Massachusetts Bay? He was the first child born of English parents in the New England colonies.
Answer: *Mayflower*.

3) Which 2 bodies of water are directly connected by the Suez Canal, which opened on November 17, 1869?
Answer: Red Sea and Mediterranean Sea.

4) Give the four fourth roots of 16.
Answer: 2, -2, 2*i*, -2*i*.

5) The Pentagon denied any connection between mysterious illnesses reported by Gulf War vets and the detection of nerve gas and mustard gas by Czech authorities in 1991 in which Mideast country where U.S. soldiers were sent to protect Kuwait from Iraq?
Answer: Saudi Arabia.

6) Saturn's Titan is the second largest satellite in the solar system. Name the 5th planet from the sun, whose satellite Ganymede is the largest.
Answer: Jupiter.

7) Pakistan ended martial law in 1987. Spell *martial*, meaning "military."
Answer: M-A-R-T-I-A-L.

8) President Clinton once persuaded both sides in an airline strike to agree to submit their dispute to an impartial person for settlement. Is such a process called *aspiration, arbitration, connotation*, or *interrogation*?
Answer: Arbitration.

9) If Paula had 54 rabbits and she sold 4/9 of them, how many rabbits did she have left?
Answer: 30.

10) Identify the French king after whom Louisiana was named by La Salle.
Answer: King Louis XIV.

11) For her efforts to preserve the Everglades, President Clinton awarded 103-year-old Marjory Stoneman Douglas the nation's highest civilian award. Name it.
Answer: Presidential Medal of Freedom.

12) Identify the solemn promise of loyalty to the U.S. whose authorship is attributed to Francis Bellamy.
Answer: Pledge of Allegiance.

13) On November 19, 1919, the Senate failed to ratify the Treaty of Versailles, crushing President Wilson's goal of U.S. leadership in the post-WWI era. Spell *Versailles.*
Answer: V-E-R-S-A-I-L-L-E-S.

14) What is the geometric term for an oval space such as the one between the White House and the Washington Monument where the National Christmas Tree is placed each year?
Answer: Ellipse.

15) Name 2 of the 4 classic films released in Hollywood's golden year, 1939. The U.S. Post Office featured these 4 movies on stamps in 1990.
Answer: *The Wizard of Oz, Gone With the Wind, Beau Geste,* and *Stagecoach.*

16) An American won the Nobel Prize for chemistry for discovering a genetic process important in recovering DNA from fossils. In which summer 1993 movie was a fictionalized account of this process seen?
Answer: *Jurassic Park.*

17) Which work by Robert O'Brien has as its subject a group of very intelligent rats who escape from a medical laboratory to help a family of mice?
Answer: *Mrs. Frisby and the Rats of NIMH.*

18) In which Russian building, whose name comes form the Russian word for "fortress," did President Boris Yeltsin entertain Queen Elizabeth in 1994 at the first black tie event held there since the 1917 revolution?
Answer: The Kremlin.

19) Researchers have started using a new group of synthetic hormones to reduce damage after brain injury. Identify the biblical figure raised from the dead for whom these new hormones are named.
Answer: Lazarus (the hormones are called Lazaroids).

20) Which area once ruled by King Philip II and his son Alexander the Great became a Roman province in 148 B.C.?
Answer: Macedonia.

21) For the first time in 96 years, the Los Angeles City Council did not have a float in the 1993 New Year's Day parade in Pasadena because women and minorities were not part of the parade's executive committee. Which flower is featured in this parade?
Answer: Rose.

22) In which 2 cities were the first battles of the Revolutionary War fought in Massachusetts on April 19, 1775?
Answer: Lexington and Concord.

23) Name the South American country on the equator that in 1994 suspended new licenses for tourist operations in an effort to protect the Galapagos Islands off its coast.
Answer: Ecuador.

24) John bought a television he found on sale for 20% off. If he saved $62.80 by buying it on sale, what was the original price of the television?
Answer: $314.00.

25) In 1995, after Madrid posted $350,000 bail, which country released a Spanish trawler and its crew charged with fishing illegally off Newfoundland?
Answer: Canada (off the Grand Banks).

26) To which of the 3 classes of rock does slate belong?
Answer: Metamorphic.

27) Name author Washington Irving's native state, where he died at Tarrytown in 1859. The Adirondack Mountains are located there.
Answer: New York.

28) DuPont agreed to let an archaeological team search for a 1702 French colonial settlement and cemetery on its property north of Mobile, Alabama. Spell *archaeological*.
Answer: A-R-C-H-A-E-O-L-O-G-I-C-A-L (or A-R-C-H-E-O-L-O-G-I-C-A-L).

29) Mrs. Jones expects 5 guests for dinner. In how many ways can she arrange her guests at her circular dinner table if she does not eat with them?
Answer: 24 (accept 4 factorial).

30) Hermann Goering presented Charles Lindbergh with a medal Lindbergh insisted on keeping. Identify the Nazi secret police force founded by Goering.
Answer: Gestapo.

31) Name the country whose Little League baseball team was defeated 3-2 in 1993 by a Long Beach, California, team in the world championship game. It is located on the isthmus joining Central and South America.
Answer: Panama.

32) Name the "Mother of the Civil Rights Movement" who was inducted into the National Women's Hall of Fame for prompting the Montgomery, Alabama, bus boycott in 1955.
Answer: Rosa Parks (Women's Hall of Fame is located in Seneca Falls, New York).

33) In which Parisian cathedral did Napoleon crown himself emperor on December 2, 1804? A famous Catholic university in the U.S. bears the same name, meaning "our lady."
Answer: Cathedral of Notre Dame (or Notre Dame).

34) If the length of a rectangle is 2 times its width, what is the width if the perimeter is 24 feet?
Answer: 4 feet.

35) Name the world's deepest trench, which is located in the Pacific Ocean.
Answer: Marianas Trench.

36) Of the 20 political regions of Italy, which one in the northern part of the country has a name that literally means "foot of the mountain"?
Answer: Piedmont.

37) The Justice Department once subpoenaed a senator's diaries. What is the silent consonant in the word *subpoena*?
Answer: B.

38) A U.S. court ruled that salvagers who spent millions to find a sunken 19th century ship were entitled to its $21 million treasure. Name the Jules Verne sea captain for whom the 2-ton robot used in the search was named.
Answer: Captain Nemo (in *20,000 Leagues Under the Sea*).

39) What percentage of the water on Earth is fresh and available for people to use: 1%, 10%, 25%, or 50%?
Answer: 1% (97% is salty; 2% is frozen in ice caps).

40) CIA memos released in the 1990s indicate the agency suspected Cuba's president of planting assassins in the U.S. about the time President Kennedy was killed. Name this Cuban leader.
Answer: Fidel Castro.

41) Excluding John Kennedy and Abraham Lincoln, name the other 2 assassinated U.S. Presidents.
Answer: James Garfield (1881) and William McKinley (1901).

42) Which state, whose name begins with M, joined the Union as a free state as part of the Missouri Compromise in 1820?
Answer: Maine.

43) Which Arizona national monument consisting of Indian cliff dwellings dating from the 1300s shares its name with the fictional Lone Ranger's Indian sidekick?
Answer: Tonto National Monument.

44) What is the sum of the solutions of the equation $x^3 - x = 0$?
Answer: Zero.

45) With which element symbolized by Pu were some people injected in early experiments conducted secretly by the government to develop safety standards for nuclear workers?
Answer: Plutonium.

46) A study found angioplasty as effective as bypass surgery in treating people with advanced coronary artery disease. What does angioplasty use to force open clogged arteries?
Answer: Balloons.

47) Which of the following designates a speech praising someone who has died: *elegy, eulogy, homily,* or *benediction?*
Answer: Eulogy (*eu-* means "good"; *-logy* means "discourse" or "words").

48) Gilbert Stuart is famous for his 3 paintings of George Washington. Give the term for a painting of a person.
Answer: Portrait.

49) What is the cube root of 64?
Answer: 4.

50) Name the American and British leaders who began a series of meetings at Casablanca on January 14, 1943, to decide the course of WWII.
Answer: Franklin Roosevelt and Winston Churchill.

51) In which city did Enrico Fermi help achieve the first controlled nuclear chain reaction at a university laboratory on December 2, 1942? This city is known for its White Sox and Cubs.
Answer: Chicago (University of Chicago).

52) President Clinton did not veto a bill his first year in office. Which President was the last to complete his first year, 1969, without a veto?
Answer: Richard Nixon (he was the 1st in 6 decades to do so).

53) The Appalachian Trail, which is among 150 areas that will benefit from $41 million approved by Congress for national park improvements, runs from Georgia to which Northern state?
Answer: Maine.

54) In how many ways can three of five people be seated in three chairs?
Answer: 60.

55) Joycelyn Elders said that drugs, alcohol, sex, and violence should be included as topics in a comprehensive health education program from kindergarten through 12th grade. Name her position when she headed the U.S. Public Health Service.
Answer: Surgeon General.

56) According to researchers, milk often does not contain the claimed amount of which vitamin called the "sunshine vitamin"?
Answer: Vitamin D.

57) A rebel attack on the Philippine government was stopped with the help of the U.S. in 1989. Spell *coup*, meaning "a violent overthrow of government."
Answer: C-O-U-P.

58) Author Gore Vidal won a National Book Award in nonfiction for his short pieces expressing a personal opinion. By what name are such brief personal compositions known?
Answer: Essays (Vidal's winning collection is entitled *U.S.: Essays 1952-1992*).

59) Give the full name of WHO, the U.N. agency that in 1988 declared December 1 as World AIDS Day.
Answer: World Health Organization.

60) Name the leader of the group of Spanish explorers who discovered the Mississippi River on May 8, 1541.
Answer: Hernando de Soto.

61) With its stars arranged in alternating rows of 6 stars and 5 stars, how many rows of stars does the current U.S. flag have?
Answer: 9 (4 rows of 5 and 5 rows of 6 for a total of 50 stars).

62) Name the only Democratic President between Andrew Johnson and Woodrow Wilson. His last term of office was from 1893 to 1897.
Answer: Grover Cleveland.

63) On November 29, 1989, which country, with the help of the Civic Forum headed by playwright Vaclav Havel, ended 41 years of one-party Communist rule? It bordered Germany, Poland, and Hungary, among other countries.
Answer: Czechoslovakia.

64) If the perimeter of a square is represented by $4y$, then which expression represents its area?
Answer: y squared.

65) The EEOC once backed a 320-pound woman who won a case giving obese people a legal stand against job discrimination. Which commission is represented by the letters EEOC?
Answer: Equal Employment Opportunity Commission.

66) What name do scientists give to the phase in which matter has no definite shape but does have a definite size?
Answer: Liquid.

67) The estate of a composer Leonard Bernstein launched a plan to make his archives, including the original score of *West Side Story*, accessible to the public via computer. Spell *archives*, meaning "a collection of historical documents."
Answer: A-R-C-H-I-V-E-S.

68) Which word identifies a room used as a photographer's studio, a display room of a museum, and the cheapest seats in a theatre or the people occupying those seats?
Answer: Gallery.

69) What is the sign of the product of negative 5 times negative 4?
Answer: Positive.

70) Which country ceded the Philippines to the U.S. for $20 million in 1898?
Answer: Spain.

71) For which person did Alexander Graham Bell send when he sent the first phone message from one room to the other on March 10, 1876, saying, "Come here. I want you"? Sherlock Holmes's admiring friend has the same surname.
Answer: Mr. Watson ("Mr. Watson, come here. I want to see you").

72) Which American—Martin Luther King Jr, Ralph Bunche, Jesse Jackson, or George Washington Carver—became the first black man to be awarded the Nobel Peace Prize? He received his award in 1950 for mediating between the Israelis and Arabs.
Answer: Dr. Ralph Bunche.

73) When the nation's white fir Christmas tree was cut from a national forest in California, was its trip to the White House about 600; 1,600; 2,600; or 3,600 miles?
Answer: 2,600 miles.

74) Solve the following equation for x. $4x$ plus 2 is equal to or greater than 10.
Answer: x is equal to or greater than 2.

75) In which Virginia city did the Pentagon become the world's largest office building when it was completed on January 15, 1943?
Answer: Arlington (it is no longer the world's largest).

76) During a total lunar eclipse, the moon can enter the inner part of Earth's shadow. Is this shadow called the *aurora*, *orbit*, *solstice*, or *umbra*?
Answer: Umbra (the penumbra is the outer part of Earth's shadow).

77) Which Ray Bradbury novel depicts a society in which books are prohibited? It was named for the temperature at which book paper burns.
Answer: *Fahrenheit 451*.

78) Complete the title of Russian-born composer Nicholai Rimsky-Korsakov's "The Flight of the _____" by naming a black and yellow humming insect.
Answer: "Bumblebee."

79) Name the German physician who discovered the germ that causes tuberculosis.
Answer: Robert Koch.

80) Which Middle Eastern city, considered the birthplace of 3 major religions—Judaism, Islam, and Christianity—did Great Britain capture on December 9, 1917?
Answer: Jerusalem.

81) If the District of Columbia became the 51st state and the stars were arranged in rows of 9 stars and rows of 8 stars, how many rows of stars would the flag have?
Answer: 6 (3 rows of 8 and 3 rows of 9 for a total of 51 stars).

82) State legislators sometimes meet for a special purpose. Is such a group of legislators with a special common interest called a *cartel, caucus, ensemble,* or *sect?*
Answer: Caucus.

83) Dutch navigator Abel Tasman discovered New Zealand on December 13, 1642. Is New Zealand off Australia's northeast, southeast, southwest, or northwest shore?
Answer: Southeast shore.

84) What is the sum of the odd integers between 6 and 18?
Answer: 72.

85) Accompanying the wartime documents the British released in 1993 is a government statement saying that early evidence shows no indication that the prime minister knew in advance of the Japanese attack on Pearl Harbor. Name this WWII prime minister.
Answer: Winston Churchill.

86) Which blood vessels in the body connect the smallest arteries with the smallest veins?
Answer: Capillaries.

87) What word beginning with the letter *O* do dictionaries use to label a word as out-of-date, though not archaic or ancient?
Answer: Obsolete.

88) On October 12, many visit Fatima, Portugal, to mark the last apparition of the Virgin Mary in 1917. Spell *apparition,* meaning "a ghostly appearance."
Answer: A-P-P-A-R-I-T-I-O-N.

89) If a machine produces woogies at the rate of 2 every 15 minutes, how many woogies will it produce in 3 hours?
Answer: 24.

90) On December 13, 1991, which 2 Asian countries signed a treaty of reconciliation and nonaggression, formally ending a war whose hostilities ceased in 1953?
Answer: North Korea and South Korea.

CHAPTER TWENTY-SEVEN

1) Identify the colorful symbol on the 29-cent stamp issued to mark World AIDS Day in 1993.
   Answer: Red ribbon.

2) In which state was London Bridge dedicated at Lake Havasu City in 1971? It is also the site of the Grand Canyon of the Colorado.
   Answer: Arizona.

3) Over 5,000 groups participated in blackouts marking World AIDS Day. Name the West Coast city whose skyline with its Transamerica Pyramid was darkened for 15 minutes.
   Answer: San Francisco (New York City and Seattle skylines were also darkened).

4) Express the following as a single term in simplest radical form: the square root of 32 plus the square root of 8.
   Answer: 6 times the square root of 2.

5) In 1993, the U.S. Army swore in its first Muslim clergyman to serve about 1,400 worshippers. Spell the word used to designate a clergyman attached to a military unit.
   Answer: C-H-A-P-L-A-I-N.

6) Which of the following is within what is considered a normal pulse rate for a 14-year-old: 130, 115, 80, or 50?
   Answer: 80 (85-80 is generally considered the normal range for this age).

7) Identify the U.S. President whose name completes the title of the 1939 Pulitzer Prize-winning play, _____ *in Illinois*. It portrays this head of state, our 16th, as aimless and disorderly.
   Answer: Abe Lincoln.

8) Complete the name of Hungarian composer Antonín Dvorák's *New _____ Symphony*, which premièred 100 years ago at Carnegie Hall on December 16, 1893.
   Answer: *World*.

9) Find the exact volume of a right circular cylinder whose height is 4 feet and whose base has a radius of 3 feet.
   Answer: 36 *pi* cubic feet.

10) What name beginning with *P* designates the area also known as the Holy Land? The League of Nations put this area under Great Britain's control on September 29, 1923.
Answer: Palestine (parts of modern Israel, Jordan, and Egypt).

11) Which former President was the third U.S. President to be knighted by Queen Elizabeth? Ronald Reagan and Dwight Eisenhower were knighted earlier.
Answer: George Bush (Reagan was knighted in 1989, and Eisenhower, during WWII).

12) An archaeologist has discovered the South Carolina site of The Oaks plantation home of Theodosia Alston, daughter of the U.S. Vice President tried for treason in 1807. Name him.
Answer: Aaron Burr.

13) Name the country in which the gulf port of Veracruz is located.
Answer: Mexico.

14) The inverse square law states that the intensity of light weakens in proportion to the square of the distance. How much brighter would light be at 1 meter compared to its brightness at 8 meters?
Answer: 64 times brighter.

15) In which Norwegian city did F.W. de Klerk and Nelson Mandela receive the Nobel Peace Prize? It is always awarded on December 10.
Answer: Oslo.

16) Name the largest muscle in the human body.
Answer: Heart muscle.

17) On January 10, 1776, Thomas Paine published a series of pamphlets entitled *Common Sense*, advocating separation from England. Spell *pamphlet*.
Answer: P-A-M-P-H-L-E-T.

18) Give the English meaning of the French word *coeur* used in the epithet *Coeur de Lion* for English King Richard I.
Answer: Heart (he is known as Richard the Lion-Hearted).

19) Name the fracture in the earth's crust that extends through much of California.
Answer: San Andreas Fault.

20) Spell the name of the country in which Allied leaders Franklin Roosevelt and Winston Churchill met in Casablanca on January 14, 1943, to decide the course of WWII.
Answer: M-O-R-O-C-C-O.

21) Which Indian word beginning with *W* identifies the small beads made of shells that were used by North American Indians as a medium of exchange?
Answer: Wampum.

22) Ellis Island in New York Bay served as an immigrant examination station from 1892 until 1943. Spell *immigrant*, meaning "one who takes up residence in another country."
Answer: I-M-M-I-G-R-A-N-T.

23) Complete the name of Kill _____ Hill near Kitty Hawk, North Carolina, where the Wright brothers made their first powered flight. This word is another name for Lucifer.
Answer: Devil (the flight was made on December 17, 1903).

24) Three interior angles of a convex quadrilateral are 80 degrees, 130 degrees, and 75 degrees. What is the measure of the fourth angle?
Answer: 75 degrees.

25) For which New York island with a greater population than that of 41 of the 50 states is the largest commuter rail system in North America named?
Answer: Long Island (it is called the Long Island Railroad).

26) What word, literally meaning "without form," do scientists use to describe solids like silicone rubber that do not keep their shape?
Answer: Amorphous (solids).

27) Which of the following means "dry" and is often used to describe land in the Middle East: *arable*, *arid*, *briny*, or *caustic*?
Answer: Arid.

28) How many strings does a violin have?
Answer: 4.

29) If a rectangular solid block of stone 7 feet long and 5 feet wide has a volume of 140 cubic feet, what is its height?
Answer: 4 feet.

30) On November 3, 1903, Panama declared itself independent from the South American country bordering it. Name this country whose capital is Bogotá.
Answer: Colombia.

31) In which year was civil rights leader and Nobel Peace Prize winner Martin Luther King Jr. buried in Atlanta: 1958, 1962, 1968, or 1972?
Answer: 1968.

32) In which state were more than 200 American Indians massacred by the U.S. cavalry on December 29, 1890, at Wounded Knee? It is the site of the Mount Rushmore sculpture.
Answer: South Dakota.

33) From which country did Venezuelan general Simon Bolívar help several South American countries win their independence?
Answer: Spain.

34) At midnight, the temperature was 27 degrees, and by 5:00 a.m., it had dropped 8 degrees. At that time, it began to warm, reaching a high for that date at 3:30 p.m. that was 14 degrees warmer than at 5:00 a.m. What were the day's low and high temperatures?
Answer: 19 and 33 degrees.

35) On the day after Easter in 1994, stocks plunged to their lowest point since October 11, dropping 42.61 points on the industrial average of 30 premier U.S. stocks. What is this industrial average called?
Answer: Dow Jones.

36) Scientists describe light intensity in terms of packets of energy known by what name?
Answer: Photons (accept light quantum).

37) In an effort to promote openness, the Energy Department acknowledged that the U.S. government concealed more than 200 nuclear tests between 1940 and 1990. Spell *acknowledged.*
Answer: A-C-K-N-O-W-L-E-D-G-E-D.

38) What name is given to the economic system in which all or most of the means of production and distribution are privately or corporately owned and operated for profit?
Answer: Capitalism.

39) By what name are the units used to measure the intensity of sound known?
Answer: Decibels (accept bels).

40) Cyprus, which was divided into Turkish and Greek sections in 1974, reopened U.N.-mediated talks in 1994. In which body of water does it lie?
Answer: Mediterranean Sea.

41) Name the scholarship awarded to students for study at Oxford University in England. President Clinton was a recipient of this prestigious scholarship.
Answer: Rhodes scholarship.

42) What group of Indians was led by Peter McQueen into battle with Andrew Jackson in 1818? Florida State's athletic teams use this name as their nickname.
Answer: Seminoles.

43) Which two Asian countries have an ongoing dispute over Kashmir? Their capitals are Islamabad and New Delhi.
Answer: Pakistan and India.

44) What integer is the sum of the reciprocals of the numbers 1/2, 1/3, and 1/4?
Answer: 9.

45) In his book *The Book of Virtues: A Treasury of Great Moral Stories*, former Secretary of Education William Bennett entitles one of the chapters with which word beginning with *P* and meaning "to stick to a pursuit or course of action"?
Answer: Perseverance.

46) What is the acronym for "sound navigation and ranging," the process in which ultrasonic waves are used to map the ocean floor?
Answer: Sonar.

47) Name the novelist whose novel *The Yearling* won the 1939 Pulitzer Prize.
Answer: Marjorie Kinnan Rawlings.

48) Spell either of the following homonyms: the one that designates "the complete authentic works of an author" or the one for "a mounted weapon that discharges heavy projectiles."
Answer: C-A-N-O-N or C-A-N-N-O-N, respectively.

49) What integer is the result of the following calculation: the product of 4 times square root of 2 and 5 times square root of 8?
Answer: 80.

50) After urging the citizens of Belarus to reject communism, President Clinton in 1994 visited the Belarus burial site of 50,000 victims of which Communist dictator?
Answer: Josef Stalin.

51) In 1989, the CPI jumped six-tenths of one percent, the biggest rise in 2 years. Identify the CPI.
Answer: Consumer Price Index.

52) In January 1935 Bruno Richard Hauptmann stood trial for the kidnapping of the baby son of which famous aviator?
Answer: Charles Lindbergh (Hauptmann was executed on April 3, 1936).

53) Name the state where scientists oversee the Hubble Space Telescope from Goddard Space Flight Center in Greenbelt. Its capital is Annapolis.
Answer: Maryland.

54) The length of a rectangle is 5 yards more than its width. If its perimeter is 54 yards, what are its dimensions?
Answer: 11 yards by 16 yards.

55) In 1993, a Memphis lawyer representing 5 people who claim to have information about the murder charged to James Earl Ray was denied permission to present new evidence to a grand jury. For whose murder was Ray convicted?
Answer: Martin Luther King Jr.

56) Calling it the biggest thing since fire, scientists at Princeton University raised hopes of commercially producing energy by the year 2035 through the squeezing of atoms together at high temperatures. What is such a process called?
Answer: Fusion.

57) *Forbes* magazine reports that the District of Columbia, Rhode Island, and Massachusetts are the U.S.'s most litigious locations. Does this mean that these sites have the most crimes, lawsuits, pollution, or poverty?
Answer: Lawsuits.

58) Name the January 6 Christian festival commemorating the adoration of the infant Jesus by the Magi who had come from the East.
Answer: Epiphany (also known as Twelfth Day, Twelfth-tide, Feast of Lights, Three Kings Day, or Old Christmas Day).

59) Lichen is a flowerless plant that consists of which 2 organisms living together as a single unit?
Answer: Fungus and alga.

60) Identify the king whose tomb was discovered in 1922 by English archaeologist Howard Carter in Egypt's Valley of the Kings.
Answer: King Tut (Tutankhamen).

61) In which Rocky Mountain state did a developer propose building a large tourist park about the American West adjacent to the spot where George Armstrong Custer made his last stand? It is known as the "Treasure State."
Answer: Montana.

62) Of which 2 states did soldier and politician Sam Houston serve as governor? One is known as the "Volunteer State," and the other as the "Lone Star State."
Answer: Tennessee and Texas.

63) On March 25, 1775, George Washington planted at his home some pecan trees sent by Thomas Jefferson, who had also planted some at his home. Name both Washington's and Jefferson's Virginia homes, near Alexandria and Charlottesville, respectively.
Answer: Mount Vernon and Monticello.

64) Solve the equation for y: $-y/5 = 8$ [READ: negative y over 5 equals 8].
Answer: $y = -40$.

65) In which African nation was a coup thwarted in 1994 when troops from 8 African nations intervened and removed rebels from the presidential mansion in Monrovia?
Answer: Liberia.

66) Give the medical name for the disease often referred to as the "royal disease." People with this affliction bleed excessively when injured because their blood clots very slowly.
Answer: Hemophilia.

67) In 1960, Senator John Kennedy phoned Mrs. Martin Luther King Jr. to commiserate over the arrest of her husband. Spell *commiserate*, meaning "to sympathize."
Answer: C-O-M-M-I-S-E-R-A-T-E.

68) Which word identifies both a popular board game and a market condition in which there is only one seller of a commodity?
Answer: Monopoly.

69) Solve this equation for x: $5^0 + 3^0 + 1 = x$ [READ: five to the zero power plus three to the zero power plus one equals x].
Answer: $x = 3$.

70) During the 1994 Winter Olympics, every school in Norway participated in a fund-raising contest to benefit which city that hosted the 1984 Winter Games and was ravaged by war in the 1990s?
Answer: Sarajevo.

71) What is the official language of Brazil?
Answer: Portuguese.

72) Which U.S. President was Vice President Al Gore quoting when he told Russian citizens that "the only thing that is necessary for evil to triumph is for good men to do nothing"? He held the presidency from 1861 to 1865.
Answer: Abraham Lincoln.

73) Is Gabon, where Albert Schweitzer established a hospital in Lambaréné in 1913, bordered by the Mediterranean Sea, the Atlantic Ocean, the Pacific Ocean, or the Red Sea?
Answer: Atlantic Ocean.

74) With a mile equivalent to 1.6 kilometers, what speed limit will replace the current 65 miles per hour on road signs if the U.S. converts to the metric system?
Answer: 104 kilometers.

75) According to a 1992 Amnesty International report, in which country are Aborigines jailed at 27 times the rate of other citizens?
Answer: Australia.

76) Give the medical name for the disease called lock jaw because of its symptoms.
Answer: Tetanus.

77) Charles Lutwidge Dodgson used the pen name Lewis Carroll. What word containing the Greek prefix for "false" designates a pen name?
Answer: Pseudonym.

78) Which famous architect designed New York City's Guggenheim Museum on Fifth Avenue?
Answer: Frank Lloyd Wright.

79) Identify the radioactive isotope of carbon that contains 6 protons, 6 electrons, and 8 neutrons. It is used to determine the age of fossils and other ancient objects.
Answer: Carbon 14 (or radiocarbon).

80) Who incorporated the Standard Oil Company in Cleveland, Ohio, on January 10, 1870? A famous center in New York City once owned by the Japanese bears his name.
Answer: John D. Rockefeller.

81) Name the annual speech each U.S. President makes to Congress about the condition of the country.
Answer: State of the Union.

82) Which Connecticut-born Revolutionary War hero organized the "Green Mountain Boys" and led them in the capture of Fort Ticonderoga from the British in 1775?
Answer: Ethan Allen.

83) Los Angeles's Santa Monica Freeway, called the nation's busiest, is part of I-10, which begins on the east coast in which Florida city, the new home of the NFL Jaguars?
Answer: Jacksonville.

84) Which measurement is 1,000 times greater than the watt?
Answer: Kilowatt.

85) The EC has changed its name for the third time in its history. What is its new name, represented by the letters EU?
Answer: European Union (formerly the European Community and the European Common Market).

86) Of the 3 main kinds of rock, which one is formed when melted mineral matter cools and hardens?
Answer: Igneous.

87) Name the queen of England who on April 4, 1581, knighted Sir Francis Drake after he circumnavigated the world.
Answer: Queen Elizabeth I.

88) Give the meaning of the French words *bleu*, *blanc*, and *rouge*, or identify the 3 colors of the French flag.
Answer: Blue, white, and red.

89) If one base angle of an isosceles triangle has a measure of 40 degrees, what is the measure of the vertex angle?
Answer: 100 degrees.

90) In which Central American country bordered by Honduras on the north did a civil war officially end on February 1, 1992?
Answer: El Salvador.

CHAPTER TWENTY-EIGHT

1) Which word derived from the Spanish word for "shade" identifies a tall, broad-brimmed straw or felt hat worn especially in Mexico and the southwestern U.S.?
Answer: Sombrero.

2) On February 28, 1919, Senator Henry Cabot Lodge spoke for 2½ hours on the floor of the Senate in opposition to which President's proposal for the League of Nations? His first and last initials are the same letter.
Answer: Woodrow Wilson's.

3) Name the country south of the equator whose capital is Wellington.
Answer: New Zealand.

4) In eight years, Joy will be three times as old as she is now. How old is Joy now?
Answer: 4 years old.

5) Which area, taken by Israel during the Six-Day War, did Syria's President Hafez Assad hope to get back in talks with Israel in 1995-1996?
Answer: Golan Heights.

6) In 1994, the FDA asked Congress for guidance on whether to regulate cigarettes as an addictive drug because of which substance in tobacco?
Answer: Nicotine.

7) Which term for "a stream with rapids" also identifies the Clintons' real estate venture investigated by a special prosecutor?
Answer: Whitewater.

8) When he died at age 99 in 1994, hundreds of thousands of people in India and Nepal traveled to the retreat of the Guru of Kanchi, one of the 5 pontiffs of which 4,500-year-old religion?
Answer: Hinduism.

9) With 8 pairs of teams playing in each of 4 regions in the NCAA Division I men's basketball tournament, what is the total number of teams that participate?
Answer: 64.

10) Crispus Attucks was supposedly the first person killed by the British on March 5 during what is today called the Boston Massacre. In which year did this event occur: 1765, 1770, 1775, or 1780?
Answer: 1770.

11) A 1994 book by Hugh Thomas gives a dramatic account of Hernando Cortés's conquest of Montezuma, in 1519. What word of Spanish origin specifically designates any of the Spanish conquerors of Mexico and Peru in the 16th century?
Answer: Conquistador.

12) Who was President in 1931 when the "The Star-Spangled Banner" became the national anthem on March 3? His first and last initials are the same letter.
Answer: Herbert Hoover.

13) Which river in the Western Hemisphere is the largest river in the world by volume? This river has the highest discharge rate of all the world's rivers.
Answer: Amazon River.

14) Give the value of x in the following finite geometric series: 9, x, 81, 243.
Answer: 27.

15) Which royal titles were held by Kristin and Hakon, who lived about 800 years ago in Norway and were represented in 1994 by the first human mascots in Olympic history?
Answer: Prince and princess.

16) In 1994, a scientist said he discovered 2 planets outside our solar system orbiting a dense star. In which galaxy that includes our own solar system are these planets located?
Answer: Milky Way.

17) What word beginning with the letter S designates a person's brother or sister?
Answer: Sibling.

18) Which word for a sleeveless, waist-length jacket worn originally by Spanish bullfighters also identifies a lively Spanish dance and a musical composition by Ravel?
Answer: Bolero.

19) Name the chemical element whose rare 235 isotope is the major naturally occurring fission fuel for nuclear energy.
Answer: Uranium.

20) Name the Flemish-born geographer who became the leading mapmaker of the 1500s.
Answer: Gerardus Mercator.

21) Which of the following foreign phrases designates a dead-end street: *cul de sac, déjà vu, laissez faire,* or *status quo*?
Answer: Cul de sac (French for "bottom of the sack" or "blind alley").

22) Which American President, the 30th, said, "The chief business of the American people is business"? He served from 1925-1929.
Answer: Calvin Coolidge.

23) In which state did Congress establish Gates of the Arctic National Park?
Answer: Alaska.

24) What is the exact value of simplified form of the square root of 108?
Answer: 6 times the square root of 3.

25) In 1994, Russia's new Parliament pardoned the hard-liners who fought President Boris Yeltsin in 1993 and the 12 communists on trial for attempting to overthrow which Soviet president in 1991?
Answer: Mikhail Gorbachev.

26) Identify the constellation between Sagittarius and Aquarius that supposedly outlines a goat.
Answer: Capricorn (Capricornus).

27) One of the lands Lemuel Gulliver visits is ruled by the Houyhnhnms (pronounced "whinnims"), a gentle and wise race of which kind of animals?
Answer: Horses (*houyhnhnm* was coined by Swift to suggest a horse's *whinny*).

28) Toward which group of people is an anti-Semite hostile?
Answer: Jews.

29) Express the square root of 72 plus the square root of 128 as a single radical in simplest form.
Answer: 14 times the square root of 2.

30) Which country between Germany and Hungary did Hitler's Nazi troops invade on March 12, 1938? It is drained by the Danube River.
Answer: Austria.

31) What name from the animal world is given to an official inside an intelligence agency who illegally reports to foreign governments? The term is derived from the name of a burrowing mammal.
Answer: Mole.

32) On March 13, 1925, in which state did the governor sign a bill making it unlawful for any teacher to teach any theory denying the story of divine creation? John T. Scopes later challenged this law.
    Answer: Tennessee (the play *Inherit the Wind* is based on the Scopes trial).

33) Between which 2 states does the Columbia River form the border?
    Answer: Washington and Oregon.

34) If the scale on a blueprint is 1/2 inch to 1 foot, then how long is a wall 3 inches long on the blueprint?
    Answer: 6 feet (accept 72 inches).

35) In 1994, the Vatican formally commemorated the Holocaust for the first time with a concert that featured a German composer famous for such works as *Eroica* and *Fidelio*, a Jewish composer known for *West Side Story*, and a Roman Catholic composer known for *Symphony No. 8 in B minor*. Name any 1 of these 3 composers.
    Answer: Ludwig Van Beethoven, Leonard Bernstein, and Franz Schubert, respectively.

36) What is the average distance between the earth and the sun?
    Answer: 93 million miles (92.96 million).

37) Which word beginning with an *E* and borrowed from French designates the practice of spying on others?
    Answer: Espionage.

38) What name is given to a ceremonial headdress used by North American Plains Indians consisting of a headband with feathers extending down the back?
    Answer: War bonnet.

39) Much current electrical research is being done on superconductors. What term is used to designate the measure of how difficult it is for electrons to flow through a conductor?
    Answer: Resistance.

40) After U.S. diplomatic intervention, Greece and Turkey avoided a war in early 1996 over an island in which arm of the Mediterranean that lies between them?
    Answer: Aegean Sea (Greeks call island Ama; Turks call it Kardak).

41) According to a 1994 story in a London newspaper, a man on his death bed confessed to using a toy submarine to help stage the famous 1934 photograph of the Loch Ness monster rising out of a lake in which United Kingdom division north of England?
    Answer: Scotland.

42) Into which country's harbor did a U.S. naval squadron under George Dewey sail on May 1, 1898, to defeat the Spanish fleet during the Spanish-American War in the Battle of Manila?
Answer: Philippines's.

43) In 1994, Catherine Destivelle of France became the fist woman to reach the 14,692-foot summit of which pyramidal peak on the Swiss-Italian border?
Answer: The Matterhorn.

44) What is the arithmetic mean of 7 and 10?
Answer: 8.5 (accept 8½ or 17/2).

45) More than 10,000 objects larger than a softball are orbiting the Earth from the debris of the 4,500 spacecraft put into orbit since the USSR launched which one in 1957?
Answer: *Sputnik*.

46) What is the term for any substance, such as alcohol, that dissolves other substances?
Answer: Solvent.

47) Which play was pulled by a New York school following complaints by the Shinnecock tribe about the "Ug-a-wug" song and such words as "squaw" and "redskin" to refer to Tiger Lily and other characters? It was written by James Barrie.
Answer: *Peter Pan*.

48) A Massachusetts man once memorized almost all of the 15,693 lines of Homer's *Iliad*. Which war is featured in the *Iliad*?
Answer: Trojan War.

49) What is the arithmetic mean of the algebraic expression $x + a$ and $x - a$?
Answer: *x*.

50) Which Spanish term beginning with the letter J identifies a group of military men serving as an interim government, such as the one ruling in Thailand in 1991 after ousting Prime Minister Choonhavan?
Answer: Junta.

51) In 1994, for the 1st time, an all female team vied to represent the U.S. in the 142-year-old competition for the trophy called America's Cup. In which sport is this trophy awarded?
Answer: Yachting.

52) Which act passed by the British Parliament on March 22, 1765, was designed to have the colonies help pay for maintaining the British army stationed in America?
Answer: Stamp Act.

53) From which site were British explorer Robert Falcon Scott and his men returning on March 27, 1912, when they died in a blizzard?
Answer: South Pole.

54) In the 1st prime-rate increase since 1989, the prime rate rose in 1994 from 6 to 6½%. In dollars, how much more is 6½% of $10,000 than 6% of the same amount?
Answer: $25 more ($10,000 x .0025).

55) With U.S. support, Colombian President César Gaviria was in 1994 elected head of which organization of Western Hemisphere nations known as OAS?
Answer: Organization of American States.

56) Name the process by which fruit in a warm place gives off carbon dioxide, leaving a solution of alcohol. This process is speeded up if yeast is added.
Answer: Fermentation.

57) Which word completes the following line by T.S. Eliot, "This is the way the world ends / Not with a bang but a _____"? This word means "a low, whining sound or cry."
Answer: "whimper."

58) On March 23, 1743, King George II of Great Britain began a tradition by standing up when he heard which chorus in Handel's oratorio *Messiah* for the first time?
Answer: "Hallelujah Chorus."

59) Which word identifies both an idle person who lives by the work of others and a bee that serves only in a reproductive capacity?
Answer: Drone.

60) On March 25, 1964, the British government donated an acre of land for a memorial to President John Kennedy in which meadow where the Magna Carta was signed in 1215?
Answer: Runnymede.

61) A scene for the movie *Murder in the First Degree* was filmed at a former federal penitentiary on an island in the middle of San Francisco Bay. Name this former prison that closed in 1963 and is now a tourist attraction run by the National Park Service.
Answer: Alcatraz (nicknamed the "Rock").

62) Name the 1964 conservative Republican presidential nominee who in 1994 urged both Republicans and Democrats "to

get off [President Clinton's] back" about Whitewater and let him do the job he was elected to do. His surname could be represented by the chemical symbols AuH_2O.
Answer: Barry Goldwater.

63) For which Virginia college, the U.S.'s 2nd oldest, was former British Prime Minister Margaret Thatcher chosen to serve as chancellor for 7 years? It is named for British royalty.
Answer: (College of) William and Mary (founded in 1693).

64) If a person has four jackets and six pairs of pants in his closet, how many different-two-piece outfits can be selected?
Answer: 24.

65) In an effort to increase tourism in Egypt, 11 royal mummies, including Ramses II, were put on display in 1994. What word designates an ancient Egyptian king such as Ramses II?
Answer: Pharaoh.

66) What name is given to all of the various glands in the mouth and cheeks that help in the digestion of starchy foods?
Answer: Salivary glands.

67) Which word completes the title of Eugene Field's poem "Wynken, Blynken, and _____"?
Answer: "Nod."

68) Spell the word that designates a Muslim place of worship.
Answer: M-O-S-Q-U-E.

69) If an 18-carat gold ring weighs one ounce and pure gold is 24 carat, what is the weight of the pure gold in the ring?
Answer: 3/4 ounce or .75 ounce.

70) The late Melina Mercouri was the first woman ever to hold a senior Cabinet post in which country on a peninsula between the Ionian and Aegean seas?
Answer: Greece.

71) Which satellite was recaptured from the space shuttle *Discovery* in 1994 after studying solar winds? Its name identifies any resident of ancient Greece's most powerful city-state.
Answer: Spartan.

72) In which year was the Gettysburg National Cemetery dedicated on November 19?
Answer: 1863.

73) Is Europe's highest peak Mount Elbrus, Mont Blanc, the Matterhorn, or Mount McKinley?
Answer: Mount Elbrus.

74) With a total of 148 points scored in the 1994 NCAA men's basketball championship game, how many points did the University of Arkansas score to beat Duke by 4 points?
Answer: 76 points (final score 76-72).

75) In 1994, C-SPAN marked its 15th year as a cable network by transmitting the re-enactment of the 1858 debate between Stephen Douglas and which competitor for the U.S. Senate who later became President?
Answer: Abraham Lincoln.

76) What is the term for a secretion such as ptyalin that works as a catalyst in changing cooked starches into sugars?
Answer: Enzyme.

77) A new line of children's clothes from Esprit de Corp. features such Dr. Seuss characters as Horton and Cat in the Hat. What is Dr. Seuss's real name?
Answer: Theodor Seuss Geisel.

78) Which Leonardo da Vinci work, a portrait of a woman with an enigmatic smile, was returned to the Louvre in December 1913 after being stolen 2 years earlier?
Answer: *Mona Lisa*.

79) What word beginning with *M* designates the first process in food digestion, the act of chewing or grinding the food with the teeth and mixing it with saliva?
Answer: Mastication.

80) In which city did Adolf Hitler commit suicide in a bunker?
Answer: Berlin.

81) Which American inventor became known as the "Father of Frozen Foods": Birdseye, Borden, Bushnell, or Cooper?
Answer: (Clarence) Birdseye.

82) Which citizens were given the right to vote in presidential elections under the 23rd Amendment, ratified on March 29, 1961?
Answer: Residents of Washington, D.C.

83) The U.S. Military Academy was founded on March 16, 1802, at West Point, New York, on which river?
Answer: Hudson River.

84) What is the mathematical name for a line that connects 2 nonadjacent vertices of a convex polygon?
Answer: Diagonal.

85) Which country's bicentennial was celebrated in 1988? This "down under" country was founded as an alternative penal settlement to the American colonies Britain lost during the Revolution.
Answer: Australia.

86) Write the number 1 trillion using scientific notation.
Answer: 10^{12} (READ: ten to the twelfth power).

87) What word completes the phrase *standing* _____ used to designate the form of applause the Gridiron Club gave Bill and Hillary Clinton for their spoof of the "Harry and Louise" TV ads opposing Clintons' health-reform plan?
Answer: Ovation.

88) Which language brought to the U.S. by European Jews combines German with Hebrew and other languages and includes words like *chutzpa*, meaning "impudence" or "gall"?
Answer: Yiddish.

89) If 2 supplementary angles are in the ratio of 3 to 1, what is the number of degrees in both angles?
Answer: 45 and 135.

90) Which European capital city surrendered to the Nationalist forces of Generalissimo Francisco Franco on March 28, 1939? It lies on the Iberian Peninsula.
Answer: Madrid (during the Spanish Civil War).

CHAPTER TWENTY-NINE

1) Give the full name for the plan known as DST, which went into effect for the first time on March 31, 1918.
Answer: Daylight-saving time.

2) Which European discovered Florida on April 2, 1513, and claimed it for the King of Spain? He was seeking a legendary spring known as the Fountain of Youth.
Answer: Juan Ponce de León.

3) 1994's winter storms, the gypsy moth, and a disease that strikes dogwoods damaged much of the area surrounding which 470-mile scenic road that winds through the Appalachian Mountains in Virginia and North Carolina?
Answer: Blue Ridge Parkway.

4) If a rectangular piece of property measures 200 feet by 300 feet, what is the area of the property in square feet?
Answer: 60,000 square feet.

5) Which disease of the small intestine spread by contaminated drinking water became an epidemic in Somalia in 1994? Its name begins with the letter *C*.
Answer: Cholera.

6) What is the name for the continuing tremors that follow an earthquake, such as the 5.3 tremor in California's San Fernando Valley centered about 6 miles from the epicenter of the 6.8 earthquake on January 17, 1994?
Answer: Aftershocks.

7) On March 30, 1842, Dr. Crawford W. Long of Georgia became the first medical person to use an anesthetic in surgery. Spell *anesthetic*.
Answer: A-N-E-S-T-H-E-T-I-C (Long used ether in surgical removal of a tumor).

8) Name the 1994 movie based on the 19th-century Hans Christian Andersen tale about a girl who springs magically from the center of a flower.
Answer: *Thumbelina*.

9) If a 3-foot-wide sidewalk is placed around the outside of a square piece of property measuring 200 feet by 200 feet, what is the area of the sidewalk in square feet?
Answer: 2,436 (square feet).

10) The IMF approves billion dollar loans to countries. What adjective beginning with *M* completes the name of the IMF, or International _____ Fund?
Answer: Monetary.

11) Name the 2 objects that represented the workers and the peasants on the flag of the former Soviet Union.
Answer: Hammer and sickle (the star represented the Communist Party).

12) Which position did Alexander Haig hold in the Reagan administration on March 30, 1981, when he said, "As of now, I am in control here in the White House"?
Answer: U.S. Secretary of State.

13) Despite a malfunction of one radar device on *Endeavour*, the other took its first images of which state's Upper Peninsula in what was an Earth-monitoring mission in 1994?
Answer: Michigan (the only state with Upper and Lower peninsulas.

14) In a plane, what is the distance between the point with coordinates (0,0) and the point with coordinates (2,3)?
Answer: Square root of thirteen.

15) In which South African city, its commercial capital, were 31 people killed in black-on-black violence during a 1994 march by 8,000 Zulus protesting upcoming all-race elections?
Answer: Johannesburg.

16) Proof that an asteroid can have a moon was found by which Jupiter-bound spacecraft as it passed the 35-mile-wide asteroid Ida in 1994? The craft is named for an Italian astronomer.
Answer: *Galileo*.

17) On April 1, 1789, the U.S. House of Representatives for the first time had enough members to conduct business. What word designates the minimum number of members that must be present for an organization to take any official action?
Answer: Quorum.

18) Spell the word beginning with *A* that designates the time of development between childhood and adulthood when the body undergoes many physical changes.
Answer: A-D-O-L-E-S-C-E-N-C-E.

19) Are geologists who specifically study rocks known as entomologists, petrologists, philatelists, or seismologists?
Answer: Petrologists.

20) Sir Francis Drake, the first Englishman to sail around the world, died on January 28, 1596. What word using the Latin prefix for "around" means "to sail around the globe"?
Answer: Circumnavigate (he died on his ship off the coast of Panama).

21) Which of the following is a meaning of the word C-I-T-E: a place for building, a tourist attraction, to summon before a court of law, or to take aim?
Answer: To summon before a court of law (*cite* also means "to quote as an example").

22) Name the Jamestown tobacco planter who on April 5, 1614, married the beautiful Indian princess Pocahontas.
Answer: John Rolfe.

23) On April 28, 1903, Andrew Carnegie gave $1.5 million for the construction of a Peace Palace in The Netherlands. In which city was it built: Amsterdam, The Hague, Rotterdam, or Haarlem?
Answer: The Hague.

24) Mr. Green wants to paint his wall, which is 3.1 meters high and 4.5 meters wide. In square meters what is the area of this wall?
Answer: 13.95 square meters.

25) The government considered allowing recreational dives at the site of which sunken Civil War ironclad that went down 16 miles off Cape Hatteras during a storm at the end of the Civil War? Its name today designates a video display unit for a computer.
Answer: *Monitor.*

26) Carbon 14 has 6 protons, 6 electrons, and 8 neutrons. What is its atomic number?
Answer: 6.

27) Which of the following means "mercy toward an offender": *clemency, indictment, jurisprudence,* or *penitence?*
Answer: Clemency.

28) Which word completes the official name of the church that Joseph Smith organized on April 6, 1830: Church of Jesus Christ of Latter-Day _____?
Answer: Saints (also known as the Mormon Church).

29) How many square inches are in the surface area of a cube whose edge is 1 inch long?
Answer: 6 (cubic inches).

30) German leader Helmut Kohl was not invited to join leaders of 9 Allied nations at the June 6 commemoration of the 50th anniversary of the D-Day invasion of which region of France on the English Channel?
Answer: Normandy.

31) Which former NBA star was named coach of the Los Angeles Lakers for the remainder of the 1994 season? He retired in 1991 after testing positive for the HIV virus.
Answer: Magic Johnson (he returned to the NBA briefly in 1992 and again in 1996).

32) To which of the 3 branches of the U.S. government does the secretary of defense belong?
Answer: Executive.

33) On April 22, 1889, in which state were about 2 million acres purchased by the federal government from Creek and Seminole tribes opened to settlers, many of whom rushed ahead of the gunfire signal to stake their claims?
Answer: Oklahoma (the "Sooner State").

34) Solve for x: $2x + 4 = 18$.
Answer: $x = 7$.

35) In 1994, a variety of which type of flower was named after Hillary Rodham Clinton and dubbed an official breed by the Dutch ambassador to the U.S.?
Answer: Tulip (it took 15 years to cultivate the variety).

36) Which word designates a plant or animal resulting from the union of 2 different species, such as the mule that results from the mating of a male donkey and a female horse?
Answer: Hybrid.

37) Name the TV series begun in 1994 based on Catherine Marshall's novel inspired by her mother who was a teacher at a mission school in the Smoky Mountains.
Answer: *Christy*.

38) How many notes are in the scale on which most Western music is based?
Answer: 8 (C,D,E,F,G,A,B,C).

39) Who was the U.S. President when Jonas Edward Salk developed the first effective vaccine for polio?
Answer: Dwight Eisenhower (in 1955).

40) Which country north of England did James VI head when he joined England and his country under his reign on April 15, 1603, and took the name James I?
Answer: Scotland.

41) Name the brittle, flat unleavened bread eaten by Jews during Passover.
Answer: Matzo (or matsah, or matzah).

42) In 1994, Illinois asked the National Park Service to send back the body of a Civil War hero to Illinois, where he lived for 20 years, if the park could not take better care of his tomb in New York City. Name this soldier, who was also the 18th U.S. president.
Answer: Ulysses S. Grant.

43) Complete the name of the island Saint _____, on which Napoleon Bonaparte died in exile on May 5, 1821. The capital of Montana bears the same name.
Answer: (Saint) Helena.

44) Give the 5 different positive prime numbers that sum to 28.
Answer: 2, 3, 5, 7, and 11.

45) In which New England state do students pause on January 28 to remember Christa McAuliffe, their state's social studies teacher who died in the shuttle explosion? She taught in Concord.
Answer: New Hampshire.

46) What is the mass of one milliliter of water?
Answer: 1 gram.

47) In the Dewey Decimal system of filing books, is fiction shelved according to title, author, subject, or date of issue?
Answer: Author (alphabetically, by author's last name).

48) Does a gerontologist specialize in the study of weather, finances, old people, or pollution?
Answer: Old people (geriatrics is the medical specialty of caring for the old).

49) Factor the following binomial over the set of integers: $35y - 7$.
Answer: $7(5y - 1)$ [READ: seven times the quantity five y minus one].

50) Which Dutch word meaning "farmer" identifies the people of Dutch ancestry who live in South Africa?
Answer: Boer (today the Boers call themselves Afrikaners).

51) What 2-word term is used to designate the cause of death when soldiers are killed by their own forces or allies?
Answer: Friendly fire.

52) Which President named Thurgood Marshall as the first black Supreme Court justice in 1967?
Answer: Lyndon Johnson.

53) In 1994, when an airplane crashed on the White House lawn, the Clintons were temporarily living at Blair House. On which street are both houses located?
Answer: Pennsylvania Avenue (the White House street number is 1600).

54) What completes the term CD-____ for the kind of compact disc that can be read by a computer?
Answer: ROM (CD-ROM).

55) In 1994, an Amsterdam museum uncovered 19 works discarded and painted over by which artist who during a seizure cut off his own ear? He painted *The Potato Eaters*.
Answer: Vincent van Gogh.

56) Spell either the homophone *humerus*, designating "the bone of the upper arm that acts as a fulcrum," or *humorous*, meaning "funny."
Answer: H-U-M-E-R-U-S or H-U-M-O-R-O-U-S, respectively.

57) Which novelist is supplementing his books with CD-ROM computer games, some of which will feature Jack Ryan, hero of *Patriot Games* and *Hunt for Red October*?
Answer: Tom Clancy.

58) Give the tense of the verb "had seen."
Answer: Past perfect.

59) According to the *New England Journal of Medicine*, overuse of which type of drug prescribed to fight infection is causing a rise in such diseases as TB, staph, and pneumonia because of their growing drug resistance? Examples are penicillin and streptomycin.
Answer: Antibiotic.

60) Name the country of Kim Il Sung, who was the world's longest-reigning communist leader at the time of his death at age 82 in 1994, the same year he died. Its southern boundary is near the 38th parallel.
Answer: North Korea.

61) In 1994, on the 20th anniversary of his record-breaking accomplishment, which baseball player recalled racially motivated death threats and hate mail, as well as the need for federal protection for his daughter, as he neared Babe Ruth's record 714 home runs?
Answer: Hank Aaron (he retired in 1976 with 755 home runs).

62) Identify the Italian explorer and navigator after whom German cartographer Martin Waldseemüller named America on his world maps published in 1507.
Answer: Amerigo Vespucci.

63) The nation's largest river restoration project at Florida's Kissimmee River began in 1994 to save which national park, the second largest in the continental U.S.?
Answer: Everglades National Park.

64) 200 is what percent of 50?
Answer: 400%.

65) In 1994, the House approved the death penalty for almost 70 additional crimes, including committing a murder while stealing a car. What 1990s coined term means "stealing a car from its occupants by force"?
Answer: Carjacking.

66) What word designates both a bone of the forearm and one half the diameter of a circle?
Answer: Radius.

67) Which word completes the proverb, "A fool and his money are soon _____"?
Answer: "parted."

68) William Raspberry, a syndicated columnist for the Washington Post, won the 1994 Pulitzer for commentary. Spell *syndicated*, meaning "sold to a number of newspapers or other publications simultaneously."
Answer: S-Y-N-D-I-C-A-T-E-D.

69) The scale of a map is 1/6 inch equals 50 miles. If 2 cities are 300 miles apart, how many inches apart are they on the map?
Answer: 1 (inch).

70) Name the African country formed on April 26, 1964, when Tanganyika and Zanzibar united. Its name is a blend of their names.
Answer: Tanzania.

71) William Shakespeare was baptized on April 26, 1564, in the town of Stratford located on which river? A brand of cosmetics marketed through home sales has the same name.
Answer: Avon (the town is known as Stratford-on-Avon).

72) In which year ending in a zero did national guardsmen kill 4 students and wound about 10 others at Kent State University as they tried to control an antiwar demonstration?
Answer: 1970 (on May 4).

73) When the Germans took over Athens, Greece, on April 27, 1941, they raised the Nazi swastika over which site, the city's highest point?
Answer: Acropolis.

74) Name the 5 smallest numbers in the set of natural numbers.
Answer: 1, 2, 3, 4, and 5.

75) In 1994, President Clinton drove his own model of which classic car, named after a wild horse, in festivities at the Charlotte Motor Speedway marking the auto's 30th anniversary?
Answer: Mustang.

76) In 1994, scientists discovered what they believe to be the last of 12 subatomic particles from which everything is made. What term completes the name "top _____" that they have used to designate this unit smaller than a trillionth of the thickness of a hair?
Answer: Quark.

77) Give the real name of the short story writer whose pen name is O. Henry.
Answer: William Sydney Porter.

78) In medieval times villagers danced around a pole while holding ribbons streaming from its top on May 1. Spell *medieval*, meaning "of the Middle Ages."
Answer: M-E-D-I-E-V-A-L (May 1 is celebrated as Labor Day in socialist countries).

79) Name the palm-sized Apple computer that was satirized in the comic strip *Doonesbury* because of its glitches. Its name also identifies the British scientist known for his laws of gravity.
Answer: Newton.

80) Which of the following German cities did the Allies bomb on February 13-14, 1945, killing between 30,000 and 130,000 people: Dresden, Berlin, Bonn, or Frankfurt?
Answer: Dresden.

81) Mattel introduced a line of dolls named for Olympic silver medalist Nancy Kerrigan. Spell *medalist*.
Answer: M-E-D-A-L-I-S-T.

82) Which country detonated the first hydrogen bomb?
Answer: United States.

83) Name the southern U.S. city nicknamed "The Crescent City" and famous for its jazz.
Answer: New Orleans.

84) If a 26-foot ladder is placed against a building 10 feet from its base, how far up the building will the ladder reach?
Answer: 24 feet.

85) Name the primates left to fend for themselves against poachers after scientists fled war-torn Rwanda's Volcano National Park in 1994, where researcher Dian Fossey worked with the rare animals featured in a film bearing their name, _____ *in the Mist*.
Answer: Gorillas (the 300 Rwandan gorillas are among 600 worldwide).

86) What is the most abundant element in interstellar gas?
Answer: Hydrogen.

87) Which 2 parts of speech do adjectives modify by limiting or describing?
Answer: Nouns and pronouns.

88) Which of the following meaning "an alliance of factions or parties" completes the name of Pat Robertson's group's name: Christian _____: *collusion, coalition, coup,* or *symposium*?
Answer: Coalition.

89) Multiply 3 squared times negative 4.
Answer: Negative 36.

90) In which country were Communist dictator Nicolae Ceausescu and his wife Elena captured on December 23, 1989, and executed on December 31? This country's capital is Bucharest.
Answer: Romania.

CHAPTER THIRTY

1) A San Francisco company reportedly coordinated illegal jumps made from the Golden Gate Bridge while attached to an elasticized cord. What is such a cord called?
Answer: Bungee.

2) Before his death, former President Nixon requested that his body not lie in state in the Capital Rotunda, where the caskets of many Presidents have been placed, including that of the President who was the last to die before Nixon, in 1973. Name him.
Answer: Lyndon Johnson.

3) In 1994, the shuttle *Endeavour* traveled at the unusually low altitude of 137 miles high in order to use its radar system to take 3-D pictures of Earth's volcanoes and forests, including which dormant volcano that is Washington's highest mountain?
Answer: Mount Rainier.

4) A floor has an area of 810 square feet. How many square yards of carpeting are needed to cover it?
Answer: 90 square yards.

5) In 1994, to which aircraft carrier, named after the U.S. President from 1953 to 1961, were 500 women assigned, in the first-ever assignment of women to a combat ship?
Answer: *Eisenhower* (women began serving on Navy repair ships in 1978).

6) Norwegian explorer Roald Amundsen made history by flying over the North Pole in a dirigible called the *Norge* on May 12, 1926. Spell *dirigible*.
Answer: D-I-R-I-G-I-B-L-E (aircraft was piloted by Italian Umberto Nobile).

7) Which of the following contains the Greek root for "currency in use" and designates "the collection or study of coins or paper currency": *numismatics*, *philology*, *philanthropy*, or *eugenics*?
Answer: Numismatics.

8) Is the Iowa-born artist known for his paintings entitled *Stone City, Fall Plowing*, and *American Gothic* named Wood, Gold, Smith, or Jones?
Answer: (Grant) Wood.

9) What is the sum of 8 numbers whose average is ten?
    Answer: 80.

10) On May 6, 1527, German and Spanish troops began sacking
    and looting Rome, thus ending its role as a center of the
    rebirth of the arts following the Middle Ages. Spell the
    French word for "rebirth" that is used to name this period of
    creativity.
    Answer: R-E-N-A-I-S-S-A-N-C-E.

11) What word designates students at the U.S. Naval Academy?
    Answer: Midshipmen.

12) In the 1995 biography *The Politics of Rage*, Dan Carter
    asserts that race relations were poisoned and violence was
    fostered by the actions and words of which former Alabama
    governor who twice ran for President?
    Answer: George Wallace.

13) In 1993, Moscow's mayor urged the government to remove
    the bodies of Soviet founder Vladimir Lenin and other
    Communists from which large plaza?
    Answer: Red Square.

14) What word is used to describe the oval-shaped path which
    most comets follow when they travel around the sun?
    Answer: Elliptical (accept ellipse).

15) Which letter of the alphabet is emblazoned horizontally on
    South Africa's new flag? It symbolizes the English word cor-
    responding to *oui* in French or *si* in Spanish.
    **Answer: Y (it symbolizes 'yes'; the flag has 6 distinct
    colors).**

16) Identify the creator of the first newspaper cartoon, entitled
    "Join or Die," which appeared on May 9, 1754, in the
    Pennsylvania Gazette. He also invented bifocals.
    Answer: Benjamin Franklin.

17) What prefix is used before *vocation*, meaning "an occupation
    or profession," to make a word meaning "a hobby"?
    **Answer: A- (*avocation*, from *ab*-, meaning "away
    from").**

18) 1994 marked the 100th anniversary of the birth of which
    choreographer who pioneered in "modern dance"? Her sur-
    name also designates a kind of sweet cracker.
    Answer: Martha Graham.

19) Which word ending in *-troph* designates an organism that
    cannot make its own food, but is dependent upon complex
    organic substances for nutrition?
    Answer: Heterotroph.

20) Which 2 countries signed a provisional peace treaty in Paris on November 30, 1782, a year prior to their signing a definitive treaty?
Answer: U.S. and Great Britain (known as the Treaty of Paris).

21) In which city was composer Richard Wagner's "Centennial Inaugural March" first played at the Centennial Exposition in 1876? This city's name bears a Greek prefix for "love."
Answer: Philadelphia.

22) Identify the signer of the Declaration of Independence who said, "We must all hang together, or assuredly we shall all hang separately."
Answer: Benjamin Franklin.

23) During the 1990s, in which state did scientists study bacteria in Lechuguilla cave, an environment they believe mimics Martian characteristics? This cave is in Carlsbad Caverns National Park.
Answer: New Mexico (Lechuguilla is considered to be the deepest cave in the U.S.).

24) If a cube's total surface area is 24 square inches, what is its volume in cubic inches?
Answer: 8 (square inches).

25) Name the South American country that is among the 6 nations that account for half the world's population of 5,642,000,000 according to a 1994 Census.
Answer: Brazil (#5; China, #1; India, #2; U.S., #3; Indonesia, #4; and Russia, #6).

26) In which century did Louis Pasteur discover that diseases were spread by bacteria?
Answer: 19th century.

27) In 1995, Richie Ashburn, Leon Day, William Halbert, and Vic Willis were inducted into the Baseball Hall of Fame in which New York city bearing the surname of the author of *The Last of the Mohicans*?
Answer: Cooperstown (named for the father of author James Fenimore Cooper).

28) The CEOs of the 100 largest U.S. companies make about 99 times the pay of their average worker. What is a CEO?
Answer: Chief Executive Officer.

29) What is 40 squared?
Answer: 1,600.

30) Which pact forged by the Soviet Union in 1955 as a counterweight to NATO was formally dissolved in 1992? Its name identifies the Polish capital.
Answer: Warsaw Pact.

31) The Roman Catholic Church designates the 40th day after the Resurrection of Jesus as Ascension Day to commemorate the day Jesus arose into heaven. Spell *ascension*.
Answer: A-S-C-E-N-S-I-O-N.

32) In which present-day state on May 10, 1869, was a golden spike driven in at Promontory Point to mark the moment when the rails of the first transcontinental railroad were connected?
Answer: Utah (the Union Pacific and the Central Pacific railroads were joined).

33) Which city, known in Africa as Al-Qahirah, is Africa's most heavily populated, with more than 6 million people?
Answer: Cairo (Egypt).

34) If *kilo-* is "10 to the third power," what power of 10 does *mega-* represent?
Answer: 10 to the 6th power.

35) How many days is the waiting period for a background check for handgun purchases as required by the Brady gun law that took effect in February 1994?
Answer: 5 days.

36) Name the 5 excretory organs of the body represented by the mnemonic device SKILL.
Answer: Skin, Kidneys, Intestines, Liver, and Lungs.

37) Which word derived from Greek history means "expulsion from society"?
Answer: Ostracism.

38) Which instrument did David, the 2nd king of Israel, play as a youth?
Answer: Lyre (or harp).

39) Which excretory organ of the body is the largest glandular organ?
Answer: Liver.

40) The Latin name of the city of Rome is *Urbs Septicollis* and is based on a geographical feature of the city. What does this name mean?
Answer: City of Seven Hills.

41) Name the first product made of totally man-made fiber. This product, made of synthetic yarn from the Du Pont Company, was put on the market May 15, 1940.
Answer: Nylon stockings (hose; nylon was developed by Du Pont's W.H. Carothers).

42) In May 1775, the Green Mountain Boys, led by Ethan Allen, captured the British Fort Ticonderoga without firing a shot. In which state are the Green Mountains located?
Answer: Vermont.

43) Identify the bay for which the British named the mercantile company they founded in 1670 to establish a fur trade in what is now Canada.
Answer: Hudson Bay (the company was named the Hudson's Bay Company).

44) 40% of what number is equal to 250?
Answer: 625.

45) With the elevation of the Veterans Administration to Cabinet-level status in 1989, how many Cabinet departments did that make?
Answer: 14.

46) Which of the following designates an inflammation of the liver: anorexia, leprosy, hepatitis, or meningitis?
Answer: Hepatitis.

47) In which literary work by E.B. White are these lines: "Wilbur admired the way Charlotte managed. He was particularly glad that she always put her victim to sleep before eating it"?
Answer: *Charlotte's Web.*

48) Identify the patron saint of sailors, merchants, and especially little children, whose feast day is still celebrated by many European countries on December 6.
Answer: Saint Nicholas.

49) Which word describes a triangle with no congruent sides?
Answer: Scalene.

50) Over which 2 mountain ranges did Hannibal and his elephants march to make a surprise move into Italy in 218 B.C.? These mountains separate France and Spain and France and Italy.
Answer: Pyrenees and the Alps.

51) President Clinton gave the 1994 commencement address at Gallaudet University, a Washington, D.C., college for people with which physical disability?
Answer: Deafness.

52) At which Civil War battle fought from July 1-3, 1863, did General George Pickett make a frontal assault against the center of a dug-in Union line and suffer heavy losses?
Answer: Gettysburg.

53) Which U.S. capital city shares its name with a Greek valley, site of the temples of Zeus and Hera and of athletic contests held in early times?
Answer: Olympia (Washington).

54) What is 20% of 50% of 200?
Answer: 20.

55) Which term designates the combination of sodium palmitate and gasoline that the Allies used in the Persian Gulf war to destroy oil trenches Iraq built in Kuwait?
Answer: Napalm.

56) O.J. Simpson's blood matched that found at the murder scene according to genetic analysis. Which 3 letters designate such analysis?
Answer: DNA (analysis; stands for *d*eoxyribo*n*ucleic *a*cid).

57) In a sentence diagram, what part of the sentence appears on the left side of the vertical line?
Answer: The subject.

58) Give the word that describes a legislature with 2 houses.
Answer: Bicameral.

59) In the 1990s, NASA began compiling a list of a few thousand female names to use in identifying new craters, chasms, calderas, and lava flows beneath the cloud-shrouded surface of which planet?
Answer: Venus.

60) Which Portuguese explorer on an expedition to India in 1500 was allegedly blown off course and discovered Brazil?
Answer: Pedro Alvares Cabral.

61) Emperor Akihito and his wife, Empress Michiko, bowed at the Atlanta tomb of Martin Luther King Jr. during a 16-day U.S. tour in 1994. Spell *empress*.
Answer: E-M-P-R-E-S-S.

62) On May 9, 1926, which specific location did Americans Richard Evelyn Byrd and Floyd Bennett become the first to fly over?
Answer: North Pole.

63) A 1995 exhibit in Houston displayed treasures from the collections of the Topkapi Saray, the principal residence of the Ottoman sultans for 400 years. In which country is the Topkapi Palace located?
Answer: Turkey (the palace is in Istanbul).

64) What is the sum of the infinite geometric series 9/10 + 9/100 + 9/1000 + ...?
Answer: 1.

65) Columbia University annually announces which awards in literature and journalism?
Answer: Pulitzer Prizes.

66) To which of the 3 classes of rock does chalk belong?
Answer: Sedimentary.

67) Name the British author who created the literary character Napoleon, the pig.
Answer: George Orwell (or Eric Arthur Blair).

68) Between which 2 Alaskan cities is the Iditarod, a 1,100-mile dog sled race, run?
Answer: From Anchorage to Nome.

69) What is the simple interest earned on $50 at 4% for 6 months?
Answer: $1.

70) Identify the Germanic tribe after which France was named.
Answer: Franks.

71) Give the formal French for "Do you speak French?"
Answer: Parlez-vous français?

72) Which U.S. President started a sports tradition by throwing out the first baseball on April 14, 1910? His surname rhymes with the word for Huck Finn's mode of travel.
Answer: William Howard Taft (Huck traveled on a *raft* on the Mississippi).

73) In which state underneath the farmland of the Cumberland Plateau have spelunkers found a huge new cave, named the Blue Springs Cave, behind an existing 450-foot cave?
Answer: Tennessee.

74) What is the sum of the solutions of the equation $x^2 - 4 = 0$?
Answer: Zero.

75) On which continent on Mt. Kirkpatrick were dinosaur bones found in 1991, a discovery experts say proves beyond question that these creatures were a global phenomenon?
Answer: Antarctica (near the South Pole).

76) Which inert gas, the most abundant in outer space, is the end product of the fusion process in stars?
Answer: Helium.

77) Which word completes the following line from Exodus 5:6-19: "To make bricks without _____," meaning "to try to accomplish a task without the essential ingredients"?
Answer: "straw."

78) Name the French impressionist who sculpted *Young Dancer* and painted *The Dancing Class*.
Answer: Edgar Degas.

79) Which type of electrical current is usually supplied by batteries and is the one in which the electrons flow in one direction only?
Answer: DC, or direct current.

80) On April 24, 1970, which Asian country became the 5th nation to put a satellite into orbit with its own rocket?
Answer: China.

81) In which city was George Washington inaugurated as the first U.S. President on April 30, 1789? It is now known as the "Big Apple."
Answer: New York City.

82) In which state in the city of Yorba Linda was Richard Nixon, the 37th president of the U.S., buried next to his wife Pat on the grounds of the Richard Nixon Library and Birthplace?
Answer: California.

83) In which 2 states is the Great Smoky Mountains National Park, the park that ranks first in the list of 1993's most visited national parks?
Answer: North Carolina and Tennessee.

84) What is the minimum number of acute angles in any trapezoid?
Answer: 1.

85) In which state did heavy rains topple the Dyerville Giant, a redwood estimated to be 1,200 to 1,600 years old?
Answer: California.

86) Name the only planets in our solar system without any satellites.
Answer: Mercury and Venus.

87) Give the name of the pirate ship in James Barrie's *Peter Pan*.
Answer: *Jolly Roger*.

88) How many years are in a millennium?
Answer: 1,000.

89) What is 10 x 1/2 x 15 x 6?
Answer: 450.

90) Name the queen of England who said as the Spanish Armada approached in 1588, "I know I have the body of a weak and feeble woman, but I have the heart and stomach of a king, and of a king of England too."
Answer: Elizabeth I.

2701) Give the Roman numerals for 2,701.
Answer: MMDCC1.

INDEX